"For bad or worse, the image of the "Indian" had been defined by dime novelists like Ned Buntline and distilled, bottled, and mass-produced by Hollywood moguls more interested in creat[illegible] white success story than mirror[illegible] lated to real history [illegible] with a gun in his ha[illegible] grunt on his lips. Wh[illegible] very good (Uncas, [illegible] haha, Old Nokomis, [illegible] he was bad he was a [illegible]lping, torturing, murdering brute who killed white people just for the heck of it. Good or bad, his extermination was justified, and his like, or his heirs, no longer existed except in the corners of musty cigar stores."

—From *The Road to Wounded Knee*

# The Road to Wounded Knee

Robert Burnette
and
John Koster

RLI: VLM 10 (VLR 8–12)
IL 9–adult

THE ROAD TO WOUNDED KNEE
*A Bantam Book / published June 1974*



*Published simultaneously in the United States and Canada*

*Bantam Books are published by Bantam Books, Inc. Its trademark, consisting of the words "Bantam Books" and the portrayal of a bantam, is registered in the United States Patent Office and in other countries. Marca Registrada. Bantam Books, Inc., 666 Fifth Avenue, New York, New York 10019.*

PRINTED IN THE UNITED STATES OF AMERICA

# Contents

## Acknowledgments

To guess at the number of persons who supplied information for this book would be ludicrous. With apologies to the many people left out owing to loss of memory or lack of space, and excluding members of coauthor Robert Burnette's family, even a partial list of Indian contacts would have to include the following: Hank Adams, Dennis Banks, the late Pedro Bissonette, Leonard Crow Dog, John Eagleshield, the late Lawrence LaMonte (also killed defending his beliefs), his mother, Mrs. Agnes LaMonte, Russell Means, Ted Means, Dale Means, George Mitchell, Ramon Roubideaux, Jeanne Shenandoah, Mark Small, Trudy Tenaya Torres, Harvey Wells, and Tom and Susie Yellowtail. Again, this list is by no means conclusive.

Among white people who provided invaluable assistance, Alvin Josephy, who figures in the story and whose help was invaluable, and Carol Bennett, who introduced the authors to one another and rendered other help, must stand preeminent. E. W. "Doc" McRoberts supplied books, personal experiences, and inspiration. Richard Rainey, Ron Stepneski, and John Walcott helped as couriers; and George Bunting, Mike Sangiovanni, and Daniel R. Holster served as critics and proofreaders.

Among the immediate families, Bea, Sharon, and Cleata Rae Burnette, and Shizuko (Obo) Koster, Mathilde (Strunck) Koster, and John P. Koster, Sr. did yeoman work retyping and proofreading.

Last but by no means least, Jean Highland did what any experienced newsman could only call a superb job of editing. Her blue pencil is one of the few whose results bear a closer resemblance to a magic wand than they do to a plumber's suction cup. In other words, the business could use a lot more like her.

# Introduction: The New Indian Wars

> We have declared war on the United States of America. . . .
>
> —Russell Means, 1972

On 2 November 1972 America and the world woke to news that seemed as incredible as a landing from outer space. A band of American Indians had seized the Bureau of Indian Affairs (BIA) building in Washington, D.C., and was holding it against the massed forces of the greatest power on earth. For the first time since the Indian wars, news about America's forgotten minority was receiving the same prominence as dispatches from Vietnam and the upcoming presidential election.

To add to the confusion, American Indians seemed as divided on the ethics and motives of the take-over as did the general public. Sympathy for the Indians rose as the government threatened violent eviction and militant leaders vowed to die defending their rights. The Department of the Interior did its best to depict its errant wards as an army of vandals, and the government trotted out a string of obedient so-called elected Indian officials who condemned the activists as urban thugs and irresponsible self-styled revolutionaries. But other, responsible Indian and white leaders supported the take-over. It seemed like everyone was an instant expert on the Indian problem. Yet the facts and purposes of the take-over remained as obscure when the protest ended as they had when the first militants charged into the building.

The take-over ended when President Nixon agreed to establish a Special Federal Interagency Task Force to review federal Indian policy and Indian needs. This task force signed an agreement specifying certain measures to be taken. The task force's recommendations, based on information submitted by all interested parties and groups, would be given to the president by 1 June 1973, together with any additional or independent views of the Indian representatives.

Some older Indians, inured to five and six decades of governmental apathy and bungling, thought it was all too good to be true.

They were right.

The federal government violated the agreement before the ink was dry and suddenly introduced a package of seven bills in Congress without consulting any of the Indian people involved in the BIA confrontation. The take-over groups, collectively called "The Trail of Broken Treaties," had another broken treaty to reckon with.

Back at the Pine Ridge reservation in South Dakota, a storm center of Indian activism, nervous BIA officials and the elected tribal leadership were preparing a warm welcome for the Trail of Broken Treaties activists. The tribal officials hated the activists who had tried to upset their applecart and had embarrassed their mentors in the BIA and the Nixon administration. A tribal court order to bar members of the American Indian Movement (AIM), the hard-core activists, from speaking or assembling on the reservation was rushed through the courts, without a random worry that the order was unconstitutional. BIA police arrested two Indians who entered their own reservation to attend a meeting of Oglala Sioux landowners. Such was the status of "law and order" among the tribal officials who tried to brand their opposition as criminal revolutionaries.

Enraged by the mockery of justice, the militants planned drastic means to regain their rights and to topple the government-sanctioned corruption and tyranny of the tribal council and chairman. They were joined by tribal elders who had suffered all their lives at the hands of heartless bureaucrats and who saw a last chance to live—or perhaps to die—with a measure of dignity and self-respect.

Thus in February 1973 a public weary to sickness

after ten years of war in Indochina was faced with the unreal prospect of a guerrilla war in America's heartland, almost in the very shadow of Mount Rushmore, the Shrine of Democracy carved out of a Sioux sacred mountain.

The catalyst came when white police and civic leaders in Custer County, South Dakota, chose to pass off the death of a twenty-year-old Indian boy at a white man's hands as a minor breach of the peace. It was an old, old story in South Dakota, but now there was a new twist. A furious mob of Indians showed up to demand equal justice and ended up burning buildings and battling police in the streets of the fatefully named hamlet of Custer. Two days later, a racial slur in a Rapid City bar set off another rampage in that capital of anti-Indian racism. Whites were beaten and more than forty Indians were jailed.

On 27 February the troubled half-sleep of America's conscience broke into the protracted nightmare of Wounded Knee. Armored personnel carriers (APCs) and self-propelled guns churned through the tall grass around Sacred Heart Church and the Bigfoot Trail, and flares and tracers seared the prairie night. AIM activists and supporters converged on the scene of America's last big massacre of Indians (eighty-three years before) and vowed to change the world or die. Their demands centered on removal of the tribal chairman and a referendum to give the Oglala people a chance to run their own lives again. While old men prayed and young men painted their faces in readiness to die, the public was numb with disbelief.

Armed Indians daring to challenge the might of the United States? War paint in the days of the B-52? Cared for from the cradleboard to the grave by an indulgent Uncle Sam, why would these people rebel? Even as nightly fire fights ripped apart the still darkness of South Dakota, as FBI men were shot and Indians killed and wounded, as real bullets plowed through real flesh and the name Wounded Knee flashed in headlines from Japan to Zambia, the public sat mesmerized as though the whole thing were a rerun of a John Ford western.

In an era of disillusionment with government, the most shocking case study of misfeasance, malfeasance, and nonfeasance remained outside the grasp of most of the American public. There was an instinctive sympathy, a nagging feeling that something was really wrong out there in South Dakota, but the facts remained clouded with the self-serving lies of government flunkies and the sometimes overblown rhetoric of the militants. The truth lurked below the rocky surface of war paint, gunfights, and FBI press releases, stirring the surface like some mythic monster—but all too real. A government that gave lip service to freedom, justice, and equality had denied the first Americans many of the basic rights that secure and preserve these goals.

With no fear of overstatement, it could be said that there was enough corruption in Indian affairs to make the Watergate bugging look like a fraternity stunt.

Because Indian people lack any real political clout, and because ignorance has immobilized even the best-intentioned portion of the public, the nation's lawmakers have seen fit to ignore the rising crescendo of unrest and anger that led to the BIA take-over and Wounded Knee. The same conditions will no doubt lead to greater violence and greater expense if this studied contempt of human rights continues. At the height of the Wounded Knee turmoil, at least ninety different groups were prepared to riot, burn, and even kill if Wounded Knee was crushed by federal forces. "Knowledgeable" white experts may not believe that "their" Indians would resort to wholesale terrorism. But six months before, they wouldn't have believed Wounded Knee was possible.

Since 1890, the facts of Indian life have been studiously, deliberately ignored. Wounded Knee is a result of that blindness.

Pulse readings of Indian outrage, such as protests where the Turtle Mountain Chippewas of North Dakota smashed the presents and Christmas trees of BIA workers because their own Christmas was just another day of freezing and malnutrition, were overlooked, even when repeated year after year.

Few national newspapers or networks paid attention to the long-drawn-out struggle between armed sportsmen and game wardens and the Indians of Washington State.

Ever since the government entered into treaties with the various northwest tribes in 1855, white citizens of the area have pressured the government to stop the Indians from using their traditional methods of netting fish. In many cases, local and state officials, including a barber acting as a part-time justice of the peace, took it upon themselves to violate federal treaties by suppressing the Indians' right to fish for food for their families. Indian "fish-ins" were suppressed with club-swinging brutality, and at least one Indian leader was shot by white thugs who neatly evaded prosecution by claiming that their victim tried to commit suicide.

Few whites had the perspective to appreciate the superb irony. The people who had virtually exterminated the buffalo and dozens of other animals sought to rob the Indians, who lived in harmony with nature, of the 2 percent of the fish harvest they needed to live, while offshore fishermen from Russia and Japan garnered most of the catch with electronic fish-finders and the latest diesel trawlers.

The seizure of Alcatraz by a small group of young Indians in November 1969 created a ripple in the media. There was a brief false dawn of concern for all things Indian—mostly women's fashions made in France or Hong Kong—on the part of professional radicals and radical actresses. By the time the federal government took Alcatraz back by subterfuge in June 1971, the day-trippers of fashionable causes had vanished like the San Francisco fog and the young Indians had nowhere to go. The fact that the island will be turned into an expensive and probably federally funded park instead of a privately funded Indian cultural center hasn't gotten much attention either.

The plea of forty-four elected tribal leaders to President Johnson for an "underdeveloped-nation loan system" was ignored by the press and the White House.

The fact that the public was oblivious to the whole "red power" movement of the early 1960s may explain the nation's shock in 1973. Sensible, intelligent, moderate Indian leaders lived and worked and died in the same obscurity that had attended the careers of such pioneer Indian activists as Dr. Charles Eastman and Carlos Montezuma at the turn of the century. Abbie Hoffman and Mark Rudd became the darlings of the counterculture, while Clyde Warrior and Richard Oakes barely rated notices on obituary pages.

The image of the "Indian" had been defined by dime novelists like Ned Buntline and distilled, bottled, and mass-produced by Hollywood moguls more interested in creating a white success story than mirroring anything related to real history. An Indian was somebody with a gun in his hand, feathers in his hair, and a grunt on his lips. When he was good, he was very, very good (Uncas, Squanto, Hiawatha, Minnehaha, Old Nokomis, Purty Redwing), and when he was bad he was a ravaging, raping, torturing, murdering brute. Good or bad, his extermination was justified and his heirs no longer existed except in the corners of musty cigar stores.

Such was the stereotype a generation was raised on. The Indian of racist mythology was somehow more real than living, starving flesh-and-blood people. The public blithely ignored horrible conditions on Indian reservations while the bitter broth of oppression rose to a boil. The national disgrace has now burst into a raging war against poverty, federally funded graft, corruption of tribal officers with administration funds, and the failure of presidents and congressmen to provide the necessary checks and balances to protect democracy and due process among Indian people.

The people of the United States must finally become acquainted with the conditions under which Indian people are forced to exist. A full and comprehensive treatment must be given to Indian affairs as they really are, with special emphasis on how a misguided and sometimes dictatorial paternalism has affected a race of people already gashed and scarred by two hundred years of betrayal, mass murder, forced removal, and oppression so great that their mere physical survival is little short of a miracle.

Wounded Knee I, in 1890, proved that the United States Army was willing to murder Indians to suppress their religious beliefs and secure their lands. Wounded Knee II, in 1973, proves that Indian people still have courage and faith, and that at least some of them would rather die than submit to another century of disgrace and penury. If any vestige of America's self-respect and national honor is to survive the pitiless scrutiny of history and world opinion, the average citizen must become a student of Indian affairs, so that, through popular demands and due process of law, the American people can salvage the lives of Indian people and the self-respect of all Americans.

Only the American people themselves can tear away the unwarranted pressures, the corrosive policies, and the stifling duress imposed on Indian people by the government, often at the instigation of corporate interests. Only the American people can alter the course of history and replace greed, racism, and corruption with love, honor, justice, and respect.

Despite bitter memories, Indian people believe in the stated dream of America, where the rights to life, liberty, and the pursuit of happiness will become a reality as they were for the first people of this land, before the coming of our white, black, and yellow brothers and sisters.

# 1
# Three Centuries of Genocide

> Tell them at Washington if they have one man who speaks the truth to send him to me, and I will listen to what he has to say.
>
> —Sitting Bull, 1867

"What," asked the reporter, "in your opinion, is the cause of the Indian outbreaks which give you military men so much to do?"

"For the past twelve or fifteen years," replied the captain, "I think the Indian Bureau has been entirely responsible, and the cause has been the enormous pilfering and stealing from the Indians."

"Who has done the most of that stealing?"

"The Indian Agents, undoubtedly. Their acts have created dissatisfaction among the savages which they have been unable to suppress. No agent can save $13,000 or $15,000 annually legitimately out of a salary of $1,500, and yet numbers of them do it. . . . It is this constant robbery which goads them to outbreaks. Treat them well, and they will be all right and make good citizens . . . we should treat the Indian as if he possessed some natural feelings. If that were done and the other reforms carried out, the Indian would soon cease troubling us, and more cheerfully give himself up to the processes of civilization."

Even when Captain Fred Benteen, who had saved what was left of Custer's Seventh Cavalry at the Little Bighorn, was going on record to the *Chicago Times* on 25 January 1879 it was no secret that something was rotten in Indian affairs.

In all fairness, the Bureau of Indian Affairs, founded in 1834, did not invent the practice of plundering and exploiting the American Indian. It merely took over an ancient and dishonorable tradition of legally sanctioned robbery and murder established by the Spaniards, the Dutch, the French, and the British and for over a century and a half, with a sugarcoating of artificial sympathy for the government's hapless Indian wards, rendered the process of land-grabbing and corrupt malfeasance more palatable to white Christian sensibilities.

By the time the BIA was moved to the Department of the Interior from the War Department in 1849, the Indians available for plunder had been considerably diminished. The Spaniards (aided, as always, by jealous Indian rivals), armed with gunpowder, horses, and a splendid disregard for honesty or mercy, had long since crushed the powerful Aztec Empire and strangled the Inca Empire, perhaps the best-governed and least brutal major power in history. The descendants of these conquerors had broken the gentle tribes of California into "mission Indians," converting people who had always lived in freedom into darker, sicklier versions of European serfs.

In Connecticut, the Pilgrim Fathers, aided by Indian allies, surrounded a sleeping Pequot village beside the Mystic River and set the town on fire.

"It was a fearful sight to see them frying in the fire . . . and horrible was the stink and stench thereof. But the victory seemed a sweet sacrifice. . . ." More than five hundred Pequots roasted. It was seventeen years since Squanto had welcomed the first passengers from the *Mayflower*.

Eight years after the Mystic bonfire, the Dutch in New Amsterdam, seeking vengeance for a single killing, lulled a peaceful tribe of Lenni Lenape (Delaware) Indians with promises of protection, then struck by night and shot or hacked to death eighty men, women, and children at Pavonia (Jersey City, New Jersey). Raids on Long Island added forty more unsuspecting Indians to the body count, and an Indian captured near the Hackensack River provided the main attraction for a New Amsterdam holiday. The Indian was publicly skinned in strips and fed with his own flesh while he tried to sing his death song, until, skinned from hands to knees, castrated, and dragged through the dusty streets by his neck, still alive and singing, he was placed on a millstone and his head crushed to a pulp. Dutch women played kickball with other Indian heads brought in from Long Island and New Jersey.

The colonists also urged Indians to kill each other—probably introducing and certainly spreading the custom of scalping by offering bounties for enemy hair. In time of war, the colonists sought Indian allies against other Indians or rival Europeans. All too many Indians shortsightedly believed they could trust whites and so unwittingly played a part in their own decimation. The Cherokees helped a frontier general named Andy Jackson defeat the Red Stick (antiwhite) faction of the Creek tribe and fought for the United States at the Battle of New Orleans. When Andrew Jackson became president, he repaid them by refusing to enforce a Supreme Court decision that would have allowed them to remain in their Georgia homeland and stood by while the Georgia Militia evicted them, with rape and murder, from their homes and drove them on the Trail of Tears. A quarter of the tribe, some four thousand people, died on their way to Oklahoma.

In California, the gold rush of 1849 brought in a swarm of greed-crazed Argonauts who, unlike the Spaniards and Mexicans, had no use for cheap Indian farm labor. They began killing off the small peaceful tribes of California with a callousness and a bloodlust not to be seen again until the era of Hitler and Stalin.

There were an estimated 300,000 Indians in California in A.D. 1500. By 1850, when the miners were pouring in, there were 100,000 left. By 1870, there were some 30,000; by 1880, 20,000; and by 1910, 16,000. Whiskey and disease helped to reduce the population, but thousands upon thousands of these unwarlike people were shot down in cold blood. In one recorded incident, some whites found a steer wounded by Indians, trailed the culprits with hunting dogs, and killed thirty Indian men, women, and children.

"In the cave were some Indian children. Kingsley

could not bear to kill these children with his .56-caliber Spencer rifle. 'It tore them up so bad!' So he did it with his .38-caliber Smith and Wesson revolver."

Many of the Indians who survived as slaves or mine-camp prostitutes were so demoralized by the senseless slaughter that they seemed to die through sheer lack of will to live. Others became hopeless alcoholics. Some fifty tribes were totally exterminated, but few whites of the era felt any sense of loss. As late as 1910, old-timers in California proudly displayed blankets made of dozens of Indian scalps.

The California genocide gives the lie to the frequent assertion that the Indians had to go because they were a menace to the whites. Most of the California tribes were so gentle as to be almost defenseless, yet they suffered the worst slaughter of any Indians in North America, precisely because they were so helpless and because their land was so desirable. When free-lance Indian-killers from California tried the same disorganized murder tactics against the fierce Apaches of Arizona and New Mexico, they were repulsed with heavy losses. The Apaches, who learned early to hate the whites, are probably as numerous today as they ever were.

By 1865, the Indians east of the Mississippi and Missouri rivers and west of the Rockies had been largely subdued or exterminated. Smallpox, tuberculosis, measles, whiskey, and intertribal warfare prompted by white traders had tragically weakened the warrior peoples of the plains and the Southwest. Yet these tribesmen, a tiny remnant of the millions of Indians who had once roamed North America, badly armed and burdened with families to feed, handed down a series of crashing defeats to the U.S. Army and won themselves a place in history that resounds from the West Point Museum down through hundreds of bad pulp novels and racist Hollywood movies. After a sneak attack on a peaceful camp at Sand Creek, where Colorado militiamen under Rev. John Milton Chivington slaughtered over two hundred Indian women and children and mutilated their bodies in ways that can scarcely be believed, the long-suffering Cheyennes and their friends the Sioux took to the warpath and cut Denver off from the rest of the nation for months. Government sources estimate that it cost the United States a million dollars for each Indian killed in this war.

When Col. William Fetterman, an arrogant braggart, boasted that with eighty men he could ride through the whole Sioux Nation, an Oglala Sioux chief named Red Cloud, aided by the young warrior Crazy Horse, saw to it that he had his chance. The army carted pieces of eighty-one white bodies away from what the newspapers called the Fetterman Massacre, and the government decided it was time to sign a peace treaty. They let the Sioux retain a huge reservation including all of South Dakota west of the Missouri River. The Treaty of 1868 was to last as long as the grass should grow and the rivers flow. It lasted eight years.

In 1874, General Custer found gold in the Black Hills, the holy mountains of the Sioux and Cheyennes. When efforts failed to buy the hills for six million dollars, the army was ordered to coerce the Indians into reporting to reservations. A chief named Sitting Bull didn't like the idea.

"I never taught my people to trust Americans. I have told them the truth—that the Americans are great liars. . . . If the Great Spirit had desired me to be a white man he would have made me so in the first place. . . . Each man is good in his sight. It is not necessary for eagles to be crows. Now we are poor but we are free. No white man controls our footsteps. If we must die, we die defending our rights."

Crazy Horse, the greatest warrior leader of the Sioux, put it even more bluntly: "A man does not sell the land on which the people walk."

The army mounted a three-pronged assault, but the prongs became uncoordinated. On 17 June 1876 Crazy Horse struck one prong that was led by Gen. George Crook, and the Indians fought the well-armed troopers and their Crow and Shoshoni allies to a draw. Crook retreated that night. Seven days later, on 25 June, Lieutenant Colonel Custer struck the main Indian camp in a decision that hindsight proved to be foolhardy. And 260 soldiers and about 38 Indians died at the Little Bighorn, which became one of the best-known battles in American history.

Unable to feed their forces, the Indians had to split up, and the outraged army beat each group separately. Sitting Bull took his band to Canada and stayed for five years, until hunger drove him to surrender. Crazy Horse, never defeated in battle, gave up because of dissension and starvation. Army and BIA officials, together with a few jealous chiefs, organized a plot to discredit him, and he was murdered while resisting arrest at Fort Robinson, Nebraska, on 5 September 1877.

It was this last gasp of Indian resistance that won the beleaguered tribes the respect of many of their adversaries. Contrasting the courage of the Indians, their skill at arms, and their loyalty to their spoken word against the naked greed, the perfidy and cowardice, and the bigotry of most of the white frontiersmen and land speculators, General Crook was forced to observe, "Greed and avarice on the part of the whites—in other words, the almighty dollar, is at the bottom of nine-tenths of all our Indian troubles. I have never yet seen [an Indian] so demoralized that he was not an example in honor and nobility compared to the wretches who plunder him of the little our government appropriates for him."

After the army had done its work, the BIA took over. The plains wars were the first in which the Indian agents became prominent. As part of the government policy, *agencies* had been established for the various tribes, often arbitrarily and without the consent of the majority of the Indians. Violence was done to the structure of Indian tribal leadership even before the wars began. The whites—soldiers and agents alike—had no concept of Indian government, which, on the plains, was one of almost total democracy, and they tried to substitute a more "American" form of government by creating, without the Indians' consent, a single head chief over all the Sioux. A few years after Bear-That-Scatters-His-Enemies was designated for this honor, he was gunned down by white soldiers in a regrettable misunderstanding.

From that time forward—the year was 1854—a

sharp division split the Indian world. Those Indians who trusted whites or sought their help came to be called *friendlies* by the whites or *loaf-around-the-forts* by the other Indians. The free Indians, who held to their own traditions and hunted for a living instead of begging were lumped together and called *hostiles* by the whites. Captain Benteen dryly dubbed them *self-supporters,* which is probably more accurate. Loaf-around-the-fort implied laziness and a certain lack of morality related to drunkenness, petty thievery, and occasional prostitution.

"If I were an Indian," Custer observed in an otherwise racist and inaccurate book, *My Life on the Plains,* "I would greatly prefer to cast my lot among those of my people who adhered to the free open plains rather than submit to the confined limits of a reservation, there to be the recipient of the blessed benefits of civilization, with its vices thrown in without stint or measure."

Yet confined the Indians were, by Custer's successors, and it was then that the BIA, now completely in charge, took over the role of cultural assassin formerly practiced by colonists and soldiers. The control of the tribes passed to Indian agents—called "Major" even if they had never worn the uniform—and white bureaucracy took charge of every facet of Indian life.

Indian agents came in three general types: thieves, religious fanatics, and men of goodwill and decent impulses. The last category was by far the smallest.

Of the thieves, on whom Captain Benteen waxed eloquent, much has been said even in John Ford westerns. During the administration of President Ulysses S. Grant, a scandal involving the sale of post traderships rocked the cabinet and led to the resignation (to avoid prosecution) of W. W. Belknap, the secretary of war. Post traders were at this time appointed by the War Department rather than the Department of the Interior, which was by then the BIA's parent department, and the traders and BIA agents had long been in collusion. Agents who sincerely wanted to be rich, as most did, would reroute goods intended for the Indians to the post traders, who substituted shoddy merchandise and then sold the government supplies on the open market at a handsome profit. The agents also forced the Indians to pay all debts—legitimate or otherwise—to the post traders, and protected their friends' monopolies by refusing the Indians permission to shop elsewhere. Post traders gouged their helpless red consumers with ridiculous prices—around 1900, one educated Indian complained of paying fifty cents for a common sewing needle. (You could get a pretty good meal for fifty cents in 1900.) Salt or sugar was mixed with sand, flour was cut with sawdust, and cows (that no Indian ever saw) were recorded on the beef ration books. Some wags said that the post traders threw rations for the Indians through a ladder and the Indians got whatever stuck to the rungs. Thus did the first Americans learn about the glories of the free enterprise system.

The religious-fanatic or utopian agents were often equally destructive in their blind insistence that their way—religious, social, economic—was right for everybody. When the agent for the Utes, Nathan Meeker, author of a utopian novel, threatened to shoot the tribes' horses, the better to turn the Indians into farmers and merchants, the Utes panicked. Meeker and his male assistants were gunned down, his elderly wife and his daughter raped; soldiers were called in and a pitched battle was fought. In the end, the Utes were evicted from much of their best land, to the delight of the surrounding whites who wanted the mineral rights.

Sincerely religious whites, like Episcopal bishop Henry Whipple and Catholic father Jean de Smet made real contributions to saving the Indians from genocide. But many of their contemporaries and coreligionists, more interested in saving souls than lives, often let the "heathen" Indians go hungry and chose to feed only their own converts when food ran low. Such an agent, John Miles, triggered the doomed flight of the Northern Cheyennes from their pestilential Oklahoma reservation to their homeland in Montana. For five months the three hundred Indians—less than a third of them fighting men—eluded the entire U.S. Army of twelve thousand men until starvation and exhaustion compelled some of them to surrender at Fort Robinson, scene of Crazy Horse's murder. To coerce them into obedience, the Cheyennes were confined to unheated barracks without food or water for five days. On the fifth night, they drew their handful of concealed guns and knives from under the floorboards and charged out to die, fighting, in the sub-zero Nebraska snow. The soldiers killed or wounded sixty-eight of them, mostly women and children, on the spot and tracked twenty-three others to a buffalo wallow where they shot them to pieces in an all-day gunfight. But their unparalleled courage and suffering, and the fact that they had avoided unnecessary killing of whites when they raided ranches for food and horses, won the survivors a small reservation in the Montana country they loved.

Truly good agents were rare. Tom Jeffords and John Clum, agents to the Apaches, and Thomas Twiss, who worked with the Sioux and Cheyenne, were among the best, but even the best were part of a bad system and were bound up almost to impotence in its toils.

The primary objective of BIA policy at this time was to obliterate the traditional Indian culture and religions. Religious rituals like the Sun Dance, the traditional funerals, and the giveaway were forbidden, in flagrant violation of constitutional guarantees. Indian children were separated from their families and shipped from South Dakota or New Mexico to Carlisle Barracks in Pennsylvania, where the death rate of students sometimes excelled that of children on disease-ridden, malnourished reservations. Tribal chiefs of proven ability were ignored, and whatever influence they had, for good or ill, was subverted by every means possible. Utilizing the high status that plains tribes accorded to young men bearing arms, *Indian police* were signed on from the ranks of young men willing to trade their loyalty to their people for the privilege of a blue coat with brass buttons and a surplus carbine. Thus died the tradition of rotating the warrior societies acting as police for the tribes. A centralized police force led to a concentration of power and thus to corruption.

The Indian police, not the army, murdered Sitting

Bull, last of the great warrior chiefs—not as has been charged, because he was a leader of the Ghost Dance of 1890 (he was not), but because he had the courage and the political clout to oppose the agent, James McLaughlin, who was striving diligently to uproot Indian culture. Sitting Bull, medicine man and polygamist, was the living negation of the sort of Indian McLaughlin wanted to create; but more than this, he had rallied the tribe against the Dawes Severalty Act of 1887.

There was a final act of the tragedy, and several minor epilogues, before the army relinquished responsibility for the destruction of the Indians to the BIA.

Panicked at the news of Sitting Bull's murder, a band of about three hundred Sioux under Chief Big Foot fled their reservation. Some of these Indians were believers in the so-called Ghost Dance religion, a fusion of Christianity and Indian spiritism that preached the return of the buffalo and the spirits of dead Indians and a sort of earthly paradise where the white man would have no place. The Ghost Dance cult was peaceful, but nervous frontier whites interpreted the strange trance dances as a resurgence of Indian militarism. When the Ghost Dance started at his reservation, D. F. Royer, the cowardly young agent at Pine Ridge, began to send hysterical telegrams to Washington asking for help. When Big Foot's band bolted, the Seventh Cavalry was sent to bring them in.

The cavalry, some six hundred men with four Hotchkiss quick-firing cannons, apprehended the fleeing Sioux and marched them to a place called Wounded Knee. The soldiers gave the Indians food and rendered medical aid to Big Foot, who was dying of pneumonia. But they also searched the captured Sioux for weapons.

The morning after the Indians' capture, 29 December 1890, another search for weapons began. According to the army version, two young Indians refused to give up their new Winchesters. According to most Indians, the army began to fire rifles and cannons without provocation.

The "battle" that followed the first wild shots was one-sided and brief. A handful of Indian warriors pulled concealed weapons or wrested arms from soldiers and put up a courageous fight while the women and children fled screaming across the frozen prairie. Most of the men were dead within minutes. Troopers pursued the women and children for two and three miles, firing point-blank at their backs. Many bodies were discovered with shawls pulled over their heads, showing that the exhausted women had knelt waiting for execution until the soldiers shot them in the backs of the heads. On the field, one trooper watched in shock as an eighteen-year-old girl vomited blood like a pump.

As the firing died, some of the soldiers were horrified at what they had done. Others later expressed pride at their role in the battle, although few admitted to killing women and babies. The army gathered up forty-seven badly injured survivors, including a baby with an American flag beaded on her hat, and left the dead to freeze into grotesque shapes as a blizzard closed the scene off from view. Three days later, the troopers returned and heaved the frozen carcasses into a mass grave. There were 146 bodies, more than half of them noncombatants. Only a handful of Indians had escaped.

The outraged Sioux struck back and a thirty-two-day war ensued, largely between the renowned Seventh Cavalry and the vengeful Indians. At one point, during the skirmish at Drexel Mission, the cavalry were so hard-pressed that only reinforcements from the black soldiers of the Ninth Cavalry enabled them to stand their ground. Eventually, resistance flickered out and the last Sioux holdouts trickled in from the badlands and surrendered.

Controversy raged about Wounded Knee for years. Critics charged that the Seventh Cavalry's lust for revenge of the Custer battle had motivated a wholesale slaughter of innocents. The army—with dissent from some men of conscience—maintained that the Indians had started the fight and that the cavalry had nothing to apologize for.

Accident or conspiracy, the brutal killing of women and children had the effect of crushing armed resistance by the tribes. But there were occasional flashes of the warrior spirit through the next two decades. In 1894, two young Cheyennes, Head Chief and Young Mule, shot a white rancher who had insulted them and then rode out to a rendezvous with death in which they charged a whole regiment of cavalry and were shot to pieces. In 1911, a band of Shoshonis got into a fight with some white cattlemen in Nevada and killed several whites. An irate posse moved in and took on the outnumbered Shoshonis, who turned to their bows when they ran out of bullets. The last of the Shoshonis mounted a suicide charge against the heavily armed vigilantes and were gunned down. A young girl and two children were the only survivors of the band.

The last Indian war took place in 1915. A young Ute named Tis-ne-gat was charged, on very conflicting evidence, with the unsolved murder of a Mexican sheepherder. When his father, a minor chief, refused to surrender Tis-ne-gat for trial, a posse of drunken cowboys surrounded the Ute camp and opened fire. Three Indians were killed, but a counterattack by another Indian band left several whites dead and the rest fleeing in terror. Gen. Hugh Scott was called out of retirement and eventually talked Tis-ne-gat into surrendering. The young Ute was acquitted after a sensational trial during which he received several letters containing proposals of marriage from white women. He returned to his tribe and died of tuberculosis a few years later.

These last flickers of resistance cast no glow into the dark night of the Indian who now had to contend with the BIA and its confusing but lethal tactics of spiritual and cultural genocide.

BIA tactics were based on a double-headed assumption: first, that white civilization was so incomparably superior to Indian or any other culture that the destruction of Indian culture was a favor to the Indians; second, that the Indians—"the vanishing Americans"—were doomed by some pitiless fate to disappear anyway, so there was no point in stopgap measures to help them adjust to the loss of their way of life. The late nineteenth century was the heyday of social Darwinism, when some philosophers saw charity of any kind as an untoward interference with evolution. The idea that a whole culture, even a whole race, should be allowed to perish was not repugnant to a sizable proportion of the men in decision-making capacities—an instructive example of pseudoscience as a justification for genocide that would crop up later in Nazi Germany or Stalinist Russia and China. When Helen Hunt Jackson, a spiritualist, Civil War widow, and close friend of Emily Dickinson, wrote an honest but polemic book on Indian abuse—*A Century of Dishonor*—she was roundly attacked by Theodore Roosevelt, the quintessential social Darwinist, who said, in part, "To consider the dozen squalid savages who hunted at long intervals over a territory of a thousand square miles as owning it outright necessarily implies a similar recognition of the claims of every white hunter, squatter, horse-thief, or wandering cattleman. . . . We undoubtedly ought to break up the great Indian reservations, disregard the tribal governments. . . . there has been little willful wrong-doing. . . ."

These two attitudes from the 1880s, fused together, have come to characterize all subsequent dealings with Indians. Officials nowadays usually talk like Helen Hunt Jackson while they act in the spirit of Theodore Roosevelt. Yet the work of Helen Hunt Jackson, George Crook, and such early Indian activists as Dr. Charles Eastman and Carlos Montezuma had some results. A cult of the romanticized red man, the noble savage, Longfellow's Hiawatha, or James Fenimore Cooper's Uncas had grown up in the East simultaneously with the cult of extermination that held favor farther west. Many white do-gooders who had worked for the abolition of slavery before 1865 wanted to "do something" for the Indian. Whether the something they wanted to do was always in the Indians' best interest is arguable. Still, it took real guts, even for a national institution like Longfellow, to write the following shortly after Custer's Last Stand:

> Whose was the right and the wrong?
> Sing it, O funeral song,
> With a voice that is full of tears.
> And say that OUR broken faith

Wrought all this ruin and scathe
In the year of a hundred years.*

Between 1890 and 1920, the long-predicted disappearance of the red race, wept over by eastern sentimentalists and fervently hoped for by many frontiersmen, seemed to be approaching. Even after the shooting stopped, infectious diseases continued. Before the white man came, the Indians had been literally free from disease, except for arthritis and cancer, according to skeletal evidence and native tradition, and their resistance to disease was almost nonexistent. Smallpox contracted from fishermen paved the way for the Pilgrims by nearly wiping out the New England tribes before the *Mayflower* landed. It winnowed the Mandans down from 1,500 people to less than 150 in 1837, cut the Cheyenne tribe in half, decimated the Sioux and the Blackfeet. Diseases that whites passed off with a few days in bed, like measles, were usually fatal to Indians. With reservations came crowding into small, overheated log huts, and tuberculosis followed close behind. Many Indians who had survived the cavalry saw their children die, one by one, from the coughing sickness. A probably spurious figure states that there were only 44,000 Indians left in the United States by 1876. When a Division of Medical Assistance was finally established, the official census figure read 250,000 Indians. A decade later, at the end of World War I, the flu epidemic swept through Indian country like the Grim Reaper's scythe. Indians believe it killed more of them, proportionately, than any other race.

Yet after 1920 the Indian birthrate began to exceed the outrageously high death rate by a strong margin and the impending disappearance of the Indian was relegated to the realm of myth.

In 1924, Indians were declared citizens, largely as a reward for their services in World War I, when 6,509 Indians were inducted from reservations, despite treaties forbidding them to ever take up arms again, and

*From "The Revenge of Rain-In-The-Face," by Henry Wadsworth Longfellow.

only 228 claimed deferments. In 1926, a congressional survey disclosed widespread poverty, early mortality, abysmal education—in essence, the same disclosure one would find today, but somewhat more extreme. In 1934, the Indian Reorganization Act (IRA) pushed through a Congress conditioned by the depression to extreme measures, supposedly gave the tribes back a measure of self-government, prohibited further allotment of tribal lands, gave the Indians a chance to redeem surplus government lands, and made funds available for education from a revolving credit program. This landmark decision helped move most of the reservations from the concentration-camp level to the very bottom of the poverty bracket. Ultimately, Indian holdings increased by 3 million acres—a drop in the bucket next to the losses from the Dawes Severalty Act, but a step in the right direction. But in 1942, under the same president, five hundred square miles were lopped off the Pine Ridge reservation to create a practice bombing range and the Indian residents were evacuated, sometimes under tongue-in-cheek threat of air attack. The return of the land at the end of the war was guaranteed, but thirty years later the land was still in government possession.

In 1946, the government set up an Indian Claims Commission to administer repayment to Indians who could prove they'd been swindled. One of the first cases was the Sioux Pony Claims, in which Indians who had turned over their horses to the army in 1876 were paid. There were three claimants left alive.

Under the IRA, the once all-powerful agent was pushed from his dictatorial position in favor, usually, of a chairman-council form of elective government. For the first time in fifty years the Indians were allowed to pick their own leaders. This was a radical change from the traditional tribal government which had total democracy in council, advised by a smaller council of wise elders who had to agree unanimously on every decision and even then could not force their decisions on any adult male. Built into the BIA's chairman-council system were all the weaknesses, but none of the strengths, of local government in middle America. The white agent was retained in the form of the *superintendent,* a white BIA appointee who holds veto power over tribal finances. Through the superintendent, the BIA could still tell the Indian people how many cows they could buy or sell, how much timber they could cut, and what their school curricula should be. There was no system of checks and balances, no procedure through which inequities could be righted. It was a blueprint for elected tyranny.

World War II was partly responsible for producing the first generation of Indians who were wise in the ways of white society, fairly well educated, and articulate rather than shy or sullen in the presence of whites. More than twenty-five thousand Indians, one out of every three males between eighteen and fifty, enlisted or was drafted. A disproportionate number were marines, paratroopers, or other combat soldiers, and they received far more medals per capita than the whites. The enforced closeness with whites for three and four years, the stresses of combat and loneliness, produced an understanding in the young Indians that many whites were not totally vicious or devoid of all decency and produced a new optimism that constructive activism might help Indians. In November 1944 the National Congress of American Indians (NCAI) was formed to act as a watchdog over Congress and to protect the tribes against legislation aimed at them from Washington. A generation later, in August 1961, Indian college students formed the National Indian Youth Council (NIYC), a group aimed at preserving and restoring their Indian heritage.

But the 1950s brought a two-headed monster to threaten the first fruits of the struggle for survival. Two government programs hatched in Washington and fostered by the BIA led to great disruption and fear in Indian country.

The first of these gorgons was the program called *termination.* Briefly, termination meant that the government would end its special relationship with a certain tribe, thus cutting off medical services, educational and other funding, and making land taxable. This was tried twice, under protest, against the Klamath and

Menominee tribes, and in both cases it reduced people who were nearly self-sufficient to the welfare level in a matter of a few years. Strenuous opposition by every faction of the Indian population and by friendly whites (including the Daughters of the American Revolution) prevented this destruction from falling on the heads of the Florida Seminoles (80 percent illiterate) or the Turtle Mountain Chippewas of North Dakota.

Not only was termination cruel and unusual punishment, it was a violation of the spirit and letter of the nations' 371 treaties. Actual termination ceased, but the threat of it was used to bludgeon recalcitrant tribes into line if they tried to "buck the bureau."

The second monster turned out to be a Frankenstein which ultimately turned on the BIA and rended it. This was the program known as *relocation*. Oddly enough, the name was borrowed from World War II, when 110,000 Japanese-Americans were forcibly removed from their homes on the West Coast and dumped in desert prison camps, from which the younger men were later drafted to fight for freedom. Even the names were the same. Dillon Myer, who headed up the War Relocation Office, became BIA commissioner just in time for Indian relocation, when Indians were recruited from the deserts and dumped in the cities. An Indian would apply to go to the city and the BIA would supply him with funds for transportation and a few weeks lodging and possibly enroll him in some sort of vocational course. No provisions were made for the confusion, the culture shock, or the almost inevitable job layoffs. Most Indians who sought relocation were the poorest and worst educated of the nation's poorest and worst-educated minority group. After half a century of more or less continuous unemployment, telling time by the sun, and living on surplus food commodities and whatever they could grow or shoot, they had little concept of a money economy and none whatever of punctuality. With no salable skills and no ethnic clout, jobs were hard to get, harder to keep. And the very name "Indian" connected to a large, dark, solemn male conjured up the worst terrors Hollywood could imagine for half-educated prospective employers. Too proud to humble themselves, too feared to be accepted, sometimes too shy even to ask directions in the street, Indians found that unemployment in the city was as prevalent, and far more cruel, than on the reservation. Within a few years of the beginning of relocation, Indian skid rows and slums had sprung up in Los Angeles and Seattle, Chicago and Cleveland, Minneapolis and Saint Paul, and San Francisco.

Relocation was a disaster from the Indian viewpoint, but very popular with the BIA. By 1970, somewhere between one-third and one-half of the Indians in America lived off the reservation.

"The relocation program only wants Indians from 18 to 35," said a Sioux relocated from Pine Ridge to Cleveland. "The old people can die on the reservation, but they want the young ones to move to the city, intermarry, forget their traditions, and disappear. It's another subtle form of genocide."

The relocation plan, aimed, Indians said, at destroying the tribes, had the effect instead of destroying the basic conservatism of the tribal Indians, with their often stifling tribal governments and menacing white superintendents. Urban Indians, out from under the BIA's thumb, became not only activist but downright militant. Leaders rose up who helped create a distinctive subculture, one part urban and one part Indian: shouts of "Right on!" and clenched-fist salutes combined with cowboy boots, beadwork, and Indian religion. Freed from threats of legal termination, the urban Indians had more to gain and less to lose by activism than their brothers or fathers on the reservation. And exposure to black and student radicals showed them that defiance was more apt to end in government concessions than in wholesale massacres or even mass arrests.

By the early 1960s, the Indians were no longer helpless victims and, on reservations and in cities, a new generation was preparing to renew the struggle against the destructive elements of white society centered in and symbolized by the BIA.

# 2
# The Rebirth of Indian Religion

> In sorrow I am sending a feeble voice, O Six Powers of the World. Hear me in my sorrow, for I may never call again. O make my people live!
>
> —Black Elk

The American Indian today is a product of history and of the disruptive elements of modern society. Federal policies—from the signing of the Constitution down to the present day—can be said to legislate his every waking action, for good, or, more frequently, for ill. Every behavioral problem among Indians, from alcoholism and apathy to poor school performance, suspicion of outsiders, and the recent clash of arms against the United States, can be traced directly to mismanagement and abuse meted out by the federal government and other segments of the white power structure.

Two facts show how far apart the experience of the Indian has set him: only the Indian, of all Americans, has ever been subjected to a conscious and stated policy of genocide by the United States government; and only the Indian, of all Americans, has been denied freedom of religion and suffered relentless persecution at the hands of the government or with their enthusiastic approval.

Indian religion bore the brunt of the general attack on Indian culture. There are on file orders from the Department of the Army and the Department of the Interior authorizing soldiers and agents to destroy every vestige of Indian religion, that is, to destroy the Indian's whole view of the world and his place in the universe. The spiritual leaders and healers known to the whites as "medicine men" were the focal point of this persecution, because they were the bearers of the Indian religion, the transmitters of oral tradition and ritual, and because their lives were living proof of the powers the Almighty conferred on Indian people.

The Indian's deep spirituality, permeating his life, is the key to his whole being. Early missionaries, steeped in the morbid theology of New England and in Calvinistic theories of predestination (presalvation and predamnation, so to speak), looked at the evidence of Indian spiritual power and imagined that the medicine men were minions of Satan. To the Puritan mind this justified any form of persecution. When materialism came to dominate even the religious thought of the nineteenth and twentieth centuries, and the white man's own beliefs became so nebulous as to be almost impotent, it was easier to attribute the powers of the medicine men to trickery and to discredit them as charlatans.

Only recently, with advances in parapsychology or psychical research, is it possible to postulate that Indian religion may be based on fact. The white man's recent preoccupation with the rape of the environment has already made it clear that the Indian's religion, through which he was brought into harmony with all living things, is theology of a high order. Close scrutiny of the Sioux belief, among many others, will refute the fact that Indians are "pagan savages."

Among most surviving tribes, Indian belief has actually grown stronger. One probable reason is that Indian religion relies on valid proof, rather than on a faith that is seemingly contradicted by science.

In Montana, there lives a tall, lean, handsome man who serves as a testimony to the powers that God Almighty has passed down to man through the loving heart and body of a Sioux medicine man.

For years, this man withered away, finally reduced to a mass of painful tissue. His muscles drew up and tightened until he was a helpless cripple in a wheelchair. In an effort to regain his health, he began to sell the cattle from his herd of five hundred, and he consulted the best doctors in Chicago, Minneapolis, and at the Mayo Clinic. But modern medicine could only administer drugs to kill the pain for short intervals, and he remained immobile and suffering.

Without his knowledge, his wife arranged a ceremony with a Sioux medicine man at the home of one of her relatives. She pleaded with her husband to attend, but he scoffed and said that no one could help him, he'd gone broke visiting the best doctors in the country. Deeply hurt at his outburst, she began to weep as only a grieving Indian wife can until he was overcome with sympathy for her and he agreed.

That evening she pushed his wheelchair into the house, glowing with faith. Because he knew nothing of the Sioux religion, he himself held no belief or faith in any miracle. He had given up all hope and looked forward to his final rest so that he would no longer burden his family.

The ceremony begins, in total darkness, with a beautiful Sioux song known as the "Entering Song," a prayer to Tunkashila (Grandfather), one of the Sioux names for the Almighty. The words ask Grandfather to send forth messengers from the spirit world to help the medicine man, who regards himself only as a tool for the use of the Almighty. As the song continues, one feels the presence of something far greater than man. Suddenly, tiny lights appear and begin to flicker in the darkness, first to the Heavens, then to Mother Earth, then to the East, West, South, and North, the four directions through which the changing seasons work the will of the Almighty. Sometimes the tiny lights, which are spirits, seize the drum and lift it to the ceiling, beating on it in harmony with the gourd rattles of the medicine man.

After the "Entering Song," the medicine man offers a prayer of thanksgiving for the Almighty's gifts to his people. He asks those present why they have asked Wakan Tanka (Great Spirit or Great Mysterious One) for help.

At the ceremony, the wife of the crippled rancher prayed to the Great Spirit, asking him to heal her man and promising to give thanks as is proper with Indian people. All the other relatives followed with a prayer for his well-being. The medicine man and his helpers then sang a prayer asking for the Great Spirit's directions in healing the man.

As the medicine man's song ended, all was silent. Only the hooting of owls and the cries of the coyotes could be heard. The silence was broken by the medicine man, who said, through an interpreter, that he would treat this man. Within thirty days, the medicine man said, the rancher would be loading heavy bales of hay onto a flatcar in a nearby town.

Racked with pain, the rancher nearly laughed out loud. He stifled the bitter laugh for fear of hurting his wife, who held such great faith in the Sioux religion.

Because of his desire to please his wife, he allowed the medicine man to treat him. To his amazement, his body began to respond to his brain impulses.

Twenty days later, he was loading bales of alfalfa on the train. Today, at seventy, he looks and acts like a man of forty-five, with no visible signs of ever having been a cripple. And, as an Indian who loves life, he never fails to stop on the hills near his ranch in the Bighorn Mountains to smoke a cigarette as a tobacco offering while praying the Indian prayer to the Heavens, Mother Earth, East, West, South, and North, for these directions represent the world that the Great Spirit has given to the Indian people and to their brothers, humans and animals, who live in this universe.

This religion, which Indian people naturally find so beautiful and good, is feared by many so-called Christians who will not admit that the miracles of the Great Spirit are the same for the Indian as for the white man. Some Christians have finally come to admit that the Almighty will aid the Indian, but many of them have brought discredit on their own beliefs by persecuting others.

One man who finally achieved tolerance was C. R. Whitlock, agency superintendent on the Rosebud Sioux reservation in South Dakota. For years, Whitlock, a faithful Episcopal churchman, ridiculed the leading medicine man—a tall, dignified Sioux called Chips. Like most medicine men, Chips wore his hair in long braids and devoted his life to helping Indian people. He continued to practice his religion despite arrest. No one ever told him that the United States Constitution guaranteed his freedom of religion and speech. In the days of the 1930s, the superintendents ruled their reservations like half-pint Hitlers and administered "justice" as they saw fit. The BIA had openly promulgated a law called the "Indian Offenses Act" forbidding the practice of Sioux religion and of the rites of the Native American Church, better known as the Peyote Church, which is a fusion of Christian and Indian beliefs. Any Indian who practiced either religion could be sentenced up to six months in jail or fined $360, more than most Indians' yearly incomes in those times.

Despite harassment from Whitlock and ridicule from other whites and those Indians who had sold out their culture, Chips kept up the old ceremonies. On one occasion, he gave the white superintendent an example of the power of Indian religion.

A little girl from the Kills Enemy family slipped and fell into the Little White River when it was swollen from the spring rains. Her grieving relatives were unable to locate her body and asked the agent for help.

Whitlock took this as an opportunity to prove that Chips and his religion were poppycock, so he ordered his Indian police to bring in the medicine man. With thinly veiled contempt, Whitlock offered to provide all the necessary ingredients for an Indian ceremony, thus violating the law himself. He wanted the ritual held in his office. When Chips agreed, Whitlock was sure he had trapped the man that many of the Sioux had in reverence. In the darkened BIA office, Chips performed a ceremony to find the child's body.

Whitlock was told that in two days a dog would bark at something from the river's edge, and a man with a cigar in his mouth would look up from raking his garden and go to investigate. The man would see a colored object floating toward the shore where he stood, and he would wade out to hook the object which would be the clothing of the drowned little girl.

The agent laughed with glee trudging home from the

ceremony. He could visualize exposing Chips as a fake before the whole Sioux Nation and dealing the Indian beliefs a blow from which they might never recover.

Two days later, Whitlock picked up his telephone to hear Mr. Steth, a teacher at the Soldier Creek Day School recite Chips's very description of discovering the little body.

Stunned, but still not convinced, Whitlock jumped at the chance when another drowning occurred. An Indian named Miller, just returned from the army, disappeared. After days of searching, his uniform was found beside the river, with the shoes missing.

Again the police hauled Chips in to perform his ceremony. Chips told Whitlock to have all the men return to the site of the drowning and to drag the north side of the river. He said before sundown a man would scream as he pulled one foot out of the water after hooking the shoe.

The next day, the superintendent personally supervised the search. As predicted, a man screamed as the body was found by the hooking of an army shoe.

Whitlock stopped scoffing and began to ask Chips seriously for advice. On many occasions he sent other whites to Chips for help.

Bizarre as these stories sound to whites who live in a world of rationalism and materialism, anyone who has spent time among Indians has heard stories like them, and most white friends come to accept their validity. Before the attempts to suppress Indian religion, they were even more common.

Students of military history and frontier lore are familiar with the story of Sitting Bull's vision before the Little Bighorn fight. While fasting and praying as part of the Sun Dance ritual, Sitting Bull lapsed into unconsciousness and saw, as in a dream, bluecoat soldiers and enemy Indian scouts falling into camp upside down—meaning that they were to die. At the same time, he heard a voice that said, "I give you these because they have no ears." The vision came true when Custer refused to listen (had no ears) as his Crow scouts told him the camp at the Little Bighorn was too big to attack. Contemptuous of both the hostile Sioux and Cheyenne and his own Crow scouts' advice, he attacked and was wiped out.

A less well-known story shows how important the supernormal or psychic world was to Indians. On the evening of 25 June, the day of Custer's downfall, Gen. George Crook noticed that his Indian scouts were restless and nervous, almost on the verge of dissension. He asked them what the trouble was. At first they refused to answer, but, after he appealed to their loyalty and friendship, one leader told him matter-of-factly, "Yellow Hair Custer and all his soldiers, every one, were killed on the Little Bighorn this morning."

Writers have tried to explain this incident away, but Crook told the story so many times that there can be little doubt that he was impressed with it.

Capt. William Philo Clark, one of Crook's aides, called White Hat by the Sioux, was a hardheaded army officer and a pioneer anthropologist who wrote the classic book on Plains Indian sign language. Clark heard and repeated many stories of warriors killed on the warpath who would return, in spirit, to tell their wives or mothers of their deaths.*

In 1877 Capt. John G. Bourke, another of Crook's aides, conducted a scientific ESP test. He asked a medicine man named Sorrel Horse to guess the faces of concealed playing cards while the Indian was in a sort of trance. Sorrel Horse obliged, calling out "squaw" (queen) and forming his fingers into a diamond to indicate the queen of diamonds. In quick succession he called off several other cards, getting each one right.

Bourke, Clark, and Col. Homer Wheeler all recorded cases where wounded Indians pronounced beyond hope by army surgeons were saved by medicine men, or where limbs that doctors recommended for amputation recovered and were once more strong and

---

*Indian people also believe in ghosts (*wanigi* in Sioux), usually said to be souls not yet ready to pass into the afterlife. Ghosts are said to be able to paralyze the side of a person's face if he angers them.

useful. Part of this Indian resilience can be attributed to the natural diet rich in protein and vitamins, but Indian medicine, then as now, obviously worked some wonders.

The ceremony Chips performed for Whitlock can also be used for healing, as in the case of the Montana rancher. This ceremony, called *yuwipi,* is probably one of the oldest of the Sioux rituals. The preparations for it are a good introduction to Sioux religion.

*Yuwipi* begins when a relative of the sick person sends a sacred pipe to the medicine man to ask for a ceremony. This pipe, which whites often call the peace pipe, is the most important sacramental object in Sioux belief.

Long ago, in the dawn of the world, White Buffalo Calf Woman brought the sacred pipe to the Indian people. One of the oldest Sioux stories tells of how two warriors roaming the plains met a mysterious and beautiful woman carrying a pipe, the first that they had seen. One warrior approached her with lecherous desires and vanished into a cloud of smoke around the woman. The cloud blew away and revealed only his skeleton crawling with worms at the strange woman's feet. The second man approached the woman with respect and awe and led her to his people. She gave the people the sacred pipe and then walked away from them out on the prairie. Before the eyes of the assembled people, she turned into a young buffalo and ran away.

Before White Buffalo Calf Woman left the people, she taught them that all things created by the Almighty are sacred. Men and women, animals and birds, trees and grass and rocks all have a sacred essence. Thus when an Indian prays with the sacred pipe, he prays for all creation. Indian believers say that the original sacred pipe has been preserved by the Sioux people. Stories are still told about this pipe's great powers. When the Calf Pipe was unwrapped and displayed at a religious meeting in 1973, the dozens of Indian people present saw a little white cloud come out of a clear blue sky and stand over the medicine tipi for ten or fifteen minutes, as if it were standing guard over the Calf Pipe and the people. Then the cloud moved calmly and purposefully away.

A sacred pipe is smoked by the medicine man before he agrees to perform the *yuwipi* ceremony. The relatives then tell him the sufferer's name and where the ceremony is to take place.

Before the ceremony, the medicine man must prepare himself to communicate with the Almighty. To cleanse body and soul, the medicine man kindles a fire under selected rocks, which are then placed in an *inipi,* or sweat lodge, a little dome tent made of a tree limb framework covered with robes or quilts. Cold water is poured over the heated rocks, flooding the tent with steam. These sweat baths are often used for health reasons, but medicine men and others about to undergo a ceremony invariably begin with a steam bath that includes a prayer ceremony.

The *yuwipi* ceremony takes place after the sweat bath. The ceremony is always held at night, in a darkened house. In a modern home, the windows are closed and covered with heavy drapes or blankets to ensure total darkness. Art works or appliances are removed from the room, and people taking part in the ceremony remove their watches and jewelry, to show humility.

On the floor, what white people would call an altar is consecrated. Four small flagpoles are erected and four strips of colored cloth are tied to the poles. The flags symbolize the four directions, or Four Powers of the world. Each direction represents a race of man, a color, and a power of life. The North, whose color is white, represents the cleansing snow and ice power that puts the earth to sleep in the winter; the East, whose color is red, is the power of birth, the land where the sun is born every day; the South, whose color is yellow, is the direction of generation and reproductive power, the land from which summer comes north every year; the West, whose color is black, is the land of spirit power and of what we call death, although Indians recognize death as merely another point in the circle of the world and not as an end.

These four directions, the Mother Earth, and the Father Sun are the Six Powers of the world, which are really one power, the Power of the Almighty.

During the *yuwipi* ceremony, the four flagpoles are bound with a rope that holds 405 tobacco knots, little pinches of tobacco in pouches. These represent the 405 types of trees and plants known to the Sioux, many of which have healing properties. The circle inside the rope of tobacco knots is covered with earth, and the medicine man sometimes draws a picture on this earth carpet to show his desire to meet with the Almighty.

The ceremony begins as the medicine man fills a sacred pipe with tobacco and prays to each of the four directions, thanking them for their bounty and blessings to man and to the world. This prayer cannot be reproduced in English. The air and everything in the room is purified by burning a braided rope of aromatic sweet grass. A clean, pleasant fragrance pervades the room.

Assisted by his helper, the medicine man is then wrapped in a blanket or star quilt and bound with forty feet of tough rawhide rope. *Yuwipi* means "tied up." The medicine man is tied up so that the spirits may use the energy of his inert body to communicate with the living.

The spirits manifest themselves in many different ways. In addition to the tiny lights that float and sputter around the room and objects that move by themselves, people at a *yuwipi* ceremony often hear the cries of eagles and feel the breeze from their wings as if the birds were circling at five thousand feet instead of in a closed and shuttered room. Hands that reach out to catch them close on empty air. Small voices whisper in people's ears, and people feel a touch on the ear or nose or pats on the head. Those in tune with the ceremony may feel an indescribable feeling of mystical contact with the Almighty.

The sights and sounds of a *yuwipi* ceremony have been experienced by many non-Indians. Some whites have argued that the *yuwipi* rite is borrowed from white spiritualistic séances. However, *yuwipi* existed long before white people became interested in spiritualism, and other people, especially in Asia, have similar ceremonies.* In 1838, a Cheyenne medicine man named Elk River used his knowledge of this spirit ceremony to tell the Cheyenne people that five of their warriors had been killed by the Pawnees at one of the streams that runs into the Solomon River. A spirit named Sun Flower brought this information. The story of the lost war party was later confirmed in every detail by a captured Pawnee girl. George Bird Grinnell, the pioneer anthropologist, recorded the story around the turn of the century.

This intimacy with the spirit world explains why Indians have little or no fear of death. As one older woman said recently, the Indian thinks of the body as a robe, easily discarded when it becomes old and worn out. Indian people often indulged in wild grief in mourning for a loved one, cutting off their hair and slashing their limbs, but this was mourning a temporary separation, not an eternal bereavenent. In some cases—the prospect of death in battle, for instance—Indians roused themselves to a pitch of religious fervor that caused them to take unbelievable risks and to keep fighting even when they were horrendously wounded.

The Sun Dance, probably the most famous Sioux ritual, seems to be of more recent origin than the *yuwipi* ceremony. Sioux legend says that the Sun Dance was discovered by a man named Kablaya (Spread) long after White Buffalo Calf Woman brought the sacred pipe. The ceremony is a flesh sacrifice by votaries who ask a blessing for themselves and for their whole tribe and all living things. Men who pledge the Sun Dance are pierced through the skin of their upper

---

*A ceremony similar to *yuwipi,* including an earth altar with four flagpoles, tied together with leafy branches rather than tobacco knots, is practiced in Japan. This ceremony can be seen in the motion picture *Rashomon.* Japanese Shintos also pray to the sun and the four directions. The Vietnamese practice a spiritualistic ceremony called "trance dancing" which seems to resemble the Sioux Ghost Dance of 1890. Whatever the scientific explanation, most Asian peoples also describe the same type of lights seen at *yuwipi* ceremonies as messengers from the spirit world.

chest and tied to a center pole by rawhide thongs hooked into their flesh. Women or older men sometimes offer tiny pieces of flesh cut from their arms.

The old Sun Dance was a pageant. The cottonwood selected for the center pole would be surrounded by warriors on horseback who would charge it, "counting coup" as they would on a human enemy. The bravest warrior of all was chosen to "kill" the tree ceremonially. The tree was then cut down by virgins, chosen for their pure character and good manners, and carried to the dance grounds by six grandfathers known for their wisdom. During the Sun Dance, children were allowed to enjoy themselves by making all sorts of mischief and were treated even more permissively than usual. Indian parents usually disciplined their children with affectionate teasing. In extreme cases, they might tie the child up for a little while. But during the Sun Dance, the children had free rein.

Most white people know the Sun Dance through the twisted and incorrect version in the movie *A Man Called Horse,* in which the ceremony was depicted as a sort of initiation to the tribe. This was totally false and most Indians found it degrading.

The Sun Dance was a symbol of solidarity—all the various bands of the Sioux Nation would assemble for the ritual. Because of this, the Sun Dance came in for a heavy dose of suppression by white authorities.

The Sun Dance was forbidden for many years, although traditionals risked jail or beatings to hold small ceremonies in secret. More recently the Sun Dance has been practiced openly, but some nontraditional Indians have tried to capitalize on it by allowing concessionaires to set up hot-dog stands and carnival rides just outside the consecrated dance circle. At Pine Ridge, a tribal politician named Dick Wilson, later to win fame or notoriety at Wounded Knee II, organized a rodeo as part of the Sun Dance celebration. Many older Indians found this, and the charging of admission to old Indians who wanted to watch the dance, more insulting than the government's previous suppression. The traditionals and some of the young activists took to holding their own Sun Dances away from the fair-grounds and carnival atmosphere.

There are seven major rites of the Sioux religion, most of which have counterparts in other tribal religions. In addition to the *yuwipi* ceremony and the Sun Dance, the others are *inipi,* purification in the sweat lodge; *hanblecheyapi,* the vision quest; *hunkapi,* the making of relatives, or adoption ceremony; *ishana ta awi cha lowan,* preparing a girl for womanhood; and *tapa wanka yap,* the throwing of the ball, a sacred ball game.

The sweat lodge is used in many ceremonies, and a Sun Dance takes place every year, usually in August in Sioux country. The Cheyenne, the Crow, the Shoshoni, and the Blackfeet also have some form of Sun Dance today. *Yuwipi,* or ceremonies like it, are common in Sioux country, and a few of the other tribes still have their own versions of this spirit ceremony. But many of the other ceremonies have fallen into disuse through persecution by the BIA and the missionaries.

*Hanblecheyapi,* the vision quest, was once part of every Indian boy's coming of age. In his teens, the boy would go off alone, usually for four days, to meditate without food and sometimes without water and to seek a sign from the spirit world as to what his life would be. All children were given names as babies, but a boy usually acquired his man's name from his vision.

The visions of Crazy Horse were famous. Crazy Horse saw himself riding a horse that seemed to shimmer and shake with spirit power as it galloped. The horse turned colors, showing that he would ride many horses in his lifetime. Crazy Horse's vision was that white people had no power to harm him; only his fellow Sioux could injure or kill him. Despite his reckless courage in battle and the hundreds of soldiers' bullets aimed at him, he was wounded only twice, once by an enemy Indian and once in a quarrel with a fellow Sioux. And he died because of a conspiracy of jealous Indians with whites who were afraid of his power and his influence.

Other visions might be more commonplace. If a person saw an eagle, he might take a name that had something to do with eagles. An object seen in a vision or dream was usually symbolic. Crazy Horse's nephew, Black Elk, said that Crazy Horse also had visions of the shadow, the rock, the badger, the day, and the spotted eagle. Each of these visions had a power of its own. According to Black Elk, the rock was protection against enemy bullets, and Crazy Horse always wore a small brown stone behind one ear as "medicine" against gunfire. The eagle was believed to symbolize contact between the spirit world and the mortal world. The badger may have stood for the power of prophecy, since Sioux people use a badger to foretell the future. The badger is slit open, and young men look into the slick blood to see reflected an image of how their face will look when their spirit departs from their body. If one sees an old man with gray hair, he can expect a long life.*

Many Indian people have unexpected visions. Black Elk's greatest vision came when he was a nine-year-old boy, unconscious and sick with an unknown disease. He saw that the Sioux people would endure great suffering, war, and misery for four generations and then would reach a new plateau of happiness and well-being. This vision occurred in the 1860s, and some Indian people have interpreted it as a prophecy for the generation now reaching maturity.

Because the BIA and the missionaries made every effort to separate young boys from their families, vision seeking declined in the years after the Indian wars, and today only a few young men follow the custom. But it seems to be coming back. Medicine men seek visions all the time, and, increasingly, the younger generation of Indians consult medicine men for advice.

*Ishana to awi cha lowan,* the girl's coming-of-age

---

*This can be seen as analogous to crystal gazing in Europe. It also resembles the parlor game in which people stare into a mirror in a dark room, lit by a single candle. Young girls try to see the man they will marry, and reincarnation buffs try to see their former lives. The scientific basis for this sort of shenanigan has yet to be established.

ceremony, which took place at puberty, was a simple, dignified ritual in which older women and a medicine man reminded the girl who had just become a woman of her duties to her people. She was urged to be a virtuous wife and a kind mother to the children she would bear. As part of the ceremony, the girl ate consecrated buffalo meat. The buffalo represented the symbolic feeding of the people who ate the meat of the buffalo just as a baby feeds at his mother's breast. This ceremony is also rare today. The whites exterminated the buffalo so thoroughly that for fifty years buffalo meat was worth its weight in silver. Boarding school teachers also taught young Indian girls to be prejudiced against their own people, urging them to try to qualify as third-class whites. The schools also tended to hammer away at the image of sexuality as something nasty. Today, the trend of white opinion has veered off in the opposite direction. It has all been very disruptive to the clear thinking of the Indians.

Among Indians in general, and the Sioux in particular, the number four was a number of great power. There were four directions; men and animals had four limbs; the year had four seasons; and a human being went through four ages—childhood, youth, adulthood, and old age, each with its own hardships and blessings.

An ideal person was said to possess four virtues. For a man, they were wisdom, courage, generosity, and strength. For a woman, they were wisdom, courage, generosity, and chastity. There was a special woman's society known as the Only Ones, in which only women who had come to their husbands as virgins and remained faithful could take part in the feasts and dances. If any man knew of a woman taking part in ceremonies under false pretenses, he was under obligation to throw dirt in her face. Indian mothers who weren't quite sure of their daughters sometimes made them wear chastity ropes tied with a special knot known only to women. If a boy was known to fool around with these knots, the women might band together to kill his horses or humiliate him publicly.

The greatest of all Indian virtues was generosity. Indian people displayed their wealth by giving away their possessions to the needy and the helpless or to their friends. When, for instance, in the winter of 1875, the Northern Cheyennes were burned out by Col. J. J. Reynolds and forced to flee from their village with little more than the clothes on their backs, they were completely equipped by presents from Sitting Bull's Hunkpapa Sioux. The Hunkpapas even gave away their tepees and moved in with relatives so that the Cheyennes could have some tepees of their own.

Most Indian tribes made a custom of either giving away all of a deceased person's property or destroying it. The idea of an inheritance was as unknown as the titles of king and princess. Among the northern plains tribes, some of a man's or woman's possessions would be buried or left on his scaffold with him, and the rest would be distributed or taken as keepsakes. Sometimes an entire Sioux family gave away all their possessions in memory of a lost loved one, and the whole family was left completely impoverished. Friends, of course, helped out.

This well-known Indian generosity is part of the reason that so few Indians ever amass private fortunes or six-figure savings accounts.

The BIA and the missionaries did what they could to wipe out this distinctly Indian trait. The giveaway ceremonies at weddings or funerals were banned and those who took part were persecuted. Under the infamous Dawes Severalty Act, the great reservations were broken up into small plots in an effort to ruin the cooperative economy.

Yet Indian generosity has persisted. One of the simplest and most profound manifestations is the "blanket dance," which can be seen at the many powwows or Indian fairs across the country. When Indians going to or from these get-togethers run into hard times—an automobile breakdown, an accident, discovery that they don't have enough money to get back home—some of the people hosting the event will pass a blanket around the dance circle, and other Indians and spectators toss in whatever they can afford, even if they themselves are nearly broke and the people being helped are total strangers. No one construes this as begging. It is sharing of the simplest, yet deepest, kind.

Indian religion is more than mere power for healing and for clairvoyance. It is the skein that binds the culture and makes life meaningful. Reverence runs through every aspect of life.

Indian people believe that animals are our brothers and sisters, and that they have souls just as people do. The Indian hunter kills with sadness and regret, only when necessary. Hunting for sport or for trophies was unheard of. Many tribes had specific rituals to appease the slain animal's spirit and to apologize for cutting his life short. It is this love and respect for all life that preserved the balance of man and nature for so many centuries before the white man came.

The Plains Indians, for instance, had a strong prejudice against the plow and often refused to become wheat farmers in the white mold, although they sometimes raised vegetables and fruit trees and were more than willing to herd cattle. The whites scorned the Indians as superstitious and lazy and began to rip up the virgin prairies and plains from California to Texas, destroying the rich carpet of grass that held the soil together and preserved moisture even in years of drought. They chopped down the few trees to build houses and put in new fields. In the 1930s, when most of the plains turned into a dust bowl, some of the whites considered the disaster a biblical judgment against their wickedness. Perhaps it was. The center of the dust bowl was Oklahoma. Like most of the rest of America, it was stolen from the original inhabitants.

If there was so much to be said for Indian religion, why try so desperately to destroy and discredit it?

Part of the answer, obviously, lies in the fanaticism of most of the missionaries sent into Indian country. Some honestly believed that the Indians had to be torn away from their own beliefs to save their souls. Others merely had to justify their presence by charging that Indian religion was cruel, pagan, barbarous, and satanic; thus, they overpublicized any Indian ceremony that seemed strange or cruel to white sensibilities, and they deliberately obscured the similarities between Indian and Christian ethics.

One recent example is the introduction to the *Lakota-English Dictionary* compiled by Rev. Eugene Buechel and edited by Rev. Paul Manhart, Catholic missionary at Pine Ridge. Reverend Buechel, who died in 1954, was a friendly enemy and constant rival of the medicine man Chips and did his best, without success, to convert Chips to Catholicism.

Once, Chips good-naturedly challenged Buechel to test their respective powers—a frequent practice between rival medicine men. Chips stood a large glass bottle on a hillside and asked Buechel to try to influence it by force of will. Buechel prayed, without results. Chips said he'd see what he could do. He made one broad sweep of his arm in the bottle's general direction, and it exploded.

The pen has power too. Buechel's dictionary includes a brief cultural explanation by somebody named Leo P. Gilroy, which, besides being rife with other inaccuracies and exaggerations of Sioux savagery in war, confuses the Indian religion to a remarkable degree. Gilroy says that the sun was worshiped as a god, as were animals, and that the Sioux believed each person had two or more souls—one that went to the hereafter at death and another that loitered near the body. He says there was no concept of a single deity until the arrival of the whites. This is in direct contradiction to the teachings of Indian religion. Black Elk, the great medicine man, cooperated with John Neihardt and Joseph Epes Brown on two books, both of which give an accurate picture of the Sioux religion.* It doesn't take too much imagination to guess why the Catholic Church, among others, would like to discredit Indian religion.

Yet in the last few years, some missionaries on reservations have taken to attending Indian religious rituals, particularly where those ceremonies are fused with Christian belief. On the Northern Cheyenne reserva-

---

*John C. Neihardt, *Black Elk Speaks;* and Joseph Epes Brown, *The Sacred Pipe.*

tion in Montana and the Rosebud Sioux Reservation in South Dakota, priests have begun to attend the ceremonies of the Native American Church. This is an Indian approach to Jesus; peyote, a hallucinogenic cactus bud, is used sacramentally to attain visions just as traditional religions have used fasting, pain, or dancing to reach supernormal states of consciousness.

This sudden conversion is something of a surprise to the peyote people, whose religion has been under attack by missionaries ever since it reached the northern reservations before the turn of the century. The priestly interlopers are tolerated without much enthusiasm by the Indian worshipers, who often note bitterly that the mission school, run by the priests, is fantastically rich, while the Northern Cheyenne are fantastically poor.

"I think they're just trying to figger out where we're comin' from," a Cheyenne observes suspiciously. Twenty years ago, priests who took part in the peyote cult might have been excommunicated. Three centuries ago they might have been burned at the stake.

Just as the missionaries justified themselves by denigrating Indian religion, many other people justified their own aims by denigrating the humanity of the Indians. Since the Indians seem to have an excellent case against the United States—we were, as we have all said so often, here first—defenders of the United States's right to do whatever it wants, regardless of morality, have spared no effort or expense to portray the first Americans as unworthy of the land and resources that the Great Spirit gave to them.

At its crudest, this campaign took the form of trashy potboiler novels and plays in which the Indian villains—"the red ravishers" and "pitiless pirates of the plains"—were accused of every crime imaginable, usually related to lecherous designs on white women and vicious cruelty to white men. This art form waned at the turn of the century but was quickly resuscitated by Hollywood, bringing the Indian villains and white heroes before a whole new American audience and an international one as well. The results are obvious to every Indian who has ever seen the panic in a white child's eyes when the tot learns that before him stands a real-live Indian. Even white adults are often leery of Indian men and seem to believe that it would take only a single careless word or fatal glass of beer to turn any reasonable, soft-spoken full-blood into a ravening dispenser of death and destruction.

The anti-Indian bias is mirrored in high school textbooks, particularly in older books whose authors usually seemed more interested in whipping up hysterical patriotism than in describing past events honestly. One white reporter with some knowledge of the Indian in history reviewed some fifty high school texts and didn't find one that gave an accurate history of the Indian wars and of white exploitation. Some were blatantly racist, others merely overlooked any incidents that showed white America in a bad light, and those that were mildly sympathetic still contained glaring errors of fact and judgment.

The most sophisticated form of discrimination is practiced by so-called experts—anthropologists and sociologists—who try to reduce men of blood and spirit to printed abstractions. It used to be said that a typical Sioux family consisted of a father, a mother, eight children, and three anthropologists. Many Indians resented anthropologists because their endless and rather pointless research used up millions of dollars that could have helped alleviate Indian poverty, but their real damage to Indian culture was their condescending attitude and their attempts to explain Indian religious and emotional thought in terms of "primitive" people making up myths to cope with a world they couldn't comprehend. The tendency to treat Indians with thinly veiled contempt can be shown by the position assigned to them in the warehouse of academe. Pottery, weapons, and jewelry of the mainstream cultures of Europe that white Americans consider to be their antecedents, starting with Egypt and Babylon and ranging down through Greece and Rome to medieval Europe, are housed in the Metropolitan Museum of Art, near the masterpieces of Rembrandt and Rubens. "Indian artifacts" are kept at the Museum of Natural History along with dinosaur bones and stuffed whales.* Some are tagged with labels that view Indian culture as crude and animalistic. One placard announces that a dummy is wearing the beautifully quilled and beaded war shirt of White Antelope, the Cheyenne chief. The placard doesn't see fit to mention that White Antelope was murdered in the Colorado Militia's infamous sneak attack at Sand Creek in 1864 after he refused to fight because he had sworn to keep the peace with the whites.

An even clearer reflection of America's opinion of its Indians is the custom of displaying Indian skeletal remains. In many places, the bones of Indians dead less than a century are exhumed and displayed for profit or for the interest, probably prurient, of the public at large. One Utah museum showed the bones of an Indian dead less than fifty years, wearing normal working clothes for that era. The activists call these displays "death zoos," and have protested against them heavily in recent years. At one exhibit near Los Angeles, the following dialogue took place:

ACTIVIST: "Just what do you think these Indian bones are good for?"

CURATOR (joking): "They make good soup."†

The idea of a decent burial is every bit as important to Indians as to whites, yet in the interests of "science" even high school students are encouraged to excavate Indian burial grounds in search of souvenirs. In Welch, Minnesota, in 1970, when a group of irate Indians from Minneapolis showed up to fill in desecrated graves and confiscate rolls of film, indignant students reacted as if they had been mugged by some group of thugs outside a movie theater. Their education had so conditioned them to the concept of Indians, past and

---

*Late in 1973, the Metropolitan Museum of Art finally held an Indian art show.

†Clark Wissler, generally considered a pro-Indian anthropologist, in his *Indians of the United States,* passed off the Trail of Tears, where four thousand Cherokees died: "We spare the reader's sensibilities by not recording the brutalities and inhumanities of this whole affair. . . ." Thus the truth was rendered palatable to white patriotic sensibilities.

present, as some strange species of fauna that they didn't recognize the right of all people to rest in peace.

One could make a halfway convincing case for the theory that some of today's Indian activists are interested in flirting with death because the mainstream society has subliminally convinced them that real Indians are dead Indians. Costumes in glass cases and specimens in death zoos, together with cinematic distortions, are more real to most Americans than living Indian people.

Today, Indian religion is growing stronger again, but the mode of living has changed tremendously. This shift in values—from a spiritual relationship with every living creature and the earth itself to a monetary relationship with the dominant culture—coupled with white cultural bias has created a new and dangerous schism between the older Indians and the young people. Actually, it is a three-way schism. The very old cling to the beauty of the past and the traditional way of life. Many of their children, the middle-aged Indians of today, have been so indoctrinated by the whites that they have turned away from the old beliefs. But the young people in their turn have rejected a sterile, materialistic culture, even as many young white people have tuned out of the mainstream society.

The worst problem seems to be with those young people who have either not yet found pride in being Indian or don't know enough about their own culture to be able to return to it. Many have tried to escape from being Indian because their culture is synonymous with poverty, oppression, and ridicule. Young Indians who go to college or to high school away from home are often ashamed to bring their friends home. Shame leads to hatred for those they love because of the failure of the old people to cope with the problems of adapting to a dominant and exploitative white society.

To compound this tragedy, many Indian young people who metamorphose into activists and militants seek to recapture some vestige of Indian religion by attacks on "Christianity," by which they usually mean the various organized denominations, rather than the actual spirit of Jesus. This is sadly ironic, because the spiritual leaders of the Indian nations invariably expressed respect not only for Christianity but for all religions. Black Elk, perhaps the greatest of the traditional medicine men, said that he believed both in Jesus and in the sacred pipe, and saw no contradiction. And the Native American Church, which commands the allegiance of about one Indian in four and is the largest single denomination on the reservations, is by definition an Indian version of Christianity.

The Indian has always accepted Jesus's teachings of love, brotherhood, honesty, and humility before the Creator and in fact had developed similar ethical systems on his own. It is not the love of Jesus, but the hatred Indians have seen in the hearts of factional bigots that has caused opposition to various denominations. Those Indians who have not been emotionally poisoned by cruelty, in the name of the white man's religion, are wise enough to recognize that all true religions teach a message of love. To the Indian, this extends to every living thing in the universe. To be in tune with all things in the universe is not easy, but even to attempt to do this is to be on the good red road, the path to greater things. The old Indians always said that it was hard to be an Indian. But they knew it was worth the trouble.

# 3
# Indian Education: The Big Whitewash

> Let me be a free man—free to travel, free to stop, free to work, free to trade where I choose. Free to choose my own teachers, free to follow the religion of my fathers, free to think and talk and act for myself—and I will obey every law or submit to the penalty.
>
> —Chief Joseph

For better or, probably, for worse, the model for a century of Indian education was set up at Carlisle, Pennsylvania, in 1879 by an army officer named Richard H. Pratt.

Lieutenant Pratt first went west with the Tenth (black) U.S. Cavalry after the Civil War. His experience as a jailer of Kiowa and Comanche prisoners deported to Florida around 1875 showed Pratt that good results in dealing with Indians could be achieved by kindness and vocational training, and he and his wife were enthused with the prospect of starting a vocational school. In 1879 the government gave Pratt the use of a condemned army barracks in Pennsylvania, and the Carlisle Indian School was born.

The lieutenant had problems convincing his superiors that saving Indians was worth the expense, for at least one segment of government opinion held that it was cheaper to kill them. However, some sympathetic soul compiled figures to show that each Indian killed in Red Cloud's War (1866–68) cost the U.S. one million dollars and that the cost of a cavalry regiment in the field was two million per annum. Confronted with figures like this, the secretary of the interior, Carl

Schurz, a German-born ex-radical, was willing to listen to Pratt's pitch.

"Feed the Indians to America," Pratt urged. "America will do the assimilating and annihilate the Indian problem."

Pratt got his program funded. His barracks at Carlisle soon had dormitories, classrooms, shops, a hospital, a bakery, a laundry, a chapel, a YMCA office, a central heating plant and, for the stubborn in mind and body, a jail. Indian students were forbidden to speak their own languages, to sing Indian songs, or to practice Indian religion. Those who spoke no English —most new arrivals were straight from the high plains or mountains—were sent from place to place like packages with address tags tied to their jackets.

Those of Pratt's packages who didn't succumb to infectious diseases were subjected to a pioneer before-and-after technique. Pratt had learned about precarious government funding during his negotiations with Schurz, and he set out to launch a public relations campaign similar to future muscle-building and bust-development courses. As "wild" Indians entered the school, they were photographed in their tribal regalia, which, because of their recent capture or surrender, usually consisted of blankets and white men's cast-off shabby trousers. Photos were taken a year or so later, showing short-haired young men in military frock coats and proper young ladies in uniform dresses. Here was the final solution to the Indian problem. Isolate the Indians in boarding schools, destroy their culture, and digest them as second-class whites.

Despite the middle-class poses of the Indian lads and lassies photographed by Pratt's assistants, Carlisle was never a college. Classes in Indian schools ended at the sixth grade until the 1920s. It was strictly a vocational school—more accurately, a reform school for those guilty of being born Indian. The inmates learned to be blacksmiths, barbers, and seamstresses. They studied agriculture by laboring on neighboring Amish farms where some learned pidgin German, about as relevant to their former lives as most of the school's regular curriculum. Carlisle's school song was set to the German Christmas carol, "O Tannenbaum" (Oh Christmas Tree).

The school's main claim in history would be several superb football teams and two fine athletes: Jim Thorpe, a Sauk and Fox who was probably the greatest athlete of his era, and Louis Tewanima, a Hopi who scored for the U.S. in the 1908 and 1912 Olympics.

The Carlisle Indian School closed when the barracks was returned to the army as America entered World War I, and it never reopened. But Pratt's good intentions were to have a malignant influence on all subsequent Indian education, especially on the BIA systems.

Pratt's success was attributed, possibly wrongfully, to the military aspects of the school, although most of the Indians who attended remembered Pratt for his kindness rather than his sternness. The BIA school staffers who sought to emulate him forgot about his concern and went full ahead in their attempts to eradicate Indian culture.

A good example of the kind of BIA school based on Carlisle was the Rosebud Boarding School, established in 1884 on the Rosebud Sioux Reservation. The school was run along military lines through the 1930s with high-collared Prussian-style uniforms, and the students had to march in formation to classes, to meals, to chapel, and even to the movies. Students were grouped by how much education they had previously endured, and it was not uncommon to find teen-agers in kindergarten. Needless to say, they usually dropped out rather than to go to class with six year olds.

The single greatest impression these boarding schools made on their Indian inmates was one of overwhelming brutality. The tone was set by the staff member—called the *disciplinarian*—whose task it was to keep the students in line. Sometime around World War II, the job title was changed to *boy's adviser*. Shortly before this, the brass-studded harness strap that went with the job was replaced by a rubber hose, which didn't usually leave marks, although some children beaten on the hands were crippled for life.

The disciplinarian delegated authority to the older boys, who were allowed to whip the younger children with impunity. Students who misbehaved, even to the extent of getting their shoes wet, were forced to "run the belt line," which meant to crawl between the legs of other students, who lashed at them with their belt buckles. At girls' boarding schools, the matrons did the whipping with lengths of rubber hose. Those who were caught speaking their own languages had their mouths washed out with lye soap.

With the tone set by the authorities, the major interest among the students seemed to be fisticuffs. Man-to-man punch-outs between boys not yet in their teens occurred daily. Some boys learned to wear rings with the stones left out, so that the sharp edges would rip their opponents' faces. The school administration blithely ignored these brutal fights and subtly encouraged them, especially when the fights seemed to consist of mixed-bloods persecuting full-bloods, who suffered the most because they were shyest and spoke little or no English. The school authorities hoped to destroy Indian culture by holding the full-blood children up to ridicule. They set the pattern for the full blood versus mixed-blood conflict that was to characterize so much of internal Indian politics for generations to come. They also made a lot of helpless children very unhappy.

I can remember how, as a little boy of five, I first arrived at the Rosebud Boarding School in 1931. Standing there thin as a rail, I was suddenly alone in a strange world. It seemed like an adventure, but it quickly turned into a nightmare. I was beaten up by older boys while instructors ignored the whole thing. Like most Indian children, I had grown up in a warm, loving home where physical brutality, even spanking, was unknown, and I was a complete stranger to the bloody fistfights that raged all around me.

Our "company" was under the captainship of a mixed-blood Indian, who, under the influence of boarding school, had become the most brutal person I ever knew. He prided himself on beating hands black and blue with his brass-studded belt, and he would hit us five extra times if we jerked our hands away from his blows. Because of my small size, I came in for a double dose of torture.

The little boys who arrived at the school were outfitted in dress-green leather-necked uniforms, similar to Marine Corps dress greens of today. We underwent what seemed to be a constant challenge to our will to live. Every morning, after marching back from a breakfast of oatmeal with huge worms twisted in it, we were forced to swallow mysterious cod-liver oil. At the dining room, everyone acted on the sound of the bells, like Pavlov's dogs. We sat down by a bell, began eating at the sound of a bell, and left the room at the sound of a bell.*

In the buildings, the younger boys and girls were assigned to different phases of cleanup, while the older students were given the task of waiting on the school's white staffers. The older boys cut meat in the kitchen which they knew Indian students would never see—all the fine cuts went to the "club" to feed our tormentors on the staff. It was an interesting lesson in integrity.

Silent movies provided entertainment. We marched to them in military fashion. In the movies, needless to say, the Indians lost every battle. The brainwashing had been so successful that the students would rise as one and cheer as the cavalry rode to the rescue and drove off the murdering savages.

Because I was reared by parents who had always stood up for themselves, it was humiliating as well as painful to have to submit to a beating every day for no reason other than that I was younger and smaller than other boys. But after a few months there were few boys who cared to fight with me. I learned to swing hard and fast, and if my fists couldn't do the job I picked up whatever was handy.

I'll never forget the last big fight I had with a boy who was four years older than I. He had all four fingers on both hands covered with rings with the stone

---

*A staple food at boarding school was a concoction of flour, water, salt, and pepper called "government gravy." Children made up a ditty: "Government gravy/Government gravy/Makes me fat/ Makes me lazy."

sets removed, so that the prongs stuck straight out like little knives. I can't forget the terror that ran through my body as I faced this huge full blood who had been forced to fight me.

As he moved in to take advantage of his size, my body exploded while my mind went blank with anger. We fought for what must have been twenty minutes, then he suddenly broke and ran, crying under the jeers of the entire boy's building student body. By some miracle I was untouched by the ripper rings. Word of this fight got around, and the bigger boys left me pretty much alone.

Hatred that makes you want to kill is a terrible thing to inflict on children six and seven years old, and we were all victims of it. One night a drunken white man barged into the dormitory looking for the disciplinarian. After a loud and profane argument, the drunk, who was wearing brass knuckles, punched the disciplinarian full in the face so hard that blood splattered all over the walls. We little boys who watched were dancing with joy because the disciplinarian was seriously injured.

The main lesson of the BIA boarding school was hate: hate between the full bloods and the mixed-bloods, and hate for the whites who inflicted so much unnecessary suffering on children. The mixed-bloods were taught to ridicule the full bloods, who were the symbol of Indian tradition; and the full bloods learned to resent some of the mixed-bloods, who were the favored pets of the teachers—pets, in the sense of animals, for more than a pet owner's interest in the future of any Indian child would have made a BIA teacher seem weak and suspect to his racist colleagues.

In some ways, the plans backfired. Some mixed-bloods who spoke only English when they came to school lined up with the full bloods and learned Indian languages and culture for the first time.

The pattern of brutality and cultural repression obscured whatever the schools were trying to teach. Usually, the curriculum consisted of learning to count, recite the alphabet, and read from primary readers.

A good example, if extreme, of the kind of education

these schools offered is the case of George Kills Plenty, who underwent eighteen years of boarding school education and finally graduated from the sixth grade when he was twenty-four years old: he was barely literate. By today's standards, he would have scarcely been qualified to enter first grade.

The BIA boarding schools have blundered along in this mold from the 1880s to the present day. George Mitchell, a sensitive, gentle Chippewa who was to be the cofounder of the American Indian Movement, remembered Wahpeton Boarding School, a North Dakota BIA academy, in the 1940s, as being substantially the same as the Rosebud Boarding School in the 1930s.

"They made us line up and march everywhere, even to the shows," Mitchell said, "and they did their best to beat the Indian out of us. Actually, I think they beat the Indian *into* us, at least in my case. We had Chippewa and Sioux there, and a lot of Cree who spoke Cree or French, and before long we could all speak one another's languages, even though they beat anybody they caught speaking Indian."

Plans to whitewash the Indians backfired in another way. Most of the violent activists of the 1970s went to BIA schools in the 1950s. In a very real way, the BIA's senseless attacks on Indian culture sowed the seeds that sprouted into the violence at Wounded Knee and at the BIA offices in Washington.

The BIA schools were so heavily vocation oriented that many Indians didn't realize there was any other type of education available. When the BIA appropriated $250,000 for Indian scholarships as part of the 1934 Indian Reorganization Act, they stipulated that only $50,000 should be used for college scholarships. Needless to say, the scholarships went almost exclusively to those with the right BIA or church connections. Today the money has increased tremendously, but the practice of using it as a bridle on Indian students hasn't changed. On Standing Rock Sioux Reservation, in the late 1960s, a young man just returned from two years at an eastern college was told to stop knocking the BIA by the BIA education supervisor in the area. He didn't stop, but his scholarship did. His case was one of many.

Sparked perhaps by the early stirrings of Indian activism and by President John Kennedy, the first president in recent memory to take an intelligent interest in Indian affairs, there were some improvements in Indian education in the 1960s. Kennedy's murder hit Indian people especially hard, and those who knew him almost unanimously felt a sense of personal loss.

President Johnson was less concerned with the Indian problem, but he made one noteworthy suggestion. Shortly before he left the White House, he recommended that the BIA form Indian school boards for all federal Indian schools. Little came of the suggestion for several years.

In 1969, a Senate Special Subcommittee on Indian Education, chaired first by Sen. Robert Kennedy and after his murder by Sen. Edward Kennedy, submitted a final report distilled from almost five thousand printed pages of notes and testimony. The report read, in part, as follows:

> We are shocked at what we discovered.
>
> Others before us were shocked. They recommended and made changes. Others after us will likely be shocked, too—despite our recommendations and efforts at reform. For there is so much to do—wrongs to right, omissions to fill, untruths to correct—that our own recommendations, concerned as they are with education alone, need supplementation across the whole board of Indian life.
>
> We have developed page after page of statistics. These cold figures make a stain on our national conscience, a stain which has spread slowly for hundreds of years. They tell a story, to be sure. But they cannot tell the whole story. They cannot, for example, tell of the despair, the frustration, the hopelessness, the poignancy, of children who want to learn but are not taught; of adults who try to read but have no one to teach them; of families which want to stay together but are forced apart; or of 9-year-old children who want neighborhood schools but are sent thousands of miles away to remote and alien boarding schools.
>
> We have seen what these conditions do to Indian

children and Indian families. The sights are not pleasant.

We have concluded that our national policies for educating American Indians are a failure of major proportions. They have not offered Indian children—either in years past or today—an educational opportunity anywhere near equal to that offered the great bulk of American children. Past generations of lawmakers and administrators have failed the American Indian. Our own generation thus faces a challenge—we can continue the unacceptable policies and programs of the past or we can recognize our failures, renew our commitments, and reinvest our efforts with new energy.

It is this latter course that the subcommittee chooses. We have made 60 separate recommendations. If they are all carried into force and effect, then we believe that all American Indians, children and adults, will have the unfettered opportunity to grow to their full potential. Decent education has been denied Indians in the past, and they have fallen far short of matching their promise with performance. But this need not always be so. Creative, imaginative, and above all, relevant educational experiences can blot the stain on our national conscience. This is the challenge the subcommittee believes faces our own generation. . . .

In 1968 there were 152,088 Indian children between the ages of 6 and 18. 142,630 attended one type of school or another. Most of these—61.3 percent—attended public, non-Federal schools with non-Indian children. Another 32.7 percent were enrolled in Federal schools. Some 6,616 school-age Indian children were not in school at all. The Bureau of Indian Affairs in the Department of the Interior, the Federal agency charged with managing Indian affairs for the United States, was unable to determine the educational status of some 2,842 Indian children.

The Bureau of Indian Affairs operates 77 boarding schools and 147 day schools. There are 35,309 school-age Indian children in these boarding schools, and 16,139 in the day schools. Nearly 9,000 of the boarding-school children are under 9 years old.

In its investigation of any and all matters pertaining to the education of Indian children (S. Res. 165, August 31, 1967), the subcommittee thus was compelled to examine not only the Federal schools, but the State and local public schools and the mission schools as well.

What concerned us most deeply, as we carried out our mandate, was the low quality of virtually every aspect of the schooling available to Indian children. The school buildings themselves; the course materials and books; the attitude of teachers and administrative personnel; the accessibility of school buildings—all these are of shocking quality.

A few of the statistics we developed:

—Forty thousand Navajo Indians, nearly a third of the entire tribe, are functional illiterates in English;

—The average educational level for all Indians under Federal supervision is 5 school years;

—More than one out of every five Indian men have less than 5 years of schooling;

—Dropout rates for Indians are twice the national average;

—In New Mexico, some Indian high school students walk 2 miles to the bus every day and then ride 50 miles to school;

—The average age of top-level BIA education administrators is 58 years;

—In 1953 the BIA began a crash program to improve education for Navajo children. Between then and 1967, supervisory positions in BIA schools increased 144 percent; administrative and clerical positions in the BIA schools increased 94 percent. Yet, teaching positions increased only 20 percent;

—In one school in Oklahoma the student body is 100 percent Indian; yet it is controlled by a three-man, non-Indian school board;

—Only 18 percent of the students in Federal Indian schools go on to college; the national average is 50 percent;

—Only 3 percent of Indian students who enroll in college graduate; the national average is 32 percent;

—The BIA spends only $18 per year per child on textbooks and supplies, compared to a national average of $40;

—Only one of every 100 Indian college graduates will receive a masters degree; and

—Despite a Presidential directive 2 years ago, only one of the 226 BIA schools is governed by an elective school board.

The subcommittee ended its report by recommending a "Marshall Plan" to improve the lot of the Indians as the original Marshall Plan had rebuilt Europe after World War II.

The BIA's indifference to their recommendation is attested to by the perpetuation of the same policies of whitewashing and cultural genocide that the bureau espoused in the 1880s.

The BIA's inaction in response to the report was predictable. An earlier report undertaken independently by Ralph Nader, before he attacked the Corvair, had come to almost exactly the same conclusions, and it changed nothing.

The best example of the BIA's flair for domestic fascism is probably the Intermountain Boarding School near Brigham City, Utah. A massive institution surrounded by a chain link fence, it looks very much like the military installation it once was. The school is seven hundred miles from the Navajo reservation it was created to serve. Many of the staff members are Mormons, whose religion teaches them that the American Indians are Lamanites, the remnants of the Ten Lost Tribes of Israel, condemned to wear dark skins and to wander for their sins against God. The Mormons, of course, are entitled to their beliefs, but anyone except the BIA might pause before asking believers in this sort of racist myth to exercise a sensitive control over Indian destinies.

The BIA does not pause, because, like Pratt, they want to feed the Indians to America. A pamphlet issued by the Intermountain school information office spells this out.

"The essential difference [between Intermountain and public schools] is that public schools have the task of preserving the prevailing customs of our society, namely the same language, same costume, same diet, housing, social customs and civic responsibilities. *The task of the Intermountain school is to change language, change diet, costume, housing, manners, customs, vocations, and civic duties.* [Italics added.]

"Changing people's habits and outlooks is one of the most complex tasks in human affairs," the pamphlet concludes.

Indeed. Particularly when the people don't want to be changed, at least at the expense of their dignity and mental health.

The first contact that many Navajo children have with Intermountain is the destruction of their medicine bundles, little pouches in which they carry objects of religious significance, usually given them by their parents for spiritual protection and comfort. The next step is a jail-style haircut, repeated as a disciplinary measure. Students who misbehave might have their heads shaved—like recruits in basic training or people about to go to the electric chair. The disciplinarian—known at Intermountain as the *instructional aide*—is very much in evidence. Students who hesitate to perform menial tasks tell of being beaten or slugged. Those who get into fights with the instructional aides, even in cases of self-defense, say that they are frequently jailed in Brigham City. Thus, a disproportionate number of male students acquire criminal records before they even graduate from high school.

Student mail has reportedly been opened and inspected by the guidance staff before distribution.

One girl, dressed up for a date, says she was told to scrub the shower stalls with her good clothes on. When she refused, the principal's wife threw her into the shower stall and turned the water on her, party dress and all.

Another popular method of discipline is handcuffing, a practice that has permanently scarred some Intermountain graduates.

Leaving the school grounds is known as "going AWOL."

The most controversial practice is the use of Thorazine, a powerful tranquilizer used on drug flip-outs, as a placebo for obstreperous students. School authorities maintain that Thorazine is used only when the student is a danger to himself or people around him, usually because of drunkenness.

The *Physician's Desk Reference,* a pharmaceutical guide used by doctors, states that Thorazine is a dangerous drug if misused and that use in the presence of alcohol is inadvisable.

In 1971, the National Indian Youth Council filed suit against Intermountain, charging that such practices had caused damage to the lives of students and asking for damage payments in cash so that an Indian-run school could be set up for Navajo students closer to their homes. The results of the suit, if any, are pending.

In light of the Senate subcommittee's report, and of President Nixon's famous 8 July 1970 message promising the Indians more self-determination, one would think that association with Intermountain would be the kiss of death of anyone's career in the BIA. But the opposite has proven true. In 1970, Wilma Victor, a Choctaw who served as Intermountain's superintendent through most of the 1960s when the school's flagrant abuses of human rights and dignity were in full flower, was promoted. She became acting director of education for the entire BIA. After a few months at this post, she was transferred to the BIA area office in Phoenix, Arizona, where she also headed an education program. She stayed put until March 1971 when Rogers Morton, the secretary of the interior, selected her as his special assistant on Indian affairs.

"I have a long record as an educator, and when you get to be my age you just say, 'There is my reputation, take your shots at it,'" Miss Victor said.

In September 1971, sixty Indians from AIM and NIYC barged into the BIA's Washington office and said they wanted to put a citizen's arrest on Miss Victor. Their leader, Russell Means, unkindly characterized her as "a dictatorial sadist." The activists were beaten and arrested by General Services Administration police and urged to get out of town by BIA officials who went so far as to get them released from jail and pay their way back home with federal funds. Miss Victor stayed put.

Despite the poor quality of BIA education, the cost to the taxpayer is by no means a bargain. In 1971–72, according to the BIA's own figures, almost 70 percent of Indian youngsters in school on or near Indian reservations went to public schools; about 5 percent went to mission schools run by various religious groups, mostly Catholic; and only 25 percent went to federal (BIA) schools. Figures for 1971–72 indicate that the BIA operated 199 schools—78 were boarding schools and 121 were day schools. Enrollment was 50,000.

The BIA also operated 19 dormitories for 4,025 Indian youngsters going to public schools. Yet, in their 1974 budget, the BIA requested $181.9 million for the education of Indian children.

By 1972, a few changes had been noted. All federal schools finally had Indian advisory boards. However, these boards are not actually empowered to make independent decisions.

Figures for 1972 indicate that 197,000 Indian youngsters were attending school. These figures covered only those Indian families who had a federal relationship, a group that numbered about 488,000 and did not include urban Indian populations which are estimated at anywhere from one-half to one-third of all Indians now living, including a preponderance of the young adults. In 1972 there were 1,958 graduates from BIA high schools, and 299 students received certificates of completion from BIA postsecondary schools (in most cases, vocational schools). The BIA was appropriating $20.9 million for Indian higher education.

Although the BIA admitted that two surveys conducted in the late 1960s indicated a high school dropout rate of 42 percent (all schools), they guessed (probably optimistically) that the dropout rate was down to 35 percent by 1972.

No similar figures are available for nonreservation Indians, since the BIA prefers to act as if they didn't exist.

The BIA figures don't scratch the surface of the world of the mission school except to point out that only about 5 percent of all Indian students actually attend mission schools. This contradicts the many brochures that reach the white public, most of which strive to give the impression that mission education is the only education available to Indian youngsters.

At one time, religious missions were indeed responsible for almost all Indian education. This epoch reached its zenith in the mid-nineteenth century. The missions actively competed for Indian souls and sometimes issued propaganda attacking the conflicting beliefs of rival Christians as well as of the "heathens."

Initially, missionaries were treated with the typical Indian respect for anything spiritual, and the Indians kept them mentally separated from the soldiers and settlers with whom they often swapped bullets. This respect may account for the many times that clergymen showed up at treaty conferences in which the Indians lost so much land.

In April 1873 the Reverend Elecazear Thomas was one of the peace commissioners sent to help pry the small but intractable Modoc tribe of Oregon and northern California away from their chosen lands. The conference was memorable. The Modocs sensed a double cross coming and double-crossed the commissioners first, shooting down Thomas and Gen. Edward Canby and wounding three other whites. The killers were hanged and the rest of the tribe evicted after a war in which the tiny Modoc tribe held up a thousand well-armed troops for six months.

In August 1876 the Episcopal bishop, Henry B. Whipple, was one of the commissioners sent to break the Treaty of 1868 and take the Black Hills goldfields away from the Sioux. Whipple himself was sympathetic and prayed for justice, but his fellow commissioners stole the land anyway.

In 1887 Rev. Samuel Hinman was sent along as a "special interpreter" for the Department of the Interior to the conferences that led to the Allotment Act and the breakup of the Great Sioux Reservation into the present fragmented islands of Indian land. By this time the Indians had lost all faith in Hinman's spirituality, for he had been officiating at treaties since the early 1860s.

The conduct of clergymen like Hinman led a modern Indian to comment, "When the white men first came to Indian country, they had the Book and we had the land. Now they've got the land and we've got the Book."

Possibly because of the services of people like Hinman, the government was eager to have churchmen move onto the reservations, thus making the separation of church and state an empty passage in a forgotten document. Today, one finds a broad spectrum of white religions represented on every major reservation.

The bulk of the full-time religious school system, however, is Catholic, coordinated from Washington, D.C., by the Bureau of Catholic Indian Missions. Historically, the Protestants were more willing to leave schooling to the government, and they never built up church-school compounds as the Catholics, with a long history of parochial education among whites, chose to do.

As of 1972 the Bureau of Catholic Indian Missions operated 45 schools on reservations, of which 12 served mainly as boarding schools. The boarding schools had about 3,000 students enrolled, with annual operating expenses of about $850 per pupil. The 32 day schools enrolled some 4,400 pupils at a yearly cost of about $500 per pupil. The schools are entirely church funded, except for federal subsidies, which, where state laws permit, cover the cost of school lunches and some textbooks.

The mission school system employs about 650 teachers, most of them clergy. Lay helpers are said to receive minimum wages.

The mission school most familiar to whites is probably Saint Labre in Montana because of its fantastically large and efficient fund appeal through the mails. Perhaps one white household in ten can boast a genuine Saint Labre napkin holder or a wall hook with a plastic papoose's head on it.

The Saint Labre Mission is a complex of buildings set in a bend of the Tongue River on the Northern Cheyenne reservation and run by the Capuchin Order of the Catholic Church. The brochures sent to whites all over the country portray the mission as a tiny institution teetering on the brink of financial ruin. Under pressure, the staff admits to a yearly intake of $800,000 to run the school, which deals with about nine hundred students from first grade to high school.

Every Indian connected with Saint Labre swears that the school is a multimillion dollar operation, and one widely quoted figure, from a white man who worked in the upper echelons and left, states that the school took in seven million dollars in 1967.

Indian critics break down the school's finances thusly: it costs the mission 25 cents to make every dollar they take in, owing to postage, plastic souvenirs, stationery, and labor involved. Most of the menial workers are Indians who receive the minimum wage. The mission, which receives 75 cents of each dollar, passes on about 15 cents to the Indian children in the form of academic education. Some 60 cents on every dollar is said to be used for matters other than education.

These Indian estimates of the school's intake could be seen as motivated by envy or antiwhite prejudice. But prejudice cannot explain the fact that the supposedly impoverished school has its own airport and private jet or that the teachers live in a splendid air-conditioned building while the surrounding Indians live in poverty.

The brochures fail to mention that the Indian students pay forty dollars tuition per semester and buy their own diplomas and class rings. Even this minimal tuition is often a hardship on Cheyenne families, for their reservation is one of the poorest on the north plains and most families are large.

And yet, many Indians are grateful for the Saint Labre Mission. The general quality of education there is better than at the BIA or public schools also available to Cheyenne people, and there is little or none of the brutality that has made Intermountain a name that rings in Indian ears like "Gestapo." The school also provides some adult education, and the plastics factory that manufactures souvenirs for fund raising gives many Indians a chance to earn a slim living, not available at many other places on the reservation.

Nevertheless, the bright promises held out by education are never fulfilled. The Northern Cheyenne reservation hasn't produced a college graduate in sixty years. Alcoholism and suicide are rampant, and employment opportunities other than opening donation envelopes or working in the souvenir factory are almost nil.

"I just keep my mouth shut because there is plenty of people who leave with loose mouths," says one Cheyenne woman who earns roughly the minimum wage. "Where else am I going to be able to work if I don't work here, the factory, or some other place in the Mission? The tribe doesn't have that much money. I don't have to worry about things as long as I keep my mouth shut and do my job. It is good money and you don't have to work too hard."

A Cheyenne student took a dim view of the social values that the school imposed on the Indian students.

"They are taking good care of us, but they want us all to be good middle-class American people. One chick really threw me when she got so hung up with this thing that she wanted two different color school jackets. She blew her top when her mother said she couldn't get what she wanted, and ran away. They are giving us everything and giving us nothing. I don't think I'll graduate, maybe I'll go to Spokane. These guys bore me with their power trips."

Still, some of the older people approve of the mission, at least contrasted to the alternatives.

"They honor us," one older man says. "The whites around the reservation want our land. The mission treats us good and accepts our ways. Our medicine is dying, maybe the mission is the only thing to help us. They put up a recreation center and other things, maybe some day we'll be able to run it."

Saint Labre, and its role on the Cheyenne reservation as practically the only employer of Indians, is a rather extreme case. Some missions have pioneered in starting Indian-studies courses and in working out Indian-English dictionaries in the various tribal languages. But, generally speaking, their fund-raising circulars vastly overrate their importance to Indian life on the reservations they claim to service. Those Indians trying to preserve traditional beliefs are often angered at the attempts of the missions to co-opt Indian religion for their own purposes while they simultaneously try to root out the power of medicine men. And mission leaders who claim to speak for "their"

Indians are in effect supplanting the suffocating paternalism of the BIA with the suffocating paternalism of their respective religious orders.

What of the Indian students who attend neither BIA nor missionary schools? Their numbers were estimated at 197,000, or 73.5 percent, by a U.S. Office of Education report in 1972. Allowing for Indians missed in the survey, the figure is probably closer to 80 percent.

The federal government pays for a large portion of Indian education that goes on in public schools, largely under the Johnson-O'Malley Act, which provides funds for the BIA to grant to state and local schools boards that accept Indian students. Johnson-O'Malley funds totaled $16.5 million in 1970, and the federal government in that year contributed an additional $17 million under the Elementary and Secondary School Act, aimed at helping school districts having a large percentage of Indian students.

The Office of Education paper cited a survey by Dr. Robert J. Havighurst of the University of Chicago, completed in December 1970. His figures indicated that the Indian dropout rate was 43 percent for grades eight to twelve—against 32 percent for children of all other races.

Havighurst also found that Indian children, more than the children of any other minority group, believe themselves below average in intelligence and have the poorest self-concept, and that they felt misunderstood in schools.

The ironic footnote to these findings is that transcultural IQ tests conducted at several locations for the past three decades show that Indians and Orientals test slightly higher than either whites or blacks.

The principle in operation here, recently studied by white educators working with black ghetto children, is one of projection. The teacher forces his impression onto the child through mental suggestion. The child expects to do badly, and he does.

Testing of Indian children in schools shows that, although they fall below the norms in national education tests in the first grade, they begin to reach and surpass the norms through the lower elementary grades and into junior high school. Here, a few continue to work on a superior level but most begin to decline and fall back to well below the norms. Indian educators say that the slump begins when the child realizes that he is an Indian, that his schooling is contrary to Indian culture, and that he is expected to fail.

Realizing this, the Indian child performs as expected. As the Senate subcommittee survey showed, Indian children are only about one-fifth as likely to enter college as whites, and only three Indians graduate for every hundred that enter college. One in a hundred college entrants gets an advanced degree.

The IQ tests show that this atrocious rate of failure is not solely the fault of the Indian student. Phrased bluntly, a large part of the problem is the white teacher and, even more, the white-oriented curriculum.

Schoolteachers, particularly in the Middle West, plains states, Southwest, and working-class California, where they are most likely to encounter Indian students, are generally products of working-class or aspiring lower-middle-class backgrounds. With a few rare and fortunate exceptions, their general concept of "Indian" is a vague swirl of images including tepees, torture, and Custer's Last Stand. All too many probably equate dark skin with dirt. Where they are not actively hostile, they are almost certainly ignorant of Indian culture and personality. Most of them see Indians as stoic, solemn, even savage, where actually, Indian youngsters are—at least initially—shy, affectionate, and gentler than their white counterparts who are much more apt to act "like wild Indians."

Such is not the case forever. Once the Indian youngsters learn what conduct is expected of them, they adopt the chip-on-the-shoulder stance of the militants, or they quietly drop out.

"I guess I was sort of what you'd call a boy named Sioux," AIM activist Russell Means said of his peregrinations among BIA, mission, and public schools. "Every time some wise guy would mouth off I'd figger I had to defend myself for bein' Indian. I got to know what it was like to hate to see it rain."

Besides teasing Indian students about rain dances, their white counterparts often do imitations of Tonto or flap their hands over their mouths in phony war-whoops, a practice that doesn't necessarily end in grammar school—which may be another indication that the IQ tests aren't mistaken. Even where it is not meant maliciously, this sort of teasing is taken very much to heart by Indian students who are already self-conscious about their race and culture. Studies of the Pine Ridge Sioux indicate that, at the all-Indian Oglala Community High School, hostility on the part of the mixed-blood girls from influential families (those with BIA jobs) forced many of the shyer, less sophisticated full-blood and near-full-blood girls to withdraw from socializing activities or even to quit school. It might not be too bold to guess that something similar happens in clashes between Indians and non-Indians of off-reservation schools in cities and suburbs.

Social life at high schools is important, too. The same surveys show that many Indians list social activities as their main reason for staying in school. Athletics, on or off the reservation, are pushed especially hard at Indian students, often at the expense of academic studies by teachers who believe devoutly, if secretly, in the myth of the Indian as a superbly coordinated wild animal. Recently, the staff of one largely white public school in South Dakota was sincerely outraged when Indians charged the school with discrimination. After all, one teacher asserted, the school's top athlete for the past two years had been an Indian.

Situations vary, but usually where the Indians have been at the mercy of white school boards the picture has been bleak and sometimes sadly ludicrous. In the South, where most Indians have no relationship with the BIA, they were subject, until recently, to the vagaries of segregation, and they became men in the middle between the whites and blacks.

In the case of the Houma, a small tribe in coastal Louisiana, the tribe had no school service whatever until about 1937. White schools refused to admit them, and the Indians didn't wish to go to black schools. Missionaries took up the Houma children around 1937, and the neighboring parish (county) eventually built them two separate-but-equal schools, one of which closed in 1964. Most students, especially boys, drop out of whatever schools are available to them before they leave grammar school.

A similar situation existed with the Tuscaroras or Lumbees of North Carolina who refused to go to either white or black schools and demanded their own schools.

White school boards often judge Indians arbitrarily by white standards. In 1972, a well-publicized incident took place in Pawnee, Oklahoma, when three Pawnee students were suspended for wearing long hair and refusing to cut it to white standards. The mitigating fact that they needed the long hair because they earned part of their tuition as Indian dancers didn't win them sympathy from the administration.

Since Indian education in Oklahoma is funded partly by federal funds from the Johnson-O'Malley Act, in May 1972 a federal court issued a restraining order that allowed the Indian boys back in school provided that their hair was braided. The mother of one boy, Mrs. Lilly Cummings, had run for the board of education, and the issue began to have serious implications over and above teen-aged hair styles. It became a sort of shadow battle for Indian rights to cultural pride.

The Indians went so far as to call in Dr. Gene Weltfish, a friendly anthropologist who testified that long hair was indeed a part of Pawnee culture. But the shadow battle ended in May 1973 when the U.S. Court of Appeals for the Tenth Circuit ruled that although Indians may want to wear their hair long for religious reasons, such displays of cultural pride are not protected by the Constitution. Several Indian boys have since refused to cut their hair and are not allowed in school.

A better situation exists at the Onondaga reservation near Syracuse, New York, an enclave where some two thousand Indians have lived autonomously, surrounded by whites, for the past 150 years. They still preserve many of their traditions, including their original form of tribal council, unscathed by the Indian Reorganization Act or by BIA meddling. The Onondagas have an elementary school on their own land, and high school students go to a white school in the neighboring town of Lafayette. By remaining free of the BIA's services and paternalism, the Onondagas have undoubtedly been blessed. The one unfortunate part of their independence is that their high school graduates cannot qualify for BIA scholarships, and the state scholarships they do qualify for are too small to permit attendance at most colleges.

The worst problems Indians encounter with public schools undoubtedly exist in big cities, where everybody else is having problems with schools too.

Young Indians in urban schools are up against a double racial barrier. In most cases, whites tend to group the Indians with blacks, and blacks group them with whites. The youngsters, already highly sensitized to their precarious situation, become the pivot point for racial conflict between the two segments of the dominant society. White attitudes tend to create most of the problems. Conservative whites often tout the Indians as a sterling example of Americanism and brag about their vast affection for the first Americans, as if loving Indians excused them for disliking blacks. This irritates the blacks, who sometimes—though not always—take it out on the Indians. White liberals, on the other hand, tend to view all racial problems as motivated essentially by skin pigmentation, and they assume that, since the Indian is lighter complexioned than the black, his problems are far less urgent and can be solved by the same measures.

Urban Indians, in the middle of the white-black confrontation, often tend to get it from both sides. Blacks and Spanish-speaking peoples, with larger communities and better relationships with the urban poverty czars of the federal bureaucracy, get a much higher priority than urban Indians when funds or jobs are doled out.

This tendency is passed down into the educational system. When publishers finally realized that their school books ignored the role of both blacks and Indians in American history, they began to grind out slick-paper supplements covering the role of minorities in America. The sections on blacks used the writing of Richard Wright and Langston Hughes. The Indian sections, much smaller, used two white authors, Conrad Richter and Peter Farb, thus ignoring both living Indian writers and the many excellent accounts of traditional Indian life recorded by John Neihardt, Dr. Thomas Marquis, and James Willard Schulz, all of whom translated first-person accounts by Indians.

The textbooks themselves are another dose of bad news for the Indian student. School readers, portraying the drama of our history, show blond pioneer boys crouching behind tree stumps that bristle with arrows as their mothers quail hysterically inside the fort, remembering how the Indians killed their other sons. Squalid savages offer to swap their papoose for the blond baby of a clean-cut, handsome white couple and, when his parents won't trade, sneak back and steal the white infant. In high school history texts, the whites are refered to as "conquerors," and the texts state charitably that Indians were children of a primitive culture and cannot be judged by higher standards. One learns that frontier whites called Indians "dirty, lousy, cruel, treacherous, polygamous, lazy, and thieving." The illustrations show whites huddled in their log cabins ready to defend hearth and home with their trusty flintlocks, and the narratives harp on the Custer "massacre" and rarely mention the Trail of Tears, Sand Creek, Wounded Knee, or the 371 treaties signed and broken by the government. The nefarious Dawes Severalty Act, in reality a public spectacle of white greed, cruelty, hypocrisy, and dishonesty, is pictured as a boon to the Indian by a kind-hearted administration. Sitting Bull, who once offered a cornered Crow warrior a free shot at him with his own rifle, is pictured as a coward because he allegedly sat out the battle of the Little Bighorn making medicine. History books erroneously state that the Indians at Custer's defeat were better armed than the whites, when even the army admits that most of the guns the Indians used were junk.

How is an Indian child supposed to feel when he sits

alone among twenty white classmates and reads some would-be historian's tongue-in-cheek gibes about the "mumbo jumbo" of medicine men and the Indians' low resistance to alcohol? If he turns on the TV, he sees his ancestors portrayed as comic idiots ("F Troop") or rapacious savages. Even in those movies that try to treat the Indian with a measure of respect, the white hero always gets the Indian "princess" and the Indian hero always gets killed. To the urban Indian child's peers, Indian culture is something Boy Scouts study somewhere between knot tying and Morse code.

Is it any wonder that Indian school children have a low self-image? To justify three hundred years of genocide, white history virtually has to portray the Indian as something so evil that his destruction has been essential to civilization. The reaction of the American Legion or the VFW—let alone the Klan or the John Birch Society—to any textbook that bore more than a vague resemblance to the reality of American history doesn't even bear thinking about.

A less obvious reason for Indian failure in the white academic world is the difference in motivation. The white student goes to grammar school, high school, and college to make more money when he graduates and to better his status in the community. The Indian student goes to elementary school, usually, because it is compulsory, and he continues to high school and (rarely) to college because his parents want him to and because his peers also go. The most common reasons that male Indian students gave for staying in school were because their friends were there and because they enjoyed playing basketball. This does not mean the Indian is less intelligent than the white. It merely means he is more dedicated to his friends and less greedy.

Success, per se, is actually unpopular on some reservations. People have refused to renovate their houses on the Apache reservations because they don't want to seem better than their neighbors. Navajo students have been known to engineer mass flunk-ins in which an entire class blows a test because they know that some students couldn't pass and they don't wish to single anyone out for humiliation. Such people find it hard to understand corporate backstabbing.

The Sioux, with their warrior traditions, go about their failure somewhat differently. Among teen-aged boys, a large number leave school after smashing up government property, stealing BIA vehicles, or getting drunk and becoming otherwise rebellious. Others go through phases of contradicting the teacher at every turn until, in exasperation, the teacher eases them out. Few teachers have the intelligence, or the patience, to recognize this daredevil stage as a rite of passage rather than an outburst of juvenile delinquency.

Virtually the only reason an Indian can respectably state for going to college is "to help my people." Professions of enlightened self-interest, in the white mode, would be scorned. And once the young Indian is away from his peer group and his family, isolated at a white college, he loses his two major motivations for continuing his education.

Those Indians who succeed in higher education are often isolated from their own communities, if they weren't isolated to begin with. And, once educated, they often find little outlet on the reservation or in the urban settlement. The "Indian leaders" most acceptable to whites—those who are educated and do things by the book—are often those least accepted in the Indian community.

One graphic example of this ivory-tower syndrome was brought before the public on 16 October 1972, about two weeks before the Trail of Broken Treaties reached Washington and the BIA building. NBC decided to cap a week of documentaries about the American Indian by showing some live specimens, and they invited four Indian guests on the show. The first three were, to a large degree, academic Indians, dressed in suit coats and wearing thunderbird tie clips. The fourth man was Russell Means, soon to become famous, or infamous, at the BIA and Wounded Knee. Means wore braided hair, a flowing red shirt, cowboy boots, and a hairpipe-and-weasel-tail necklace. He spent the first ten minutes scowling as the three academics hashed around abstractions about what it means to be an Indian, et cetera. Finally, Means had enough.

"Look, I want to say one thing," he cut in. "This Indian education deal is the biggest rip-off goin'. You can see that right here with yourselves. There isn't one of you that's gone back to the reservation or done anything for our people!"

The rest of the interview consisted of the three nervous-looking academics prefacing their every statement with "Russ is right when he says . . ." and agreeing with just about everything else he had to say.

White viewers probably realized they had witnessed an intellectual mugging by one of the greatest living experts in the art, but the full significance escaped them. The three academics were very good at getting university grants and having books published, but, in terms of activism, they couldn't have led a corporal's guard to the latrine. Means, an unknown quantity to white publishers, was able to stage the storming of buildings even though he had never gotten his academic ticket punched. To the mass of down-trodden, ill-educated Indians, Means was something of a folk hero, and the author's guild was a sideshow for gullible whites.

The implication is not that Indians reject education. They need it to survive. But to succeed, it must teach Indian values by Indian methods. Like every profession, pedagogy is protected by a screen of jargon designed to keep outsiders from realizing how little the supposed experts really know. These experts would probably explode with indignation at the idea of Indians without reams of certification and diplomas guiding the destiny of their own school system, but the idea is not without precedent. Less than a dozen years after the remarkable Cherokees had been exiled from their Georgia homeland to the Oklahoma plains, they had set up a working elementary school system and a male and female seminary that functioned on a junior college level. A white lady who toured these schools in 1888 was amazed to find Indian students, under largely Indian teachers, studying at schools run by Indian school boards.

> Here Indian girls learn Latin, literature, mathematics, the sciences, mental and moral philosophy, rhetoric, and the various lesser branches supposed to lead up to these scholastic heights. . . . In the Male Seminary nearly as many boys are drilled daily in practice at arms, and study a somewhat more elaborate curriculum. Greek as well as Latin is taught here, and a wider range of science, while trigonometry and surveying are made much of.*

The Cherokees were more ready for white society than white society was for the Cherokees,† and the school system was confiscated when Oklahoma became a state, never to be returned to Indian control. Today, 120 years after the Cherokees set up this model academy, the U.S. government is beginning to grope its way back toward Indian control over Indian educaton.

Education is the least controversial area of Indian-white relations today, because it doesn't involve the conflict-of-interest problems inherent in land rights, treaties, government, or law and order. Because Indian schools provide jobs for large numbers of college-trained whites, Indian education doesn't encounter the same sort of resistance as do efforts to reestablish Indian control over Indian land. And because it is readily acceptable to the white middle class, education tends to be one of the brighter frontiers of Indian progress. In 1955, there were a grand total of 5 Indian students in college in South Dakota, and less than 150 across the nation. Today, there are about 15,000 Indian students in college, many seeking advanced degrees. However, there are at least 16,000 Indian school-age children not in school at all. Only 1 percent of Indian children in elementary schools today have Indian teachers or principals. And one-quarter of the elementary and secondary schoolteachers

---

*Anna Laurens Dawes, "An Unknown Nation," *Harper's News Monthly*, vol. 76, 1888.

†Around 1820, a Cherokee named Sequoya, who was himself illiterate, devised a phonetic alphabet for the Cherokee language. Within a year after his invention, most of the tribe had become literate in their own language, on their own initiative.

who work with Indian students say they would prefer not to teach Indians. Small wonder that Indian education is still warping the self-image of young Indians and will probably do so for many years to come. Progress has been made; but when you start at rock bottom you have a long way to climb.

# 4

# Health and Welfare: The Politics of Hunger

> **Is it wise to urge upon the Indian a foreign social form? Let none but the Indian answer. Rather let the white brother face about and cast his mental eye upon a new angle of vision. Let him look upon the Indian world as a human world; then let him see to it that human rights be accorded to the Indians.**
>
> **—Chief Standing Bear**

Modern Indian activist mythology declares that, before the white man came, this continent was an earthly paradise.

The alternate myth, of the white scientist, holds that before the white man introduced European medicine, life was nasty, brutish, and short, much as it was for the Europeans in the Age of Discovery from 1492 through 1688.

Oddly enough, the Indian myth is supported by fact, while, under analysis, the white scientific myth appears to be part of the justification for conquest that colors most of America's history.

Virgil Vogel, the great expert on Indian medicine and health, has produced evidence that the Indian viewpoint is largely correct.* Before the white man came, North America was almost totally free of infectious diseases. Skeletal remains, artifacts, and legends substantiate the fact that there was no smallpox, measles, mumps, diphtheria, cholera, or tuberculosis. Contrary to older sources, there was no venereal disease

---

*Virgil J. Vogel, *American Indian Medicine.*

either. The legend that Columbus's sailors brought the clap back to Europe from America is another racial slander. Syphilis existed in the Middle East in biblical times, but didn't arrive in America until the white man came; blaming the Indians was another attempt at guilt projection to take the weight of genocide off the white man's shoulders.

The accounts of the early explorers, who saw the New World through eyes not yet tinted with racism based on greed, support the notion that virgin America was, if not a paradise, at least a country populated by handsome and healthy people. Giovanni Verrazano, who landed in the coastal area that is today New York and New Jersey, wrote of the Indians he met in 1524.

> This is the goodliest people and of the fairest conditions that we found in this our voyage. They exceed us in bigness, they are the colour of brasse, some of them inclined more to whiteness, others are of yellow color, of comely visage, with long black hair, which they are very careful to trim and decke up, they are black- and quick-eyed, and of sweete and pleasant countenance, imitating much the old fashion. I write not to your Majestie of the other parts of their body, having al such proportion as apperteeneth to any handsome man. The women are of like conformitie and beautie, very handsome and wel favoured, of pleasant countenance, and comely to behold; They are as wel manered and continent as any women, and of good education.*

Sketches by settlers in Virginia and other colonies depict the Indians as people of stalwart physique and almost invariably show them to be bigger than the whites, as Verrazano said. That they were completely free of disease is also constantly remarked upon. To this day, scientists who encounter Indians not yet in contact with whites in the jungles of South America or the mountainous regions of Mexico often note that they

*Irving Skull, A.M., *New Jersey: A History* (New York: American Historical Society, 1930).

are not only free from infectious diseases but often nearly free of cancer, high blood pressure, ulcers, and tooth decay.*

Needless to say, the coming of the white man changed all this drastically. Smallpox, the deadliest killer, wiped out a far greater number of Indians than all the wars with the United States. Smallpox helped clear the way for the Pilgrims before they even landed by laying waste most of the Indian population around Plymouth. The Indians seem to have caught the disease from sailors who landed to pick up fresh water, or sometimes to carry off Indians as slaves. Samoset and Squanto were probably so friendly to the Pilgrims because there was no one else left to talk to.

In most cases, the whites spread the smallpox involuntarily, merely by relentlessly moving into Indian country. But in at least one case, they may have spread it deliberately. During the war of Pontiac's Conspiracy, just after the French and Indian War, the British were taking a pasting from a coalition of Indians rallied around Chief Pontiac. Lord Jeffrey Amherst, the British commander, ordered his subordinates to send blankets infected with smallpox among the Indians "as well as to try every other method that can serve to extirpate this execrable race." No one is quite sure whether the plans were carried out, but an epidemic did break out among the Indians in question around the time of Amherst's letter.

Smallpox also had its heyday among the tribes of the plains. Because they had never experienced infectious diseases, the Indians had neither developed natural immunities nor had a chance to search for herbal remedies that were effective in controlling the few diseases they knew about. The sedentary farming tribes along the Missouri River were hardest hit. The Mandans, Hidatsas, and Arikaras contracted the disease from white traders in 1837. It spread through

---

*Recent excavation at the so-called Koster Site in Illinois indicates that prehistoric Indians were healthy and had plenty of leisure. The Koster Site owner and coauthor Koster are not apparently related.

their earth-lodge villages and was almost invariably fatal. As they watched their loved ones die, a longing for death seemed to overtake even those few Mandans who survived. Warriors cut their own throats, jammed arrows down their windpipes into their lungs, or shot themselves. Women killed their children and hanged themselves in a frenzy of grief. Sick people, burning with fever, leaped into the Missouri River. Of the fifteen hundred Mandans who lived around Fort Clark at the beginning of 1837, fewer than a hundred survived the smallpox epidemic. Today, their descendants live among the Three Federated Tribes of North Dakota (Mandan, Arikara, Hidatsa) whose population even after 150 years doesn't equal the total number of Mandans alone before the smallpox hit.

The spotted sickness spread from the Mandans to the Assiniboins and from them and the whites to the other tribes of the plains. The Cheyennes lost half their tribe. This was to be fortunate for the whites, for the Cheyennes became one of the fiercest tribes on the plains. The Crees are said to have lost seven thousand people. Because so much of the death and suffering took place out on the prairie, the full toll will probably never be known. A white trader, wondering why his regular Blackfeet customers hadn't come in to barter, rode out to search for their camp. He came upon a silent village, with hundreds of rotting bodies sprawled around the doors of lodges and two sick old women crawling demented among the dead.

The Blackfeet fared worse than any other tribe, except the Mandans. Estimates of their deaths from smallpox range from a low of seven hundred to a high of eight thousand. The result was that their lands were open to the fur trappers, and the tribe was so reduced that, almost alone among the major plains tribes, they never fought a war against the cavalry.

Late in the fall of 1837, the Skidi band of the Pawnees took some Sioux women and children prisoners in a raid. Unknown to the Pawnees, the Sioux had smallpox. The older Pawnee people had been partly immunized by a previous epidemic in 1830–32, but the young children had no such protection. About a quarter of the Pawnee tribe died.

The great epidemic of 1837 burned itself out, but it was not the last time disease would stalk the tribes. In 1849, half the Kiowa and Comanche tribes died of cholera. In the 1870s, the Blackfeet were hit with another smallpox epidemic which spread to some other tribes.

In California, in addition to the other scourges and the outright murder of the Indians by miners and ranchers, venereal disease, largely spread by rape and forced prostitution, was a major killer. Prostitution and venereal disease had been unknown in California before the Spanish and the Americans came. During the first twenty years after the gold rush, venereal disease was a factor in 40 to 80 percent of all Indian deaths in California, according to anthropologist F. S. Cook.* Smallpox, measles, chicken pox, typhoid, influenza, bad whiskey, and bullets took care of most of the rest.

Disease killed many more Indians than were killed by soldiers' bullets. The "justification of the conquest" school of history uses this as an excuse for seizure of Indian lands by alleging that the Indians were "weak" and "primitive." The charge is not really fair. It would be interesting to speculate how the history of Europe might have changed if the Mongols had arrived at the same time as the Black Death. Even if the white man's diseases weren't responsible for conquest by weakening the Indians, they undoubtedly made it easier.

The second wave of disease that swept through Indian country was even more directly the fault of the white man, more specifically the BIA. During the first two decades after the reservations were set up, the Indian service set their minds to moving the Indians out of tepees or wickiups and into white men's log cabins. Many of the Indians resisted. The base of the

---

*Theodore Kroeber, *Ishi In Two Worlds* (Berkeley: University of California Press, 1962).

tepee was round, the sacred shape of continuance and eternity—a circle with no beginning and no end. The sun, the moon, the bowl of the sacred pipe, and the bird's nest are all round. The cabins were square, which was not a good shape.

The agents scoffed at this as superstitious nonsense and forced or cajoled the Indians into log cabins and shacks. Respiratory diseases began to spring up like wildfire. Thousands of Indians, mostly small children, died of tuberculosis and pneumonia. Their naturally low resistance to strange diseases, lowered further by malnutrition, combined with the overheated, airless cabins to create a condition that virtually guaranteed infection. This was the era in which white sympathizers called the Indians the "vanishing Americans" —with their children dying faster than they were born, it seemed like only a matter of time until the Indians disappeared completely.

What the Indians had known, and the agents had forgotten, was that the tepee was a superbly designed dwelling.* The "ears," or smoke flaps, at the top and the door flap at the bottom created a steady flow of air keeping the tepees ventilated and cool in the hot weather that made the army's Sibley tents unbearable. In the winter, an inner tepee wall could be added to the lower part of the lodge, providing a dead air space for insulation and making the tepee a snug cold-weather dwelling.

Fortunately, the Indian population plunge was reversed, slowly at first, and it began to climb phenomenally. Indians in the 1950s and 1960s became the nation's fastest-growing minority group. Better health care, better nutrition, somewhat better housing, and, perhaps most of all, a return of the will to live may yet lead the Indian population back to the same size as before 1492.

Just what the population was is open to question.

---

*Indian people who can afford them still use tepees for summer houses and for sentimental reasons. At the Crow Fair held each year on that tribe's Montana reservation, a tepee village of over two hundred lodges is set up. Many, however, belong to white hobbyists.

Estimates of the number of Indians who once lived in what is now the United States fluctuate wildly. George Catlin, the remarkable artist-explorer who lived with a number of tribes in the 1830s, estimated it to be sixteen million. Most historians consider this wildly inaccurate. The most frequent estimates are between one and three million.

Later figures are also based on guesswork, though perhaps the guesses are more educated. The Indian population in the year 1800 is usually estimated at about one million. The high birthrate of the plains and mountain tribes are thought to have made up for the early inroads of bullets and smallpox on the eastern tribes.

Shortly after 1800, the decimation began. Actually, decimation is too weak a word, for the Latin root means to kill one out of ten, and the years that followed saw more than nine out of ten Indians die. Smallpox epidemics, the Indian Removal Act, where thousands of Cherokees and Choctaws died, Black Hawk's War, and the havoc miners wreaked in California all took place between 1800 and 1860. By 1860, the U.S. Census reported an Indian population of 44,021. This figure is questionable, since one doubts the census takers touched bases at every plains village. But it does reflect the horrendous losses the Indians suffered owing to disease and cruel government policies.

Between 1860 and 1870, the Indian wars got under way in earnest. Little Crow's uprising in Minnesota, the Sand Creek and Washita massacres, battles with the Apaches and Navajos, and more free-lance murder by civilians in California piled up Indian corpses. The census figure for 1870 is 25,731. Again this figure is probably far too low, for, aside from the difficulty, it would probably have been fatal for census takers to go around asking hostile Sioux, Cheyennes, and Apaches to count noses. But it does reflect another huge drop in population.

The wars went on through the 1870s. In 1877, the Sioux were pursued through snowstorms and cornered at Wolf Mountain, where they fought a great delaying action. His people starving, Crazy Horse came in, never having been completely defeated in battle, and he was duly set up and murdered. The same year, the Nez Percé Indians under Chief Joseph, the friendliest and least violent tribe on the plains, were pushed into a war by venal white settlers and blundering diplomacy. The Nez Percés scrupulously avoided killing civilians and taking scalps, but the army turned cannons on their women and children anyway. In 1879, the Northern Cheyennes tried to escape from Oklahoma back to their home in Montana and almost made it before the soldiers caught them, jailed them, and foiled an attempted escape by shooting down eighty men, women, and children in the snow outside Fort Robinson, Nebraska.

Yet in 1880, the census takers reported 66,407 Indians. The huge rise certainly doesn't reflect the cooperation of the army. Most of the tribes were now on reservations and could be counted more easily.

By 1890, the Indian wars had almost petered out. There were, between 1880 and 1891, the last flare of Apache resistance under Geronimo and Nana and the shameful Wounded Knee Massacre. In 1890 the population had soared somehow to 248,253. Even given a phenomenal birthrate, this is hard to explain. But at this point the figures begin to show some statistical logic.

After 1890 came the years of housing reform and resultant tuberculosis. The population actually decreased in those years—from 248,253 in 1890 to 237,196 in 1900—despite the presumably high birthrate. By 1910, the population, having staggered, was starting to recover and reached 265,683. In 1918–19, the influenza epidemic hit. Bodies were piled up that winter like cordwood because they couldn't be buried fast enough in the frozen ground. The population by 1920 was reduced to 244,437, lower than in 1890.

Despite terrible hardships, the 1930 census showed a healthy growth from the dark years of 1918 and 1919. The Indian population by 1930 was 332,397. Around this time, the Indian Reorganization Act and the New Deal depression-relief projects made life a little more bearable. At the same time it became much easier for Indians to leave the reservations, where some of them got lost in white society. Census takers in 1940 were told not to ask questions about race, but to use their own judgment as to who was of one-quarter or more Indian blood, therefore legally an Indian by United States definition. Thus the census for 1940 shows an increase of only about 1,500 people, from 332,397 to 333,969.

World War II took most of the available Indian manpower away from the reservations for three and four years, and, after the war, many of them remained in the mainstream society. Thus the 1950 census of 343,410 reflects losses through the lure of city lights, as well as a near-stagnation of the birthrate for several years.

The 1960 census shows the first tendency of the population jump, with 523,591. If one adds the 28,078 Eskimos and Aleuts counted separately, the total becomes 551,669.

According to the 1970 census, there were 792,730 Indians living in the United States. Added to the 34,378 Aleuts and Eskimos, native people total 827,108. Of these, 488,000 reside on reservations. Many Indians claim that a large number of Indian people have been overlooked in the census and that the actual total is already more than 1,000,000.

What are health conditions like for the descendants of those who lived through the smallpox, the diphtheria, and the bullets?

The answer, according to everyone including the BIA itself, is—miserable.

The BIA states that the life expectancy for an Indian child born today is 66.5 years, against 70.4 years for all other races in the U.S.* What they don't state is that the life expectancy for all Indian people now *living* is somewhere between 43 and 46 years. On some reservations the life expectancy is under 30 years. The infant mortality rate is 23.8 for every 1,000 live births, 1.2 times the national average, the BIA

---

*Life expectancy, and other conditions for Indians, are even worse in Canada, and statistics are even more unreliable.

says. In 1955, before the Public Health Service (PHS) took over Indian health from the BIA, the infant mortality rate was 62.5, more than twice that of all other races. On some reservations, however, the rate of infant deaths is 100 for every 1,000 live births, twice that of the worst black ghettos and four times that of white babies.

In 1973, one Indian child in six died before reaching the age of fifteen, as against one non-Indian child in twenty. A study by Dr. Helen Wallace of the University of California showed that the survival rate of Indian children is 83 percent from birth to age fifteen, whereas the survival rate for non-Indians (including the poor and nonwhite) was over 94 percent. The statistics were even worse for Eskimos. This figure is especially poignant because the lives it deals with are not yet much affected by the factors of suicide, homicide, and alcoholism.

The leading causes of death are (1) accidents, with an age-adjusted rate of 186 per 100,000 people; (2) heart diseases, 182.6 per 100,000; (3) cancer, 84.4 per 100,000; and (4) cirrhosis of the liver, 66.8 per 100,000. The figures for accidents and cirrhosis are tied in with alcoholism; and the heart disease figure is linked with poor nutrition and the starchy, fatty diet of most reservation Indians.

Other important causes of death are suicide and homicide. The Indian suicide rate is double the white rate, with 21.8 Indians (compared with 11.3 whites) committing suicide for every 100,000 people. But suicide plays a disproportionate role in Indian lives because so many of the people who commit suicide are young. Although the figures for Indian-white society are about two to one, an Indian from 15 to 24 years old is four times more likely to kill himself than a white man. From the age of 25 to 34, the Indian suicide rate is still more than that of the white population. But after the age of 35, the suicide rate for Indians is far lower than that of whites.

The main reason for the high suicide rate among young men, other than miserable living conditions, is cultural clash. Because of the brainwashing he has received in school, the Indian is sometimes ashamed to be Indian. Contact with the prejudices of the white world convinces him that he doesn't fit in anywhere. If he is unable to externalize his rage against white society, he turns it inward.

For the same reason they have a high suicide rate, Indians have a homicide rate between two and three times that of the national average. Crime for gain is rarely a factor in Indian homicides. The usual forms are automobile accidents and fights with guns or knives, and alcohol is involved in both cases far more often than not. Another form of homicide that affects Indians is the killing of Indians by whites, who are rarely convicted. The modern code of the West might be stated as this: it's no big deal for an Indian to kill an Indian, or for a white man to kill an Indian; if an Indian kills a white man, no matter what the provocation, he's lucky to make it to his trial alive and luckier still if he only gets life in jail.

The basis of the Indian health found by the first white men was good nutrition. The basis for the sickness and early death today, other than psychological factors, is bad nutrition, often malnutrition.

Indians in every part of America had found some sort of balanced diet. The tribes of the East and Southeast had perhaps the most varied fare. From their fields, the women brought corn, beans, squash, and pumpkins. Men hunted and fished, and children gathered nuts and berries. Both sexes gathered clams and other seafood, and maple syrup was taken as a tonic. These were the people who made such an impression on Verrazano and other explorers.

When an American painter who had seen Indians all his life traveled to London and was shown a statue of Apollo Belvedere, the personification of strength and manly beauty, he is said to have remarked, "How like a Mohawk warrior!"

In the Southwest, the farming tribes lived mainly on the same crops and the meat of the deer and other animals. Oddly enough, their diet, which should have been deficient in calcium, was amply supplied with this vital mineral from the rub-off from the limestone corn grinders they used to grind flour for their daily bread.

In the Northwest, fish and other seafood were the main staple. The fishing Indians remained self-sufficient long after the hunting Indians were left destitute, and even today, the same forces that wiped out the buffalo are trying to cut these fishing tribes off from their food supply.

The buffalo-hunting tribes of the plains were probably the best nourished of all. Buffalo meat has more protein and less fat than most beef and a better flavor. The buffalo was the staff of life to the Plains Indians, and their culture revolved around the yearly buffalo hunts. When the meat wasn't eaten fresh, it was dried in strips called jerky or pounded with berries, nuts, and rendered fat into pemmican for use in the winter months. There was hardly a part of the buffalo that the Indian didn't use. Hides with the hair left on were used as cloaks or bedding, and tanned cowhides were used to make tepees. Intestines were used as water bags, bones as paintbrushes, tails as flyswatters. The horns were used for spoons.

The buffalo-hunting tribes varied their diet with greens, berries, wild turnips, other game, and sometimes with corn, and they prospered mightily. Soldiers who served on the frontier were impressed with the size and strength of the plains tribesmen, and rightly so. Of one draft of 159 white soldiers sent west in 1865, only four were six feet tall, and many were a mere five feet three. Among the tribes they met in the plains, the Cheyenne averaged five feet nine, the Crow and Arapaho five feet eight, and the Sioux five feet seven. Two Moon, a Cheyenne who fought Custer, was six feet four; and Wooden Leg, an eighteen-year-old warrior at the Little Bighorn, was six feet two and not considered especially big. The Indians gave the buffalo full credit for their strength and vigor.

The white man is said to have viewed the buffalo on strictly economic terms, but this is not entirely true. To the white man, the buffalo was the symbol of the free-roaming Indians, and using the politics of hunger, the destruction of the buffalo was intended to break the Indians' will to fight. It was, in fact, one of the first examples of what has come to be called the military-industrial complex.

Before 1870, buffalo hides were regarded as untannable, and those that reached the East were used mostly as sleigh robes or for belts in pedal-driven machinery. But in 1871 John Mooar, an inventive Yankee businessman in the West, sent his brother Wright in the East a load of hides for experimentation, and Wright reported that a way had been found to tan buffalo hides so that they were as good as any leather. This discovery touched off the era of the professional hide hunters. Within a few years, those buffalo accessible to the whites had been slaughtered and stripped of their hides, and the carcasses left to rot. Having exhausted the buffalo supply on the land already claimed by the whites, the owners of the larger buffalo-hunting companies cast their eyes on the lands that had been promised to the Indians in perpetuity. They took their case to Gen. Philip Sheridan.

Sheridan's best-known quote is, "The only good Indians I ever saw were dead." But when the buffalo hunters began to cry on his shoulder about lost opportunities to get rich quick, he made a statement whose implications were even more widespread.

"Boys, if I were hunting buffalo, I would go where the buffalo were."

Between 1870 and 1875, white buffalo hunters racked up something like 12.5 million kills. A hunter named Frank Nixon claimed to have gunned down 120 bison in twenty minutes. The wholesale killing glutted the market to the point where a good hide only brought $1.25. The great southern herd was completely exterminated. When early conservationists objected to this wasteful slaughter, Sheridan exploded.

"Protect the buffalo, hell! The hide hunters have done more to solve the Indian problem than the army has done in 30 years. Let them kill, skin and sell until the buffalo is exterminated as it is the only way to bring about a lasting peace and let civilization advance."

By 1880, with the Sioux on reservations, civilization advanced into their territory. In 1881, 50,000 hides were shipped out of Bismarck, Dakota Territory; in 1882, the number was reduced to 200,000; in 1883, there were 40,000, and in 1884, only 300. Prices soared during these years from $5 to $30 per hide, and by 1885 a buffalo hide was so rare that a good one was worth $75.

During the years when the buffalo was abundant, the slaughter was amazingly casual. Expeditions set out from the East to take potshots at buffalo from railroad coaches, not even bothering to pick up the hides and choice tongues. William F. Cody and "Medicine Billy" Comstock, two white scouts, held a refereed contest to determine which one had the right to call himself "Buffalo Bill." In eight hours, Cody killed sixty-nine buffalo and Comstock forty-six. Indians later killed Comstock while he was scouting for the army, but Cody went on to become a self-made legend.

As the buffalo dwindled, the hunters became more meticulous. During the last great slaughter in 1883, the hunters built fires along the river banks and guarded every water hole until the thirst-crazed bison had to come forward and brave the rifle fire in a doomed attempt to reach the water.

With the buffalo gone, the agents cajoled the Indians into surrender with the promise of food. Like the other promises, the guarantee of food was frequently broken. Once the "Indian troubles" were over, a heartless Congress cut back on appropriations, reducing the Indians to such a level that even tough old soldiers like General Crook and General Sherman were disgusted. This was the era in which Indian health, like Indian freedom, was broken. The promised beef rations were replaced by whatever food was cheapest and most convenient. Venal agents made a pile by falsifying contracts and further undercutting the amount Indians received.

By the early 1900s, Indian food had become fairly standardized. The tribesmen waited in long queues to receive their rations: bacon, lard, flour, navy beans, baking powder, and dried prunes. A nutritionist would note that everything except the prunes consisted largely of starches and fats, the root of most of the Indian health problems. Quantities were also insufficient, and most of the time the Indians got by, if they were lucky, on potatoes. Reservation cooking gravitated to fry bread—dough fried in liquified fat. Fry bread is tasty, but it probably explains why so many older Indians are obese, why the second major cause of death among reservation Indians is heart disease, and why so many young men have skin problems.

One of John Kennedy's first acts as president was to expand the surplus commodities program to include rice, skim milk, peanut butter, and tinned luncheon meat for the reservation people. Indians received all these foods as well as occasional boned turkey or chicken, cheese, butter, oranges, and tomatoes. The diet was still skimpy and full of starch. The surplus commodities program was terminated in 1974 because of a lack of surplus. At this date, no documentation exists on how this drastic, but quiet, action affected Indians and other poor people.

Inadequate diet is the direct cause of many of the diseases that shorten Indian lives and make them miserable. The incidence of tuberculosis, for instance, is currently 9 times as high as for the population in general. Deaths from tuberculosis are 3.7 times as frequent among Indians as among the rest of the nation.

Low income is also linked to bad health. The BIA says that the average per capita income for Indians on federal reservations is $1,115 (1971 figure). But this is deceptive, because it is an average based on extremes. A small number of Indians, mainly on a few reservations in California and New York State, receive a relatively good income. The average per capita income on the Navajo reservation, the nation's largest and most populous, is said to be about $300 per year. Some tribes are even poorer. The reservation is so barren that supplemental vegetable gardens are next to impossible, and the Navajos live mostly on the sheep they raise. Even here the BIA managed to interfere, agitating against the Navajo custom of eating every part of the sheep's body, until independent studies proved that this was the only way to maintain any semblance of a balanced diet. Still, the Navajos suffer an extremely high rate of digestive disorders and kidney problems from eating too much fat.

The reservations are a living museum of diseases seen nowhere else in America. Kwashiorkor, a disease of protein deficiency, and marasmus, a wasting disease caused by protein and calorie deficiency, are usually associated with tropical Africa, but both exist on the Navajo reservation, among others. Indian reservations are probably the only place in the United States where either disease is ever seen. Otitis media, a middle-ear disease that causes deafness, and trachoma, a contagious eye disease, are also seen on reservations and nowhere else. Even death by starvation is not unknown, particularly in winter when people who live far from the agency towns can't report for their rations.

The Indian health problem more whispered about and stereotyped than any other is alcoholism. Two of the four most frequent causes of Indian death—accidents and cirrhosis—are directly linked to alcohol abuse; and homicide, suicide, and other diseases are also tied in to it. Mark Small, a Northern Cheyenne who headed the American Indian Commission on Alcoholism and Drug Abuse, said in 1971 that alcoholism was the single major health problem on most reservations, and that 80 percent of all Indian families were affected by it in some way. Part of the Indian's susceptibility is because of the absence of cultural conditioning. The Indians, with few exceptions, had no alcoholic beverages and never developed a concept of "social drinking." Only the Apaches, who made a sort of corn beer called tiswin, ever produced alcohol in North America, although some tribes in Central and South America did brew liquors. The Indians learned about liquor from white soldiers and frontiersmen who drank strictly to get intoxicated whenever they could afford it. This, rather than wine with dinner, created the cultural norm as far as Indians were concerned.

Alcohol, with smallpox, was a major cause of Indian defeat and cultural disintegration all through the history of Indian-white relations. Many Indian leaders made efforts to stop the flood of liquor. As early as 1650, Oratam, a chief of the Delawares in New Jersey, was authorized by the Dutch to arrest any trader bringing liquor across the Hudson to the Indians and to transport him back to Manhattan for punishment. When the English took over New Amsterdam, they rescinded the prohibition. Excessive drinking was a major cause of the Delawares' downfall and a major reason for their immigration west, out of reach of the liquor traders.

In 1794, a coalition of tribes from the Ohio area shattered the army of Maj. Gen. Arthur St. Clair and routed the larger force of regulars and militia in the greatest defeat the Indians ever inflicted on the U.S. Army. A dozen years later, future president William Henry Harrison referred to these same tribesmen as "the wretched scum of the earth" and was able to oust them from their homeland without a battle. The Indians had weakened themselves with excessive drinking, which, coupled with disease, made them an easy prey to venal white diplomacy.

Several wars were touched off by incidents in which one or two drunken, brooding Indians shot whites who offended them. Whites retaliated by killing every Indian they could get their hands on. Two notable incidents were the Pavonia Massacre, in which the Dutch retaliated for a white man's murder by killing eighty peaceful Delaware men, women, and children, and Little Crow's War, where four Sioux hunters, all apparently drunk, killed five settlers to prove to one another that they weren't afraid of whites.

Liquor spread out ahead of the mainstream of white invasion. Some white traders mixed sugar with the whiskey to lure the Indians into tasting it. The whiskey they sold to the Indians was a concoction of raw alcohol doctored with tobacco juice (for color), pepper and snake heads (for bite), and fusel oil (for taste). Often it killed Indians outright.* When the liquor came in, many of the old virtues went out. In

*Such whiskey was called "40-rod," because forty rods was said to be the maximum distance one could stagger after imbibing.

1830, Porcupine, war chief of the Cheyennes, knifed a fellow tribesman while drunk and was exiled, the usual penalty for killing a brother Cheyenne. His departure deprived the tribe of their best war leader at a time when they needed him. In 1880, Little Wolf, perhaps the greatest of all Cheyenne chiefs and a man who made fools of the entire U.S. Army for months during the tribe's flight from Oklahoma, was exiled from his tribe after he killed another Indian while drunk. The tally continues, and several promising Indian leaders of today have had their careers or lives destroyed by liquor.

Perhaps the best-known story is that of Ira Hayes, a Pima Indian from Arizona. Hayes served in the marines in World War II and was one of the six men who raised the flag over Iwo Jima, a scene that became the most famous photograph of the war. Hayes toured the nation selling war bonds and found himself in a totally unreal situation, lifted overnight from poverty to adulation. A painfully shy man, he began to drink heavily to overcome his embarrassment. After the war, he went back to the desolate reservation and a life of unemployment. Ten years later, he drowned while drunk in two inches of water at the bottom of an irrigation ditch. In life, Hayes had become a symbol of the nation's valor. In death, he became a symbol of the betrayal that so many Indian veterans felt when they returned home to poverty and oppression after fighting for America.

Indians who drank were commonly regarded as dangerous to whites. Perhaps because of this, until about twenty years ago, it was a federal crime to sell or give liquor to an Indian. During the Korean War, when many young soldiers were denied beer, the "old-enough-to-fight, old-enough-to-drink" issue created something of a furore. Perhaps because of this, the Indian prohibition law was lifted in 1953. This created a whole new industry for the white towns just outside the borders of the reservations. The reservations usually remained dry, but the surrounding white towns became decidedly wet. The ready availability of liquor probably had a detrimental effect on Indian health, and the necessity to drive long distances, usually at night, and return while under the influence contributed to the horrendous accident rate that is the single major cause of Indian deaths.

The exact scope of Indian alcoholism has never been determined. Some sources say that about one Indian man in four and one woman in eight is afflicted. Problems with alcohol seem to be even worse among urban Indians than among those on the reservations.

The reasons that Indians have drinking problems are obviously as varied as the individual personalities involved. Mark Small, former director of the American Indian Commission on Alcoholism and Drug Abuse, had a list of forty-two possible reasons for Indian alcohol problems, some of which he considered probable.

Among the most important were the following:

1. Defiance of prohibition. Because the Indians were constantly warned against drinking by missionaries, they drank as a form of defiance, proving themselves independent.
2. Peer pressure. Many young Indians grow up with the mistaken idea that to drink is to be Indian, and vice versa. The fact that most of the great chiefs of the past—Tecumseh, Crazy Horse, Sitting Bull—were opposed to liquor is not generally publicized.
3. Boredom. In the days before reservations, Indians spent most of their time earning their livelihood. Religious ceremonies, dances, and warfare also occupied their time. On the reservations, with religious ceremonies and dances forbidden by the BIA, and with nothing to hunt and no place to work, boredom became a major problem and the Indians killed time by drinking.
4. Cultural repression. Most Indian cultures taught people, expecially men, to control their feelings and hide their emotions. Drinking became attractive, particularly after the white invasion, because it allowed people to express their feelings. Many Oriental people, notably the Chinese and Japanese, who cultivate a facade of calm detachment, are also noted

for their uproarious behavior when drunk. But because they have not lost control of their own destinies and have other outlets for their energies, their drinking rarely becomes alcoholism.

5. Genetic weakness. The theory is that there is something in the Indians' body chemistry that predisposes them to alcoholism. Indians, like Orientals, do tend to get drunk on less liquor than whites. Nutrition is probably a more important factor than genetics. Recent experimental work has linked chronic alcoholism to nutritional problems, of which the Indians have more than their share. It may well be that the sense of elevation often created by drinking provides Indian people who are malnourished with an illusion of physical well-being.
6. Despair. This was best summed up by a Sioux man who told Small, "When you've got no job, no money, and a house with a dirt roof you've got good reason to want to get drunk."

Small's theories were never meant to be conclusive. He did offer some solutions. The most important factor in ending Indian alcoholism, he said, would be to give the Indians the greatest possible amount of self-determination, thus removing their frustration. In the meantime, he advocated counseling by traditional medicine men as an alternative to psychiatrists or Alcoholics Anonymous, which he felt were probably detrimental to Indians rather than helpful.

Characteristically, nobody in any position of authority listened to Small, and his organization was constantly suffering from lack of funds, even though pioneer programs showed some good results.

Serious consideration of the Indian alcohol problem was obviously beyond the sensitivity, if not the intelligence, of most of the nation's legislators. A good indication of their feelings is revealed by an incident that occurred at a conference in Washington in 1972. About two hundred Indian leaders, ranging from militant activists to moderates, churchmen, and tribal leaders, were asked to come to Washington to hear presentations on four different bills related to Indian education. In the evening, the group was invited to a reception to meet the congressmen from their various western states. Instead of showing up, most of the congressmen just sent cases of whiskey to be handed out.

One Indian group that faced the problem head on is the Native American Church. Through peyote, members of the church seek visions that will help them lead a better life. Church meetings are usually held all through Saturday night—the time when Indians are most prone to go off-reservation and drink—and most often take place in a tepee. The Native American Church theology is a blend of Christian and Indian beliefs. Their four basic rules of life are (1) brotherly love; (2) care of one's family and abstinence from adultery or extramarital affairs; (3) self-reliance and hard work at one's job; and (4) avoidance of alcohol. "Peyote and alcohol don't mix" is a maxim among peyotists.

Peyote is not addictive, and the use of sacramental peyote by Indians is permitted by federal law, although in most areas it is illegal for Indians to give peyote to whites. By 1970 the Native American Church had 225,000 members, some of whom attend traditional Indian or conventional Christian services as well.

It is a favorite conceit of missionaries and bureaucrats that Indians had no knowledge of health or medicine before the white man came and that when people got sick they just died. This same school of thought holds that medicine men did nothing but perform sleight of hand and take credit for accidental recoveries. Nothing could be further from the truth. Not only did the medicine men cure their patients through spiritual or faith healing, but they worked out a system of herbal medicines that were often excellent cures for minor illnesses and the everyday problems of life. Many were taken up by the pioneers and became American folk cures. There are today herbal potions to prevent or encourage conception, break fevers, calm upset stomachs, relieve pain, and induce vomiting to cleanse the stomach. At least two herbals would probably become best sellers on the white market. One, a common herb, can induce an almost painless abortion. The other is a natural aphrodisiac. Indian medicine men rarely use either. Abortion, except to save the mother's life or to prevent a seriously deformed baby, is against Indian beliefs.

The one shortcoming of Indian medicine was in the treatment of infectious disease. Perhaps for this reason, the Indians accepted white doctors more readily than other trappings of white culture, reasoning that any doctor must have strong medicine indeed who could save a people with as many diseases as the whites. The first doctors in Indian country were army medics, who vaccinated Indians against infectious diseases, mainly to prevent the spread of infection to the soldiers. In 1832 the War Department, which would soon spawn the BIA, made an appropriation of twelve thousand dollars, thus starting the Indian Health Service.

In 1849, the responsibility for Indian health was transferred from the War Department to the BIA's new home in the Department of the Interior. By 1880, the BIA was running four hospitals and providing the services of eighty doctors, some of them on contract. In 1890, the BIA had twenty-five nurses and field-service matrons on the reservations teaching hygiene and sanitation. One of the first efforts was to get Indians to discard their cradleboards, the baby carriers that Indians of all tribes had used for centuries to protect and transport their children. The nurses seemed to think that cradleboards were some form of medieval torture, perhaps reminiscent of the iron maidens they had read about in Gothic romances. Nothing could be further from the truth. The nurses were so preoccupied trying to eradicate "savagism" that they didn't notice that babies like cradleboards. The cradleboard is constructed of a pouch that laces up rather like a shoe, to hold the infant. There is a reinforced back with one or two wooden slats; another half-circular slat, like a roll bar, to protect the child's face in a fall; and a strap. Contrary to artists' impressions, the Indian mother didn't usually carry the child tumpline fashion, with the strap over her forehead. More often, she held the cradleboard in her arms. The strap was to fasten the cradleboard to a packsaddle or a tree limb.

Cradleboards served three important functions. They kept the infant out of harm's way, so that he didn't crawl into fires or toddle away from camp, they protected his tender back and unhardened skull for the first year or so of life, and they enabled him to view the world upright before he was old enough to stand on his feet.

Owing to the influence of the field matrons and BIA bureaucrats in general, many tribes have discontinued the use of cradleboards. They may still be seen in Navajo and Apache country, and some of the other tribes are bringing them back. Ironically, the whites have capitalized on the idea with two greatly inferior devices modeled on the cradleboard but lacking the protective slats at the top and front.

The early Indian Health Service doctors were a diverse crew. Like people who went west in general, the service doctors ranged from a handful of sincere idealists to a larger crew fleeing from their past, their failures, the law, or their wives. Several of the early doctors were noted mainly for their attempts to seduce female patients. In one case an upright Indian mother buckled on a .45 and barged into the Indian Health Service clinic, ordering the doctor to marry her daughter or quit hanging around. She punctuated this demand with a few shots aimed at his feet. He chose to leave hurriedly.

One young doctor fresh from medical school held a feast for his Indian colleagues, the medicine men, when he arrived on his assigned reservation. He sought their cooperation in referring him to any patients whose diseases they couldn't handle. The medicine men appreciated his tact. The Indian Health Service didn't and upbraided him harshly for socializing with "pagan savages" and lending credence to their "mumbo jumbo." The young doctor later froze to death trying to reach a sick Indian's cabin in a snowstorm. His type was exceedingly rare.

As early as 1919, attempts had been made to transfer the Indian Health Service from the BIA to the Public Health Service. Neither the BIA nor the PHS was in favor of the idea, but the medical establishment wanted the transfer, which was authorized in August 1954 and took place in July 1955. Over 2,500 personnel, 48 hospitals (mostly small ones), and 13 school infirmaries were shifted, lock, stock, and barrel, from BIA to PHS under the Department of Health, Education, and Welfare (HEW). Policies affecting eligibility for health care have not changed.

The transfer to HEW led to major improvements, although the record is still abysmal. The main lesson involved is not how good HEW is, but how bad BIA must have been if conditions as bad as today's can be regarded as a major improvement. HEW control cut the infant mortality rate almost in half in a few years. Between 1955 and 1968, admissions to contract hospitals increased 84 percent, and tuberculosis was reduced by 33.6 percent.

HEW spent an estimated $129,149,000 on Indian health in 1970; $138,057,000 in 1971; and $156,365,000 in 1972. The care Indians received for all this money was no bargain at the price.

As of 1970 the Indian Health Service had 2,674 beds in 276 hospitals and employed about 5,500 persons in addition to some 1,000 doctors and dentists, many of them assigned to administrative posts. Of every 4 Indian Health Service employees, 3 are Indians, but most of them are concentrated in the lowest brackets as orderlies and practical nurses. In the United States as of 1972, there were only 39 Indian doctors and a single dentist.

In 1970, there were 108 doctors for every 100,000 reservation Indians as compared to 164 doctors per 100,000 people for the nation as a whole. There was one dentist for every 3,400 Indians, as compared to one dentist for every 1,900 whites.

Although the number of doctors is not outrageously low compared to the population, their level of competence, productivity, and energy is often abysmal. Most qualified doctors have no desire to live on desolate reservations, and the majority of Indian Health

Service doctors are recent medical school graduates who fulfill their two-year military obligation with the Public Health Service. A great many of these men treat the Indians contemptuously.

Every reservation has its horror stories about the incompetence and indifference of the available medical staff. The most common stories are of critically ill people, brought in by frightened relatives, who died in the waiting rooms.

At the Rosebud reservation, shortly after the Public Health Service took over, nineteen Sioux babies suffering from an infectious disease were brought in by ambulance. All were treated and released. All died within a few days.

At Standing Rock Sioux reservation, in the mid-1960s, a teen-aged Indian hunter accidentally shot himself in the foot with a .22-caliber rifle. The hospital staff put a cast on the boy's foot without bothering to X-ray or probe for the bullet that had lodged against a bone. The boy died of blood poisoning.

At Standing Rock in 1972, a Sioux grandmother was sick with a respiratory ailment. The doctors diagnosed and treated her for diabetes, then changed their minds and began treatment for tuberculosis. Finally, they discovered that the woman had pneumonia. Meanwhile, she had wasted from about 140 pounds to 70 and was preparing herself for death. While in a coma, she had a dream in which she saw her husband, who had died two years before, and some other girlhood friends. As she rose to greet them, they all turned their backs, the Sioux gesture by which one refuses conversation. She took this as a sign that she was not yet ready to die, and she recovered. Her family can hardly be blamed for not attributing her recovery to the Indian Health Service.

At the Crow reservation hospital at Crow Agency in Montana, in July 1973 an eighty-five-year-old man, Joe Hill, asked to be admitted for treatment of arthritis and other complications of old age. He was denied admission, given some pills, and told to go away. He died, untreated, a few days later.

"They give them some aspirin and tell them to go

home and come back if they feel worse," says Mrs. Susie Yellowtail, who serves as a consultant for the Indian Health Service.

> The unknown is very fearful for Indian people. They get really worried when they don't feel right. So they come in and have to wait for hours and hours because the doctors are all too busy to see them, and then they go away and don't come back until they're really sick. And the doctors say it's their fault because they don't come in soon enough.
>
> Ten or fifteen years ago we only had one doctor and he even made house visits, all over this big reservation. Now we have five and they don't have time to see people even when they come to the hospital. All these doctors come here rather than go in the Army, and the Indians sort of look down on them for it. There's been trouble about it, especially when we've had some family where they've had somebody wounded or killed in Vietnam, and they get kind of wrecked and turn on the doctors. Now with the draft over we're really gonna have a hard time. If they don't have to go in the Army, they won't come out here either.
>
> There was one doctor, when a little boy needed a blood transfusion, he offered his own blood. I take my hat off to him, he was a real human being. But we have very few of them. We have had some real conscientious ones, but a lot of them just don't care.

Mrs. Yellowtail, born in 1902, was the first Crow woman to become a registered nurse. She graduated from a Boston nursing school in 1927. She blames the problems of the Indian Health Service on the lack of funds as well of the lack of concerned doctors, but she says that the director, Dr. Emery Johnson, has made sincere attempts to improve conditions.

> He's a friend of the Indian, definitely, but when you're working for the government, your hands are tied. If you stick your neck out too far, they chop it off for you.
>
> Another problem we have is that there aren't enough dentists. They take care of the children and that's it. If they have time and feel like it, they may take care of the adults after hours. A lot of us don't have many

teeth left because of it. I have a cavity now and I feel like I'm walking around with a cellar in my mouth.*

Like many other Indians, Mrs. Yellowtail feels that more and more Indians are turning back to their medicine men who often achieve remarkable cures and are always sympathetic to the patient and always available. Her husband Tom is an herbal medicine man credited with curing many people, Indian and white, who have sought his help.

Even if Public Health Service doctors want to do their jobs, they are kept so busy with charts, forms, notes, and administrative duties, not to mention back-room politics, that they have little time for medical practice. But the most aggravating thing is their cavalier attitude toward their patients. It irks Indians when these draft dodgers act as if they were doing the reservation people a huge favor by being there.

Those Indians who qualify usually prefer to go to Veteran's Administration hospitals, where both the skills and the manners are somewhat better. But Indians generally tend to avoid white hospitals, both because of blatant racial prejudice and because they rarely have enough money to pay the astronomical bills. In Rapid City, a South Dakota town with three hospitals—two for whites, and the "Sioux San" (Sanitorium) for Indians—it is not rare to meet veteran white nurses who have never spoken to an Indian.

Although the responsibility for Indian health rests outside the BIA, the responsibility for Indian sickness resides with a broad segment of society—the exploiters who have created institutionalized poverty for their own gains.

One of the greatest hotbeds of corruption is reservation housing.

Previous to the Kennedy administration, Indians weren't qualified for public housing. Many Indian peo-

---

*Contrary to the impressions her criticism of PHS may create, Mrs. Yellowtail is by no means a militant. She is strongly opposed to AIM and personally dislikes most AIM leaders.

ple lived in abandoned cars, tents, lean-tos, and shacks made of condemned lumber and tar paper. Had they been able to afford them, they probably would have almost unanimously preferred to live in tepees.

In 1972, a decade and more after Kennedy made public housing available to the Indian people, the BIA itself revealed that of 88,450 Indian housing units, 33,453 were substandard. They said that 20,-500 of these were worth renovating. Some 4,400 others lacked one or more utilities. The BIA estimated that 48,300 new homes would be required to replace substandard homes and to provide homes for families living with other families—almost 15,000 families had no houses at all.

Meaningless in themselves, these statistics indicate that many Indians were still living in abandoned cars, tents, lean-tos, tents, and shacks made of condemned lumber and tar paper. Many of those in supposedly standard houses were hardly better off.

On reservation after reservation, rumors and charges of corruption in housing have become rampant. On the Crow reservation in Montana, a young man's public housing home had just been completed when a high wind tore the roof completely off the house, tumbling it five miles across the plains like tumbleweed.

Allocation to public housing is also rife with corruption in some cases, usually at a tribal level. Families who are unpopular with the tribal council or the BIA superintendent find every conceivable obstacle thrown in their way.

Mrs. Yellowtail told of a house, built by the One-to-One Program with government funds and Indian labor, in which the construction crew built the septic tank uphill and the well downhill, creating a perfect situation for contaminated drinking water. Despite her objections, the setup was unchanged; when the widow and her grandchildren who lived there were constantly sick, they moved out and the house was abandoned.*

---

*Among most plains tribes, camp was moved every ten days to prevent fecal contamination.

"We gave our son our old house, which was one of the oldest on the reservation," she said.

> It's down by the banks of the Little Horn River, and some day it's just going to wash away. He applied for a house and was told he didn't qualify because he didn't make so many thousands of dollars per year. He was wounded in the Korean conflict and has a total disability pension so he gets $42 a month for a family with six children. He's a heavy-equipment operator but they're scared to give him a job because of the disability and he can't get a job with the BIA. So I went to the office and said, "I thought this housing was supposed to be for poor Indians. Why can't my son get a new house?" They gave me a form to fill out, and I knew all the answers, so I wrote them in. And at the bottom I wrote a P.S. "Next time there's a heavy rain, send a man with a crane down to the Little Horn River to pull him out."

Mrs. Yellowtail attributed the failure of her son's housing attempt to the fact that she and her husband had offended people in the BIA. "I think the name Yellowtail is a kind of bad name around here."

Bad planning augments bad construction. On the Turtle Mountain reservation of North Dakota, the government built large multifamily garden apartments. Many Indians rejected them as un-Indian or disliked living too far off the ground. On the Northern Cheyenne reservation in Montana, rich in timber and coal, the contractors forced butane heating systems on the Indians.

"Now when we finish the first container of butane, we do without heat for the rest of the winter because we can't afford another one," a Cheyenne says.

The housing system is cruelest on the northern plains where winters are brutally cold and summers blazing hot. In the Southwest, where the winters are milder, many Indian people prefer to retain their own forms of housing. A great many Navajos still live in hogans, and a fifth of the White Mountain Apaches still live in grass wickiups as they did in the days of Cochise and Geronimo.

Another cause of bad health and bad housing is unemployment. Contrary to the slurs of white bigots, most Indians are more than willing to work. But opportunities on the reservation, other than employment by the tribe, are usually almost nil, and the prejudice of surrounding whites prevents a great many Indians from finding jobs within commuting distance to the reservations. Another factor that contributes to Indian unemployment is the generally low quality of education and the frequent language barrier.

In 1972, the average rate of unemployment on Indian reservations according to the BIA was 40 percent, with an additional 19 percent employed in temporary or seasonal jobs—in other words, as stoop laborers on nearby farms. The Indian unemployment rate was thus seven times the national average.

Many who do work on the reservations work for the BIA either in regular BIA jobs or through the tribal councils, which, if the chairmen are corrupt, are usually nepotistic in the extreme. Recent efforts to bring employment to the reservations have had limited success. There are 238 industrial and commercial enterprises located on Indian reservations, but they provide only 16,700 jobs, of which less than half, 7,500, are filled by Indians. This is only enough to provide work for about one Indian in a hundred.

Thus the vicious cycle perpetuates itself. Unemployment breeds poverty and the boredom that leads to alcoholism, which, in turn, leads to the poor health that contributes to unemployment.

One of the greatest problems the Indian faces today are bloodsuckers throughout the United States who derive their income from raising money to help the Indian.

Approximately 95 percent of the money exacted from a generous public never reaches the needy Indians who serve as a facade for large- and small-scale fund-raising operations.

Individuals who run these groups are able to prey on the general public because the Indians are scattered, isolated, and politically fragmented to such an extent that there is no one central agency controlling the activities of those who supposedly work for the Indians' benefit. The propaganda that various church and secular groups circulate through the mail with the aid of sucker lists they buy from one another has created the second most prevalent stereotype of the Indian—the needy child dressed in rags and dirt.

There are plenty of needy children in Indian country, but the organizations that use them as a front rarely contribute much to their income. It is well known to Indians, but almost unknown to whites, that almost every church that collects clothing for the poor sells it and does not give it away. The money is used to fund church activities. As unbelievable as it sounds, this is common practice everywhere in the West.

The ploy of using winsome Indian children to rake in funds is played for all it's worth. One Catholic school in Montana sent out a brochure describing an Indian boy as an abandoned illegitimate child. The public relations men who made up the leaflet must have photographed the first Indian child they found. The boy's parents turned out to be a highly moral couple who had been happily married for years, and they sued the church for defaming their character. The church and the couple's lawyer settled out of court for a new house and several thousand dollars.*

On a somewhat more sophisticated level, the Association on American Indian Affairs has long been noted for collecting money, to help Indians, that the Indians never see. Because the association's records are closely guarded, no one can be sure of how much they actually make. But by studying documents, one can deduce that they probably take in about a million dollars per year.

The association has a few Indians on its payroll, but it has relentlessly fought Indian efforts to take control of the supposedly Indian organization. Indians who work for the association are paid employees stationed

---

*As a corollary, one major Protestant group's Indian Works Committee forbids use of funds for "construction, major remodeling, purchase of buildings, individual scholarship, or research." One wonders what sort of project they *do* fund.

in Montana, California, and New York City. There is no tribal affiliation whatever.

To maintain some semblance of Indian image, the association imports Indians for its annual meeting. Most of these figurehead Indians don't really understand how they are being used. One speaker at their yearly bash, Johnnie Wooden Legs, was so enthralled with his sponsors that he kept turning to face the association's president instead of speaking to the audience. The president had to rise three times to physically turn Wooden Legs back to face the audience.

At the same meeting, several tribal chairmen deliberately attended to hear the finance report, but the executive director and the president did not have the courtesy to introduce the chairmen along with the imported guest. The treasurer's report was accepted by motion, without being read.

When the question of placing Indians on the board of directors was raised a few years ago, a Mrs. Smith dismissed the subject by slamming her fist on the table and shouting, "Over my dead body will an Indian serve on the Board of Directors."

When every tribe in the nation was opposing the "heirship bill" before Congress in 1962 and 1963, the association's lawyers in Washington testified in favor of the bill. This bill could have led to the destruction of reservations all over the country through termination and land sales, and it was only the direct intervention of President Kennedy that crushed it. The same association lawyers who testified in favor of the heirship bill represented several of the tribes that were opposed to it, including the Oglala Sioux of South Dakota and the Nez Percés of Idaho. The conflict of interest came about because the Indians were fighting for survival, while the association was fighting to remain the voice of the Indian.

Every major city in America seems to have an "Indian organization" that makes its living off the generosity of the American people. One AIM militant discovered a white family of four in Oklahoma who made better than twenty thousand dollars a year soliciting money for Indians and pocketing everything. He convinced them at gunpoint that they were in the wrong business.

The greatest offenders are those groups who believe they are helping the Indians by selling them cheap used clothing and other articles. A better method would be to simply give the donated clothes away, or to let the Indians work out their value through some sort of meaningful labor.

There are twenty-eight hundred organizations now raising money for "Indians," and it is safe to say that most of them are either bogus or woefully inefficient.* The deadliest of all are those that employ professional fund raisers who take a cut of the money. The Association on American Indian Affairs, for instance, relies almost completely on these professionals.

People who wish to contribute money should clear the name of any group with the Indian tribe or all-Indian organization nearest to the charity's operation. Any check should be made out in the name of the organization, not in the name of an individual, unless the individual receiving the money is well known to the donor.

The safest procedure is to give directly to the tribe or organization that operates on a reservation. In almost every case, someone is keeping a watchful eye on these organizations and on the tribes. If a check is made out in a tribe's name, it is a serious crime for anyone to take, deposit, or in any way dispose of the donation. And because tribes are under federal jurisdiction, it becomes a crime against the United States.

On nearly every reservation there is a group of Indians striving to develop business enterprise which will enable Indians to work on their own land and increase their buying power. One example is the Lakota Cooperative Association on the Rosebud reservation. This business venture will eventually become an entire shopping complex, owned, operated, and enjoyed by Indians. The Broad Arrow Investment Corporation,

---

*Several organizations are rumored to have ties with the Mafia. Needless to say, documentation of these rumors has never been produced.

headed by Charles N. Bellow, is primarily responsible for funding this dream. Under construction at present is a garage employing Indian mechanics, to be operated in conjunction with a coffee shop, gift shop, and Indian arts and crafts shop. There are plans to set up a reservation-wide grocery chain as soon as capital is available, and an Indian-made product will be manufactured for nationwide delivery. If the general public would invest in such small businesses instead of blindly mailing checks to groups making unproved claims, they could buy a piece of the American Indians' brighter future.

Anyone who wants to invest in a truly worthwhile organization could find no better cause than American Indians and Friends Incorporated, or other legitimate links with the Indian people, operated by Indians who have dedicated their lives to improving the lot of their people.

Instead of spending time and energy on meaningless federal programs, the government should heed the voice of the Indian and develop economic enterprises that will fully utilize the Indians' assets—land, water, and tragically wasted human energy and ability.

# 5
# Treaties and Land: Real Estate Deals at Gunpoint

> Brothers, these people from the unknown world will cut down our groves, spoil our hunting and planting grounds, and drive us and our children from the graves of our fathers, and our council fires and enslave our women and children.
>
> —Metacom (King Philip), 1675

One could probably write a history of the United States, not in terms of starry-eyed pioneers and noble words, but in terms of fraudulent real estate transactions, often pushed through at gunpoint.

These real estate transactions were called treaties. Between 1778 and 1871, the federal government signed and ratified 371 of them, and history tells us that each one was broken or abrogated. Instead of taking a gangster's pride in this fantastic record of swindles, the government, even today, prefers to pretend they never happened. High school students, for instance, learn about the Louisiana Purchase, but the lands marked "acquired from France" on the school-book maps no more belong to France than East Germany belongs to the Soviet Union. The lands belonged to the Indian tribes who lived on them, and the United States duly recognized this by making treaties to change the legal ownership.

Treaty making went through a series of different styles. At first, when the Indian nations were a stronger power, the United States government carried out treaty making with all the panoply of international negotiations. Later, when the whites' need for land couldn't be satisfied in small gulps, and they were after a whole continent, the treaties became stopgap measures to keep the Indians at peace until they deteriorated from smallpox, whiskey, and political corruption.

In many cases, Indians were not even consulted, especially if they were too weak, or too peaceful, to pose much of a threat to white encroachment. Nor was the profiteering always strictly in the interests of the nation alone. Documentation exists that George Washington carried through some dealings that eventually gave him title to forty thousand acres of "free land" that had once belonged to Indians.

It was Andrew Jackson, fondly remembered for introducing the "spoils system" to American politics, who brought about the infamous Indian Removal Act. In theory, this law, enacted in 1830, allowed the president to generously give lands west of the Mississippi to Indians whose homes lay east of the Mississippi, thus removing them from their ancestral homes. In fact, it paved the way for the Trail of Tears, an Indian death march on which the old, the weak, and the young perished by thousands.

The Indians evicted by this mandate were the five civilized tribes—Cherokees, Choctaws, Creeks, Chickasaws, and Seminoles—called "civilized" because of their remarkable adaptation to the white man's material and intellectual culture. The Cherokees, in fact, waged and won a battle in the U.S. Supreme Court against the state of Georgia, which had seized on the Indian Removal Act to evict the Cherokees from their land.

Andy Jackson, "the Man of the People," expressed the sentiments of the white frontiersmen when he said, "John Marshall has rendered his decision; now let him enforce it!" Thus the executive branch of the government refused to recognize the decision of the judicial branch, and the Cherokees, who won the right to their land in court, lost it at gunpoint. The Georgia Militia threw them out of their comfortable homes with murder and rape, and in 1838 U.S. troops escorted them on a death march to Oklahoma after a handful of sold-out Cherokees agreed to sell the land they had already lost. For this treason, the ringleaders of the sell-out faction were later assassinated by their own tribesmen. They didn't die alone. Most sources estimate that a quarter of the tribe, about 4,000 people out of 16,000, succumbed to the privations of the journey. Of 1,000 Choctaw immigrants in another party, only 88 survived.

Like George Washington, Jackson was not solely a disinterested patriot. He made a good deal of money selling Indian land for three dollars an acre after buying it for forty cents.

At about the same time as the Cherokee death march, the last free Indians were being driven out of the Old Northwest (the Middle West of today) in a miserable affair called Black Hawk's War. Black Hawk made the mistake of trying to live on land that had been sold, during some very shady dealings, by a small minority of Indian collaborators. The "war" consisted of a confused series of verbal showdowns and skirmishes. It ended when the Indians, trying to cross the Mississippi to escape from the whites, were intercepted by a gunboat and butchered by whooping frontiersmen. "The Indians were pushed literally into the Mississippi, the current of which was at one time perceptibly tinged with blood of the Indians who were shot on its margin and in the stream," a white general noted.

During this period, Indian matters had been handled, appropiately, by the War Department, which had authority for treaty making and war making, whichever was expedient. The various states—as in Georgia's dislocation of the Cherokees—also took a hand. When, in 1834, the BIA of the War Department was set up to take charge of the Indians, a few well-meaning souls found their way into the ranks of the bureaucracy and began to take what measures they could to stem the massacres of Indians that attended the land-grabbing of the government. The Protestant churches, particularly the Quakers, were in the vanguard of this movement to restore some semblance of humanity to Indian affairs.

The Indian Removal Act had guaranteed that the Indians west of the Mississippi would be protected by the government from further incursions. Removal beyond the Mississippi, or later, beyond the 100th meridian, had seemed a solution to the Indian problem during the early years of the Republic. After all, surveyors and spies sent out from Washington had characterized most of the land between the Rockies and the Mississippi as the Great American Desert, so public opinion decided that the Indians and the desert deserved one another. But subsequent exploration made the land look desirable. And immigrants passing through the plains to Oregon and California posed a potential threat to Indian-white relations.

In 1851, the United States government formally recognized the plains tribes as a force to be reckoned with and convoked a treaty council at Fort Laramie, Wyoming, to legislate relations between the plains people and the United States.

This council was based on a number of assumptions. One was that the "chiefs" of the various tribes had an unequivocal right to order their followers around like serfs. This ludicrous assumption had remained with the whites since the days when John Smith's henchmen jammed the crown down around old Powhatan's ears declaring him king, and John Rolfe took the "Princess" Pocahontas back to England with him. In reality, Indian tribes, particularly the plains warriors, were democratic almost to the point of anarchy, but because it was a profitable fallacy the whites maintained it. Chiefs of the white man's choosing could sometimes be influenced to sell land or otherwise do the invaders' bidding.

The other faulty assumption was that the white man's word was his bond. The Indians, who lived in a culture of extreme verbal honesty, couldn't fathom how people could lie and lie again. They never seemed to realize that the treaties were merely marriages of convenience, made to be broken whenever expedient. The pattern had emerged on the East Coast and was carried west. Whites would make a treaty and then flagrantly violate it. Indians would fight to defend their land when they had no recourse left, suffer defeat, and be forced to cede more land in another treaty which was broken again at the white man's earliest convenience.

The pattern was repeated, in classic form, on the plains. The 1851 Laramie Treaty was broken after the Civil War when the whites tried to build a road through the Sioux hunting grounds to the Montana goldfields. The Sioux under Red Cloud were vehemently against the Bozeman Trail, or, as they called it, the Thieves' Road. The resulting war lasted for three years and was conducted with great tenacity by the Indians. It grew expensive and the government ended the fighting by signing the Sioux Treaty of 1868, defining the Indians' hunting ground again and promising them that the army would keep the whites out.

This rejection of whites as neighbors was not pure snobbery. Romanticized white histories have obscured the fact that frontier whites were dangerous to have around. The Indians had never forgotten the terrible smallpox epidemics of the 1830s. Nor were the wise older men blind to the effects of white man's brown crazy water, as they called the raw alcohol that fur traders palmed off on the Indians. Corruption of Indian women, through duplicity, was another cause for outrage and figured prominently in several outbreaks. But the overriding factor may well have been protection of life and limb. In one case, in 1873, some whites and Indians got into a saloon dispute that ended with several dead Indians. Instead of being stricken with remorse over the drunken murders, the whites exposed the dead Indians' heads on fence posts with humorous signs attached to them that read On the Reservation at Last and Let Harper's Speak of My Virtues.

When Wild Bill Hickok was shot in Deadwood, South Dakota, in 1876, his obsequies were almost disrupted when some teamsters from a freight wagon shot an Indian, apparently on general principles, and exhibited the man's head from saloon to saloon for free drinks. The solemnity of Wild Bill's funeral was saved when a gambler shot one of the teamsters dead and the man's friends calmed down and lost interest. Such was the character of many of the innocent homesteaders who constantly screamed for government protection as they encroached on Indian land.

Gentlemen of this persuasion began to invade the Sioux treaty lands in 1874, after gold was discovered in the sacred Black Hills. Government commissioners offered to buy the Black Hills, the Sioux refused to sell, and the BIA, in its wrath, declared that anyone who didn't report to his assigned agency was officially a hostile. Since the Sioux were, by the Treaty of 1868, a sovereign people on their own land, it is unclear what right the BIA had to order them around as if they were domestic help. Many Indians never received the message, but most of them had determined to resist anyway.

The army closed in with three invading forces in the biggest military operation since the Civil War. One prong, under Gen. George Crook, was beaten on the Rosebud Creek bottoms. Another, under Gen. George Custer, foolishly attacked the huge Indian camp at the Little Bighorn River and five companies under Custer's personal command were destroyed to the last man. The third column, under Colonel Gibbon, arrived in time to pick up the pieces.

While the fighting raged on through 1876 and 1877, a new government commission came out to patch things up. The power of Congress to make treaties with Indian nations had ended in 1871, so that subsequent real estate transactions were called *agreements*. The commissioners rounded up the Indians who chose to loaf around the fort and told them that they had a choice: sign away the Black Hills or starve. The loaf-around-the-forts signed and, while most of the Sioux Nation was still fighting or seeking refuge in Canada, the sacred Black Hills were wrested from their control on paper.

By 1880, active warfare had ceased, with a few exceptions—the Apache resistance in New Mexico and Arizona and the shameful massacre of Sioux refugees at Wounded Knee by the reconstituted Seventh Cavalry. With the Indians at peace and many eastern whites becoming sympathetic to their plight, the exploiters began to cast about for new ways to relieve them of "surplus" land.

In 1887, a way was found. Congress enacted the Dawes Severalty Act, better known as the Indian Allotment Act. The act was pushed through by the time-honored methods established in the signing of 371 treaties and countless agreements. Accessible leaders were bribed or flattered; sympathetic eastern whites were lied to, and the Dawes Severalty Act was promulgated—as every evil act has been since—as a master plan to bring Indians into the mainstream of American society. When Sitting Bull, the last of the great old Sioux war leaders, vehemently opposed the Allotment Act, the agent at the Standing Rock Agency saw to it that he wasn't invited to the signing. The same agent later figured in his murder. Less than 10 percent of the tribe, instead of the three-fourths majority required by treaty provision, signed the act, but Congress passed it anyway.

The Allotment Act was billed as giving the Indians the right to own land individually so that they could become small farmers. That most of the land to be allotted was not suited for dry farming, and that the Indians had no capital to start farms nor any interest in agriculture, did not concern the men who framed the act. The philosophy behind the Allotment Act also violated the traditional Indian attitude toward the land. To the Indian, the land was something no man could possess, any more than he could possess the air. Land was seen as sacred, an intrinsic part of the Almighty's cosmic design for life, and spoken of as mother earth, because it was mother of all living creatures. To the whites, this was pagan as well as communistic and had to be eradicated. This moral urge to reform the Indian coincided nicely with a chance to give the rest of the Indians' land to whites.

To the Indians, the government seemed to be lurking like a giant snake that had slowly hypnotized a helpless bird and was about to swallow its victim—a metaphor used in many Indian legends is of two snakes (the United States and Canada) who were nurtured by soft-hearted Indians until they grew monstrous and devoured their benefactors. In 1900, the government, through the BIA, began applying pressure on heads of families to select the 320 acres of land that the provisions of the Indian Allotment Act entitled them to. Although many of the traditional full bloods defied the government by refusing to select allotments, many members of the half-breed element, eager to please the all-powerful white agents, were among the first to select large tracts of land that controlled vital water in semiarid land areas.

Allotment, to say the least, was an economic disaster, although some school books persist in calling it a great boon to the Indians. At the time the Allotment Act went through, the Indian land base amounted to 138 million acres. Between 1887 and 1934, 60 percent of this land passed into the hands of whites. Some 60 million acres were lost through sale as "surplus," and the rest was sold by individuals. Almost two-thirds of the land allotted to individual Indians was signed over to whites.

The benevolence of this act may also be judged by the areas affected. In Arizona and New Mexico, where the land is arid and mountainous and not particularly desirable, allotment usually didn't take place. In Oklahoma, where the land was more valuable and the land-hungry whites were numerous, the reservations were wiped out to the extent that today there are no reservations in Oklahoma, which was founded as the "Land of the Redman" by those same five civilized tribes evicted from the South by Andrew Jackson and the state of Georgia.

In 1898, Congress ordered the Cherokee, Choctaw, Chickasaw, and Creek Nations dissolved and their tribal property shared among individual members. In 1908, restrictions on land sales by Indians were lifted. Grafters moved in like a plague of locusts and the Civilized Tribes were stripped bare. During the 1930s Depression, many landless Cherokees starved to death.

Before allotment, many tribes, under the tutelage of some astute half-breeds, had begun to build up large herds of horses and cattle. As their herds prospered, some Indians actually became men of wealth in the eyes of their white neighbors. With the spread of allotment, this came to an end. The land was opened to homesteaders after the Indians had chosen their allotments. Many of these homesteaders were in fact not free entrepreneurs but in the pay of large land interests. Most agents saw to it that the Indians were not informed of their right to choose homesteads until all the land was taken.

The allotment process could be called a second slaughter of the buffalo as far as the Plains Indian economy was concerned. The big horse and cattle herds disappeared, sold by force through a state law that allowed the county sheriff to sell Indian livestock until all state and county taxes were paid in full. Although such a practice was illegally executed, since the federal government held exclusive jurisdiction over all Indian land and property, the federal agents allowed this procedure to occur in an effort to destroy the Indian economy. Gone were the annual roundups when the Indians culled out their surplus horses and cattle to be sold to surrounding white ranchers or to be shipped by rail to market as far away as Chicago. From near self-sufficiency, the Indians slumped back into poverty where they were to remain while everyone else prospered from Indian land.

Despite their treatment, the Indians rushed forward to volunteer for service in World War I, demonstrating the courage that had once led white generals to call them the "best light cavalry in the world." Their reward for this patriotic fervor came when the U.S. issued *forced patent-in-fee* title to their allotments. A forced patent-in-fee meant that the Indians now owned their lands free and clear of all government restrictions and would pay taxes like all other citizens. Of course, most Indians did not realize this until their land was sold by tax deed for failure to pay state and local taxes. More millions of acres passed out of Indian ownership, and the states enriched themselves with the sale of more Indian land.

Under cover of war, the United States Army disgraced itself by capriciously seizing a little more Indian land, proving that the spirit of Custer was not yet dead.

For generations, the Nisqualli Indians, a small, self-sufficient tribe of fishermen, had lived on their four-thousand-acre reservation along the Nisqualli River in Washington State on land guaranteed them by treaty. In the winter of 1917, soldiers from Fort Lewis, Washington, evicted them from their houses at gunpoint, loaded the hundred or so Nisquallis onto wagons, drove them off their own land, and dumped them in the wintry forest to fend for themselves. The army, it was explained, wanted the reservation for a firing range and was deporting the Indians for their own protection.

After several years without a home, the Nisquallis received seventy-eight thousand dollars from Congress to purchase new land. The only available land was adjoining other reservations far from their own ancestral land and fishing grounds. In effect, the Nisquallis, protected by a sacred treaty, supreme law of the land, had been destroyed as a tribe, at least on paper—to make room for a firing range. The Nisquallis ended up with three acres to call their own.

But some tribesmen refused to accept this illegal deportation and returned to their own fishing grounds at Frank's Landing, on a small remnant of the reservation not actually held by the army. There they continued to fish for a living, despite attacks by game wardens. These people—the Bridges, McCloud, and Siatacum families, later joined by Hank Adams—became some of the first leaders of the modern Indian activist movement. They insisted on their treaty rights, even though the state game wardens continued to prosecute them for fishing. The game wardens thus violated federal law to enforce state law, making the law-and-order issue of the case look a bit ridiculous.

During World War II, while thousands of Indians were rushing to enlist and fight overseas, a similar stab in the back struck the Oglala Sioux of the Pine Ridge reservation. In 1942, the War Department teamed up with the BIA and took five hundred square miles from the Oglala Sioux for use as a practice bombing range. The Indian owners were given anywhere from eight days to a month to evacuate and were told that if they stayed around they would either be bombed or killed by "the Japs," who were said to be just over the next hill.

The Indians were told they would be paid for their allotments, which were about half good grassland and half badlands, and that the land would be returned at the end of the war. The payment was a joke. One old man was paid $232 for 320 acres. A woman received $200 for 400 acres. When she protested, she was accused of being unpatriotic. This is bitterly ironic, for the reservation was almost completely stripped of young and middle-aged men who had volunteered for the war. Had the better-educated men been present in large numbers, they might have averted this shameless exploitation.

After the war, the government reneged on its promise. In 1965, the War Department declared the land surplus and handed it over to the General Services Administration. Today, despite two major protest demonstrations, most of the land is still under government control—the badlands section is intended to go to the Badlands National Monument, and the grasslands are slated for use by the white ranchers.

By 1928, the Indians, now duly declared citizens, began to stir against the government and to send delegations to Washington to protest their treatment and to make demands for justice. As if the Great Spirit were answering the Indian prayers, the stock market crashed in 1929. Then the great drought created a dust bowl and thousands of homesteaders moved off the reservations, leaving their plundered lands for the breadlines in the cities. The Hoover administration reeled under the depression, and Franklin D. Roosevelt swept to victory.

Roosevelt appointed Harold Ickes as secretary of the interior, and Ickes sought out John Collier, an anthropologist, as commissioner of Indian affairs. Under pressure of these New Dealers, the BIA shuffled around and prepared new legislation.

On the reservations, the Indians, inured to years of poverty, hardly noticed the depression. In some ways, the national disaster was a blessing for the Indians. Not only did it remove thousands of white homesteaders from Indian land, but some of the New Deal work programs spilled over into Indian country. The Civilian Conservation Corps (Indian division) provided some Indians with employment opportunities for the first time in their lives, creating housing on some reservations as a sort of make-work project.

But the legislation being shaped in Washington proved to be another disaster. John Collier's brainchild, the Indian Reorganization Act of 1934, was billed as a move to reform the Indians by providing them "self-government." The act was bitterly opposed by many tribes who preferred their own forms of government, but it became law anyway.

Collier hit the campaign trail to sell the act to the Indian people. Since the act provided for each and every tribe to hold a referendum before accepting it, Collier had some heavy selling to do. Indians across the nation saw the act as a scheme to throw them into the melting pot and mold them into what the politicians thought an average American should be. Wherever he went, Collier met with traditional leaders who complained of the broken treaties of the past and asked him what made him think that this one would turn out any better.

The Indians began to organize a campaign of their own to oppose the IRA. Collier, authorized by Ickes, drew on government funds to hire Indian leaders to sell the act of the tribes in their own areas. The hired Indian politicos made promises that many reservation people found hard to resist, especially if they were geared toward the white ethic of competition. The full-blood element on most reservations stood firmly opposed, although a few defected.

But, as the date of the referendum neared, the full-blood faction made a terrible mistake. Thinking in Indian rather than white terms, they urged their partisans to show their feeling by boycotting the election and staying away from the polls. On reservation after reservation, the tribes voted to accept the Indian Reorganization Act by a slim margin. In the Midwest, nearly every tribe, except the Yankton Sioux of South Dakota and the Winnebago of Wisconsin, accepted the act only because most of the opposition failed to exercise their right to vote.

The Pueblos of the Southwest, the most conservative of all the tribes, stood as one in resistance to the act and held on to their tribal government, which is closely interwoven with their religion. But across the rest of the country, most tribes succumbed to this latest assault on Indian culture.

From 1934, when the IRA took effect, through 1953, the dictatorial BIA superintendents maintained almost absolute control over newly elected puppet tribal councils. In many cases, the superintendents issued special rations to the councilmen who did their bidding. The BIA wrote the tribal constitutions for them so that nearly every act of the tribal council was subject to the approval of the secretary of the interior. The adoption of tribal members, the internal law-and-order code, the approval of land transactions, the appropriation of tribal funds, the approval of loans from the revolving loan funds for business or livestock enterprises, and the approval of release of tribal funds in the U.S. Treasury were all subject to the whims of the superintendents, most of whom thoroughly enjoyed their power while they held the Indians in contempt.

However, the IRA did put an end to the allotting of land to individuals, thus checking the loss of Indian land—on paper. But the 1887 Dawes Severalty Act still wrought havoc through the heirship problem that developed over the years following the allotment of Indian lands to individuals. The Dawes Act's concept of land ownership by individual Indians caused untold hardship within the legal fields of inheritance that automatically arose from its provisions.

The heirship problem may have been a coincidental outgrowth of the Dawes Severalty Act's mistaken attempt to force assimilation on the Indians. But many Indians, burned more than once, believe that the havoc it created was intentional. Because most Indians refused to make wills to pass their allotments on to their favored descendants, the land went into heirship status and was fractionalized into multiple ownership. In some cases, one 160-acre plot may have as many as 100 joint owners.

Multiple ownership plus trust status is one of the major causes of Indian poverty, because it prevents efficient usage of the land by the owners. In this day of agribusiness, it is obviously inefficient, even financially impossible, to farm plots of five and ten acres of dry land. Moreover, because land in trust status is held in the name of the United States of America on behalf of the Indian owner, just as tribal land is held in trust, the Indian owner cannot do anything with his land without the permission of the BIA superintendent, who acts on behalf of the United States government.

Indians cannot even collect lease income on their land for more than one year at a time. The law that prevents them from doing so was enacted in Congress in 1956, and amended the law to prevent long-term leasing because a South Dakota congressman came charging down the aisle of the House of Representatives waving telegrams from "his" Indians as he offered this amendment.

Lease incomes on Indian land today vary across the nation, depending on, among other factors, the honesty of the agency superintendent and the ability of the tribal council to cope with the outside political forces around their reservation. Less than ten years ago, many tribes were leasing tribal grasslands to whites at less than ten cents an acre with the approval of the BIA. On the Oglala Sioux reservation at Pine Ridge, the United States itself was leasing over 100,000 acres of Indian land at three cents an acre. When the tribe raised the issue of just recompense, the government generously raised the rental to ten cents an acre.

At the same time, the BIA was approving thousands of lease contracts for farmland for as little as $2 per acre while the white farmers leasing the land from Indian owners were receiving from $8 to $24 per acre from the Federal Soil Bank for leaving the same land under summer fallow. To clear an average profit of $16 per acre, the farmer had only to keep the weeds down by plowing the fields three times during the growing season. This practice was permitted by both the Department of the Interior and the Department of Agriculture.

Although a white farmer could place this Indian land in a federal agricultural program, the Indian who owned the land was not allowed to do so.

The blame of this sorry mess is not solely laid at the door of the BIA; Congress openly discriminated against Indians by refusing to allow tribes to use their own funds to purchase other lands, including the lands they lost through earlier swindles. In simple language, the Congress was impounding tribal moneys so that Indians, even if they had the wherewithal, could not enjoy economic growth along with all other corporations and individual citizens. This restriction was in force from 1934 through 1964 and may still be in effect for some tribes.

Today, the various tribes are still hindered in free operation of their lands, but not nearly as severely as the individual Indian. Federal laws are strangling the individual Indian owner in red tape (which Indians call white tape) entangling anyone who wishes to make the simplest changes in the status of his own property in a mesh of confusing and degrading legal technicalities.

Public Law 450, for instance, provides that any Indian can mortgage his land, a proviso that the public no doubt assumes to grant the Indian equal status to everyone else with a mortgage. But under the regulations and the BIA white tape, it takes an intelligent and well-informed Indian more than two years to secure such a mortgage, thanks to the enormous amount of boondoggling involved. Particularly to a people with a heritage of freedom, this creates horrendous frustrations as well as imposing an economic hardship.

The BIA has been known to refuse to give an Indian any of his lease income unless he signs power of attorney over to the superintendent. This practice occurs on reservations where *range units* are maintained in compliance with the Indian Reorganization Act of 1934. Under a provision of the act, the secretary of the interior can force the tribe and all affected individual

Indians to place their lands in range units which are advertised for public sale in huge blocks. Some range units encompass well over 10,000 acres of Indian land. On an average these range units will bring in approximately $30 per animal, and under the BIA regulations an average of eight animals can be grazed on each 160 acres. This means that every Indian who has 160 acres in the range unit will receive about $240 per year for the use of his land.

The federal government has prosecuted Indians for refusing to take part in their "range unit systems."

On land owned by the United States, grazing law consists of the Taylor Grazing Act. Much as oil companies receive special privileges, those who hold grazing permits under the Taylor Grazing Act are given a special profit-making advantage. Under this act, the federal government is only receiving thirty cents per animal per month for grazing privileges on government-owned land. To add to this legalized robbery of the taxpayers, the permit holder only has to pay for eight months out of a year. In reality, he is paying a grand total of $2.40 per year for grazing one steer, bull, or cow. On the market in 1973, this same animal will bring in from $325.00 to $650.00.

To add insult to injury, holders of the Taylor Grazing Act permits don't have to meet any competitive bidding and they may sell their permits to anyone they choose.

Here is a case where the taxpayers are losing more than a billion dollars annually while the individual states lose thousands more, for the Taylor Grazing Act provides that 25 percent of the grazing fee be paid to the state in which the land is located, so that the money may be used for educational purposes.

This legalized swindle was even worse previous to 1964, when the secretary of the interior, Stewart Udall, doubled the fees from fifteen cents per animal per month to the present thirty cents.

The point is this: if ranching interests are thus allowed to rake off a handsome profit at the expense of the majority of white taxpayers, how much easier is it for the government to permit them to abuse the reservation Indians?

One of the government's noteworthy attempts to cast a benevolent light over their dealings with Indian tribes was the creation of the Indian Claims Commission in 1946. By its very concept, this commission was an insult, for it forced the Indians to sue the government to receive payment for damages, rather than relying on the 371 sacred treaties. Thus it seemed to deny the duplicity of the past even as it sought to rectify it. Since 1946, the Indian Claims Commission has paid various tribes about $100 million. This sounds like a lot until one considers the amount of land taken from the Indian. Based on the contemporary Indian population (purely by example, since payments are made to individual tribes) it would mean that every Indian would receive about $225.

Indian lands, once considered "free," are still treated in this manner by the ranchers and other whites who reside on reservations. While the ranchers exploit Indian lands for profit, local governing bodies trespass for reasons of convenience, building roads, setting up high-tension wires, and committing other "improvements" without consulting the Indian landowners.

The government's cavalier attitude toward Indian land rights is even more evident in their failure to protect Indian natural resources. From 1778 until 1958, the Department of the Interior approved the sale of Indian lands without the slightest mention of water and mineral rights. The Rosebud Sioux Tribal Council changed this through their attempts to negotiate an oil lease on their reservation to secure money to alleviate tribal poverty. During this transaction, the assistant secretary of the interior in charge of the BIA, as well as the Bureau of Land Management (BLM), saw fit to order a new regulation that tightened up controls on minerals, oil, and gas. The new regulation required that all mineral rights be retained by the landowner in supervised sales of Indian land.

This meant that whenever the government approved of a land sale and publicly advertised the land for sale, all mineral rights would be held in trust for the Indian owners.

Previous to this legislation, minerals had caused conflicts that have haunted the Indians, the whites, and the BIA down to the present day. In one case, the government ripped off a 232,000-acre zone of grazing land from the San Carlos Apache reservation in Arizona "for mineral development only." When the so-called mineral strip proved to have no minerals worth mining, the government opened up the grazing lands to white ranchers without consulting the Apaches. Over the years, some parcels of the mineral strip have ended up on state rolls and others are under control of the U.S. Forest Service and the BLM, both subsidiaries of the Department of the Interior. This indicates how hard the Department of the Interior works to protect the Indians' land rights. Under the BLM, twenty white ranchers moved onto the mineral strip and began to consider it their home.

In 1969, an executive order, backed by the secretary of the interior, Stewart Udall, returned all surface rights in the mineral strip to the San Carlos Apaches. Four years later, the white ranchers were still illegally squatting there and defying tribal orders to leave. Finally, after the Wounded Knee take-over of 1973, the San Carlos Apaches began to hint that their patience was wearing thin and that they too owned rifles. Meanwhile, the ranchers were insisting that the BIA, which they blamed for their predicament, pay them compensation for their losses in having to vacate the mineral strip.

Water rights are another vital problem, and the absence of aggressive protective action on the part of the BIA has reduced many a tribe from self-support to dire poverty. One case is the Pima tribe, one of the friendliest tribes ever encountered by the whites in their invasion of America. Without being conquered or coerced, the Pimas became Christians and learned to farm, even raising wheat to sell to frontier whites. They were hereditary enemies of the Apaches, and they supplied scouts to the U.S. Army in the wars of Cochise and Geronimo. They accepted, willingly, a reservation that represented part of their original holdings. But whites moved in around them and began to build deep wells and pumps and dam the rivers. This took the vital water out of the Pimas' reach, and their lands dried up. When the Coolidge Dam was built, the Pimas were promised a share of the water, but they lacked the money to pay for the pumps and other irrigating equipment or to compete with surrounding white farmers, most of whom would prefer to see that things stay that way.

Another people plagued by water rights, or the lack of them, are the Pyramid Lake Paiutes. Pyramid Lake is the source of their main livelihood, but white interests are draining the lake from under them at such a rate that their way of life is seriously imperiled.

Water rights are one of the many areas where the Indians come into direct conflict with the big business interests which have far greater pull with the Department of the Interior than any tribe of Indians. It is not surprising that Indians usually get shafted. This conflict exploded into the public's attention briefly when the first AIM war party hit the BIA building on 22 September 1971. One of their demands was that William Veeder, a white expert on Indian water rights, be retained in his position instead of transferred into oblivion. Their reason: Veeder, a white man, had been doing his best to protect Indian water rights from exploitation by vested interests inside the Department of the Interior. For this, his superiors had decided to punish him.

Belatedly, on 8 July 1970 President Nixon announced that a special office of Indian Water Rights had been established. To the general public, this seemed a momentous gesture of goodwill. To the Indians, it meant that the water that was theirs by treaty was to be thrown into the political arena to be ruled on by the judicial system. With justified suspicion, Indian people looked on this move as the end of Indian water rights and the continuance of the theft of Indian resources.

More relevant was the beginning of an activist Indian movement prepared once again to defend their land in the way they know best and the only way the white man seems to understand—with guns. As events of the last two years have shown, Indian people are no longer willing to passively accept whatever dictates a malevolent government chooses to aim at them.

# 6
# Law and Disorder

> An Indian reservation is a tract of land set aside for the exclusive use of Indians, surrounded by thieves.
>
> —Gen. William Tecumseh Sherman, circa 1880

Law enforcement, like most other things in Indian life, has decayed from a sound, functional system, developed by the Indians, into a complex maze of technicalities under white control. Most federal reservations have three sets of law enforcement organizations to contend with: the FBI, their own Indian police, and the white police of the state in which the reservation is located.

It could be contended that the FBI has jurisdiction on the various reservations today because of the sex life of Chief Spotted Tail of the Brulé Sioux.

Spotted Tail, a strong and courageous man, was best known as a friend of the whites, for he realized early on that the soldiers were too numerous to be defeated, and he preferred to keep what lands he could through diplomacy. He was a skilled orator who sought peace, but he wasn't afraid to offend white commissioners by standing up for his rights and his tribe. But women were his joy, and, in the end, his undoing.

When he was a young man, hardly more than a boy, Spotted Tail fell in love with a beautiful Sioux girl named Appearing Day. His rival for her hand was the renowned warrior Running Bear, a much older and more influential man. The two men met one day outside the camp and the next day they were found sprawled across each other's bodies with their butcher knives in their hands. Running Bear was dead, with Spotted

Tail's knife in his heart, but Spotted Tail, fearfully hacked up, was still breathing. Appearing Day nursed him back to health and they were married.

Spotted Tail's next source of woe was his daughter Fleet Foot, a tall, headstrong girl whose temperament resembled her father's. Fleet Foot decided that she wanted to marry a white man—not just any white man, but an army officer. When Spotted Tail became enraged after some white ranchers had insulted him, Fleet Foot threatened to kill herself if he went on the warpath, and she actually began to cut herself with a knife. To humor Fleet Foot, Spotted Tail cooled his temper and remained at peace with the whites.

Ironically, Fleet Foot, who was fond of the whites and wanted to become an officer's bride, died of pneumonia, a white man's disease, in March 1866. She was given a full military funeral by the commander of Fort Laramie, with a guard of honor around the coffin and a howitzer fired off every half hour through the night. This honor to his daughter helped win Spotted Tail over to the whites, who were later to declare him chief over all the Sioux—without consulting the other Indians.

Spotted Tail's final woman trouble came after Fleet Foot's mother had died. He lured away the wife of a crippled Sioux named Medicine Bear, an act the Sioux took seriously. Medicine Bear's relative, a warrior named Crow Dog, swore he would avenge this breach of honor. On 5 August 1881, Spotted Tail, coming from a tribal council meeting, met Crow Dog and his wife coming from the opposite direction in a buckboard. Crow Dog swung up his gun and blasted Spotted Tail before the chief could get his six-shooter clear of its holster.

Crow Dog hid out while his relatives offered restitution in horses and other goods to Spotted Tail's family. The chief's kinsmen accepted this—Spotted Tail, after all, had run off with another man's wife, which was grounds for a shooting. But the white authorities couldn't let it go. After years of casual murder, the frontier was trying hard to become respectable. Crow

Dog was dragged off to court in Deadwood, South Dakota, and sentenced to hang.

It is mute testimony to the respect for the word of an Indian held by even the crudest frontiersmen that Crow Dog was released from jail and allowed to live with his wife on the reservation until the day of the hanging. Calmly, he gave away his horses, asked his relatives to look after his family, and returned, on the appointed day, prepared to die. To his delight, he found out that his attorney had successfully appealed the case. The U.S. Supreme Court had ruled that the federal authorities had no jurisdiction over a crime committed by one Indian against another on a reservation. Crow Dog was set free.

But white outrage over the death of Spotted Tail shortly made this immunity a thing of the past. In 1885, the Seven Major Crimes Act made the Indians on reservations subject to prosecution for murder, manslaughter, rape, assault with intent to kill, arson, burglary, and larceny. The FBI has jurisdiction in the case of these serious offenses.

Before the Wounded Knee fire fight in 1973, the reservation people had at least some regard for the FBI, which, if not as efficient as has been claimed, was not actively hostile to Indian people and therefore preferable to the various state agencies.

One case the FBI was particularly proud of was the murder ring they broke up in Osage County, Oklahoma, in the 1920s.

The Osages had been shunted down to Oklahoma from their original hunting grounds during the Indian wars, and they were as poor as most Oklahoma tribes for many years. But about the time of World War I, oil was discovered on their land, and leasing arrangements set up by the government made them among the richest people, per capita, in the world. Among the hordes of sharpers, crooks, prostitutes, pimps, and mountebanks that moved in to help the Osages spend their money came William K. Hale, a banker who made money by filing fraudulent liens against the estate of every Osage that died, for goods allegedly purchased and never paid for. This worked for a while. When Hale began to tire of the slowness of this process, he began to hire men to kill off the Osages. His most grandiose plot was to wipe out six members of the same family so that his nephew, who was married to one of them, could collect their total inheritance.

Hale is believed to have murdered at least seven Osages and three non-Indians. After one gruesome triple bombing—which killed a white man—the FBI took an interest in the case, and four undercover investigators penetrated Osage County. After six years and four different trials, Hale was convicted of hiring men to kill Henry Roan Horse, a full-blood Osage, and in 1929 was sentenced to life imprisonment. He was paroled in 1947, which means he served about eighteen months for each death he instigated.

Aside from their control over the Indians' own tribal police forces, the BIA had special agents to prevent the sale or distribution of liquor among Indians. Some idea of the high quality of the personnel employed may be discerned from the career of Richard James Hart, special officer to the Indian service for the Winnebago and Omaha tribes. Hart earned a reputation for brutality among these tribes, and he was transferred to Sioux City, Iowa, where he was charged with killing an Indian, allegedly a bootlegger, in a saloon brawl. He was freed and transferred to Coeur d'Alene, Idaho, where he was again tried for murder but again freed. Subsequent probing into Hart's career showed that he was in reality Al Capone's older brother, Jim Capone. It sort of made you wonder who took care of the hiring and firing at the BIA.*

Most minor crimes on the reservation are covered by the Indian police, a group that might be called the unnatural offspring of Gen. George Crook and the old tribal warrior societies. Before the whites took control of Indian lives, the various warrior societies of each of the plains tribes took care of police work, and the councils of chiefs acted as judges. Crimes against property were never a serious problem in Indian society.

---

*John Kobler, *Capone* (New York: G. P. Putnam's Sons, 1971).

Anyone who stole from his neighbors was held in such contempt that theft was almost unknown. The main duties of the camp police were to separate people who got into fights and to prevent overeager young men from spoiling the communal buffalo hunts by charging the herd before the rest of the hunters were ready. Laws were as few as crimes were rare. If anyone was crass enough to steal anything, he was forced to restore it to the owners. Anyone who murdered a fellow tribesman would be punished, sometimes by death, more often by exile, a cruel fate on the lonely plains. Adulterous wives would usually be cut across the face or have their noses cut off, generally by their husbands, and subsequently be cast adrift. A flagrantly promiscuous girl would be thrown out of camp, usually by the other women. Public opinion preserved the morality of the tribe.

When the tribes were first placed on reservations, the army kept order. This was a bad idea. The constant presence of soldiers was an embarrassment to the proud warriors, reminding them of defeat and oppression. Also, the younger men, especially those who had never taken part in battles and raids, often tried to show their courage by defying the soldiers. The soldiers themselves were a problem. Many of the old-timers hated Indians with a passion; young recruits were often terrified of the tribesmen and interpreted every act as a threat of renewed warfare.

In the 1870s, when General Crook was pacifying the Apaches, he used Apache warriors themselves as a sort of tribal police, thus preventing the kind of army-Indian friction that led to the massacre at Wounded Knee, among other disasters, and the BIA began to consider expanding the idea all across the country. In 1877, the commissioner of Indian affairs wrote the following:

> I would recommend that the force be composed of Indians, properly drilled and officered by white men, and where capable Indians can be found, that they be promoted to command, as reward for faithful service. The army has used Indians for scouts with great success,

> and wherever employed the Indian has been found faithful to the trust confided in him. I would also recommend that the police force be supplied with a uniform similar to the style of clothing which I shall hereafter suggest to be furnished all Indians, with the addition of a few brass buttons by way of distinction. The employment of such a force, properly officered and handled, would, in great measure, relieve the army from doing police duty on Indian reservations. I am thoroughly satisfied that the saving in life and property by the employment of such a force would be very large, and that it would materially aid in placing the entire Indian population of the country on the road to civilization.

"Placing the Indians on the road to civilization," of course, meant destroying the old ways, especially of the warrior societies which were tradition oriented and a mainstay of the power of the old chiefs and medicine men. The BIA would be served, and in 1880, Indian police forces were formed on forty different reservations. The Indian police reported directly to the agents, or "majors," who ruled the reservations as petty fiefdoms.

The Indian police won the respect of many whites. One service they did for the tribes was to prevent the white cowboys from cutting the barbed-wire fences around the reservations to rustle cattle and horses or to graze their own stock in Indian grass. They also provided some of the younger men with an outlet for their martial spirit, which might otherwise have been channeled into furtive raids and escapes from the reservation.

But the cumulative effect on the tribe's traditions was almost all bad. Most tribes regarded the Indian police as a band of renegade sellouts or, at least, as a bunch of misguided and not very well-bred young men. On the Northern Cheyenne reservation in the 1890s, the Indian police were powerless to keep the people from butchering stray cattle. In desperation, the agent called out the old warrior societies who put down the cattle butchering in short order. They resorted to the methods they had always used to punish lawbreakers

—destroying the violator's property and killing his horses, with a beating for good measure if he put up a fight. The butchering stopped, the agent returned control of law and order to the Indian police, and the butchering started again. The warrior societies went back to team plowing, a job they did with vigor but without much relish.

The Indian police were never reticent about firing on their own people. The Sioux called the Indian police "metal breasts," as much in comment on their hardheartedness as on their shiny badges.

In 1887, Wraps-Up-His-Tail, a medicine man from the prowhite Crow tribe, began to say that he was bulletproof, and he demonstrated his power to cut down trees by pointing his saber at them. He said he could do the same thing to white soldiers. Nervous settlers ran to the agent, and the troops were called out to arrest the medicine man. When they arrived, the Crow Indian police struck the agitating Crows first. Wraps-Up-His-Tail was shot in the arm and gave himself up. Crazy Head, one of the Crow Indian police, then shot Wraps-Up-His-Tail in the head, proving that the medicine man hadn't really been invulnerable. For years after, most of his fellow tribesmen scorned Crazy Head for shooting a fellow Crow.

In 1894 on the Northern Cheyenne reservation, two young men got into some trouble trying to impress one man's girl friend. Head Chief, a young Cheyenne, was visiting a girl who regretted that she had no food to offer him. He rode out with his friend Young Mule and butchered a white man's cow to impress the girl and feed her family. While the two Indians were carving up the beef, a white man named Hugh Boyle rode up and made some rude remarks to the young Cheyennes. "He calls us dogs," Young Mule translated. In a fit of rage, Head Chief shot the white man. The two boys hid out in a remote part of the reservation and sent word to the whites that they wanted to fight the soldiers. The army was called out and the two young men, dressed and painted for death, attacked the troops and the Indian police. Head Chief rode through the soldiers' firing line before he collapsed with three bullets in him. Young Mule's horse was shot from under him, and he fought from a clump of brush until he was killed. The Indian police fought along with the soldiers.

The Indian police were given additional jobs that made them unpopular. When Indian children ran away from the brutality of boarding school instructors, the Indian police were forced to act as truant officers and bring them back hog-tied in buckboards. On at least one reservation, they were sent to break up the sacred Sun Dance. Fearing that the dancers would resist with guns, the Indian police went to the dance ground painted for death and wearing their best clothes, in the tradition of warriors about to meet their Maker. Fortunately, the dancers didn't have the heart to fire on their own people. For years after, until the 1950s, the Sun Dance was either discontinued or held secretly, and the big Indian holiday on the reservations became the Fourth of July. Incongruous as this celebration of independence may have been to the tribes, the BIA superintendents found it more acceptable.

Between 1890 and 1930, the Indian police were often active in attempts to break up the power of Indian religion. Medicine bundles were confiscated and burned, sacred pipes were broken, and medicine men were jailed for practicing Indian healing or holding the old ceremonies. This was done under the so-called Indian Offenses Act, which meant, quite simply, that Indian religion was a crime. Since most of the Indian police of this era were recent converts to the white man's religions, usually Catholicism, they did their job with zealous enthusiasm.

One interesting BIA policy carried out by the Indian police was to give a haircut to any arrested male Indian. Braids or other long hair were considered the marks of savagery, or at least of defiance. Many Indians were more resentful of the haircuts than of the sentences imposed by the superintendent.

Under the Indian Reorganization Act of 1934, police jobs became subject to direct or indirect nepotism. Direct nepotism meant that the tribal chairman and his councilmen appointed their relatives to jobs in the tribal force. Indirect nepotism meant that when a mixed-blood administration came to power the tribal council harassed the full bloods off the force and gave their jobs to mixed-bloods, and vice versa. Morale sagged because of this blatant favoritism, and many dedicated Indian policemen became obsessed with holding onto their jobs by whatever means necessary.* During the 1950s and 1960s, a favorite pastime on at least one reservation was a sort of peekaboo game in which they took pictures of one another sleeping on duty so that anyone charged with negligence in a job shuffle could have evidence against his accusers as well. Some feared losing their badges because they dreaded retribution by fellow tribesmen.

State jurisdiction over reservations depends on where the reservation is located. Most places where Indians live east of the Mississippi have no federal status as reservations, and in these cases the states maintain law and order. Most of the Indians involved dislike this system, because states have an even worse reputation than the federal government for protecting Indian rights. Indian people have no choice in the matter. Neither did the tribes in the five western states that assumed jurisdiction over the reservations during the era of termination. With a stroke of the pen, on 15 August 1954, Public Law 280 gave the states of Washington, Oregon, Nebraska, Minnesota, and Wisconsin jurisdiction over the reservations within their borders, with a few exceptions. This was a disaster for the Indians. In Washington and Oregon, the state police and game wardens began to interfere with the fishing rights of the Indians on their own reservations. Nebraska, which had always borne a dark name among Indian people for racism, became even more bigoted as the police there began to assume more power over Indian lives. In Minnesota and Wisconsin, state authorities used their new powers to break up Indian families by removing children from the custody of their parents and placing them in foster

---

*During the turmoil on Pine Ridge reservation after Wounded Knee II, AIM supporters blamed BIA police for several killings and many beatings of AIM supporters.

homes. In theory, this was done to provide the children with a better environment. In practice, it was a method of breaking up the culture and of penalizing Indian mothers who applied for welfare assistance to feed their families. The most arbitrary standards were sometimes applied—too many children in a single room, inadequate plumbing, and the like. In many cases, children from unbroken homes were removed. The white foster homes they were sent to received a per capita payment for each child, so that boarding Indian children became a business to many whites far less qualified to care for the children than their natural parents.

By 1970, the ratio of Indian to white children in foster homes was ten to one in Montana, seventeen to one in North and South Dakota, and twenty-four to one in Minnesota. Many of these children were not unwanted by their families—they were forcibly removed by outside interlopers.

Ten years after Public Law 280 had been foisted off on the Indians of Washington, Oregon, Nebraska, Wisconsin, and Minnesota, the South Dakota state legislature tried to extend it to the Sioux reservations. The Sioux didn't want to subject their children to "Indian kidnapping agencies," nor did they want the often callous state troopers to invade their domain. Three months after Governor Archie Gubbrud signed the state jurisdiction into law in March 1963, Sioux tribal leaders presented him with a petition forcing the question of Public Law 280 onto the ballot.

The projurisdiction faction of whites, led by ranchers who utilized Indian land to fatten their cattle, tried to portray the jurisdiction law as a measure to "give the Indians full citizenship." This ploy had been used to justify every theft of Indian land since the Dawes Severalty Act of 1887, including the huge losses of Indian land after the Citizenship Act of 1924. But this time, the Indians were ready to resist. Every tribal faction, full blood and mixed-blood, Christian and traditional, young and old, began to mobilize and to muster their own ranks to vote the jurisdiction act down. They were helped by South Dakota's Council of (Protestant) Churches and by Father Joseph Karol of the Catholic Church. The Episcopal Church declared that, in Christian conscience, it had to oppose the state jurisdiction, and the Sioux found out that, at least in the eastern part of South Dakota, they had more white friends than they realized.

Election day was 3 November 1963. An amazing 90 percent of all eligible Sioux turned out to vote. The previous record was below 40 percent. Across the state, the Sioux and their white allies defeated the state jurisdiction attempt by nearly a four-to-one margin, with 201,389 votes opposed and only 58,289 in favor. On every reservation in the state the Indians held dances of triumph to celebrate their victory.

The Sioux were no strangers to the dual standard of justice that is the new code of the West. State police were barred from the reservations, but the Indians who went off-reservation to buy groceries and clothing or to drink had sampled their brutality for decades. White South Dakota police had won the state the sobriquet "Mississippi of the North" among Indian people.

In 1959, when Public Law 280 had been in effect on some reservations for six years, I testified before the Interior and Insular Subcommittee on Indian Affairs about the effect of the law on Indian people.

> Indians are arrested wholesale, because officials are paid mileage fees for each arrest on a reservation.
>
> Indian women have been attacked sexually while in jail. A fifteen-year-old girl became pregnant after such an attack.
>
> Indian men are brutally beaten and chained while in jail.
>
> Jail sentences for Indians are grossly disproportionate when compared with similar convictions and sentences for whites.
>
> Indian life is cheap in the eyes of the local authorities. An Indian who murdered another Indian was sentenced to four years in the state penitentiary. A white man, "Nig" Ryan, killed an Indian and was sentenced to a one hundred dollar fine and 30 days in jail and did not serve one day of the sentence or pay one dime of the fine.

Another white man shot an Indian in the back seven times, killing him, and received two years in the penitentiary, of which he served six months.

Since reservation Indians are not on the tax roll, they are excluded from jury duty, and therefore it would be futile for an Indian to expect trial by his peers.

When the *New York Times* broke a story on the treatment of Indians in South Dakota, conditions became worse instead of better. Police in the white town of Martin once jammed forty-two Indian prisoners into a filthy cell intended for eight men, and they were known to handcuff men to their bunks. In Winner, South Dakota, a state patrolman fired his tear-gas gun into a cell in the city jail crammed with Indian men and women. In Todd County, law officers passed jail keys around to police and nonpolice alike. Members of this "key club" were allowed to enter cells and rape female prisoners. In another incident, the police set a police dog on six Indians in a jail cell.

The classic case of separate-but-unequal justice in South Dakota took place in 1967. On 24 March of that year, two young Indians, Thomas James White Hawk and William Stands, broke into the home of James Yeado, a jeweler in Vermillion, South Dakota. Stands said later that both young men were drunk and they entered the house with intentions of robbery, but not murder. But White Hawk, an obviously unbalanced young man, shot the jeweler twice with a .22 and then broke an iron skillet over his head. Stands fled in terror. White Hawk, completely berserk, broke into the bedroom of Yeado's wife, allegedly raped her, and then crawled into her closet to hide. Police found him there the next morning, cringing under a pile of blankets.

White Hawk, the nineteen-year-old slayer of Yeado, was arrested and by January 1968 had been sentenced to death. Under pressure from Indians and church groups, his sentence was later commuted to life.

The law enforcement situation, on and off the reservations, has probably worsened in recent years. The double standard of justice is one of the few points on which all Indian people seem to agree. Murder, unlike philosophies about land use or politics, is never negotiable. Recent events, which have inflamed Indian people across the country, show how little justice has progressed since the violent days of the frontier.

• In Rapid City, South Dakota, whose population of 40,000 includes 4,400 Indians, there have been fifty unsolved murders of Indians in recent years.

• In Nebraska, perhaps the most anti-Indian state in America, fourteen Indians have been recent victims of fatal accidents in which they were run over while walking beside the road. In most cases, the motorists involved turned themselves in and got off scot-free. The nature of the deaths in some cases seemed suspicious. In one series of accidents, three brothers died in the same area. In another area a hundred miles away, two brothers were killed at different times almost at the same spot.

• In Gallup, New Mexico, city police arrest an average of one thousand Navajos per day, mostly for liquor-inspired offenses, and house the arrestees in a garage.

• In California in 1972, Richard Oakes, an Indian activist who was the guiding spirit of the Alcatraz take-over, was shot to death by a white YMCA director who is a free man today. Oakes was completely unarmed, and he had been partially crippled for more than a year as a result of a beating he had suffered.

• In Philadelphia, early in 1972, Leroy Shenandoah, an Onondaga Special Forces veteran who had served in Vietnam and guarded Kennedy's grave, was shot to death by two Philadelphia policemen. Two other Indian high-iron workers were wounded when the police invaded their hotel room and fired on the unarmed men. The two policemen were acquitted, but four Indian men involved in the incident, including the two who were wounded, were given jail sentences for interfering with the police. These sentences were overturned by appeal.

• Early in 1972, Elijah Leaureaux, a Chippewa, was killed in Grand Rapids, Michigan, when he ended up under a passing school bus after an argument with a white man. The white man was arrested for manslaughter but acquitted.

• Late in 1971, Michael "Bunky" Ferris was shot to death, while unarmed, by a white bartender in a bar in Willow Creek, California. Although Indian witnesses reported that the bartender said, "I got one of you black son of a bitches; if any more of you want the same, come and get me," he was not arrested. Instead, Indians say that police at the scene told them, "Well, you Indians finally got what you wanted."

The picture of injustice off the reservation is unchanged since the murder of Robert Francis a decade ago. In 1963 three Massachusetts businessmen on a hunting trip to the Passamaquoddy reservation in Maine tried to break into the house of a crippled Indian, shouting that they wanted to "have a squaw." Robert Francis, a young neighbor of the crippled man and his wife, came to their aid and threw the three hunters off the property. As the hunters were leaving, they shot Francis to death. None ever served time in jail for the murder.

"It's a worse crime in Maine to shoot a moose out of season than it is to kill an Indian," said a white friend of the Passamaquoddy tribe.

While law enforcement off the reservation continues with flagrant injustices, law enforcement on the reservation is withering because of the breakdown in the federal system. The United States district attorneys, the chief federal law enforcement agents of each state, are failing to prosecute serious crimes committed on the reservations.

Meanwhile, under the Nixon administration's so-called self-determination policy, the once-potent BIA police forces on the reservations have been reduced to shambles. The rank-and-file BIA policemen live in fear of losing their jobs without notice because of the Nixon policy of contracting all federal services to Indian tribes, despite laws against this. Like other federal employees on the reservations and in the BIA area offices, the policemen fear termination of federal services.

Indians on the reservations are also denied their day in court because the tribal court systems are not separated from the tribal councils. And federal courts usually refuse to accept appeals from the tribal courts, contending that accepting Indian appeals would clutter up their calendars. All other citizens of the United States can appeal a case from their respective state courts into the federal courts.

Across the nation, Indians are beginning to abandon the patient attitudes of the past and to react to the lack of any due process by taking the law into their own hands. On one reservation a councilman who was stealing his people blind had twenty-one of his haystacks burned mysteriously. The arsonist was undoubtedly trying to tell the councilman that he didn't like the way the tribal lands were being exploited. In another case, a councilman's store suffered a mysterious fire. After the blaze, the councilman seemed to have sold out to the tribe's powerful chairman. He later borrowed money from the tribe to refurnish his store, with the tribal chairman's approval.

The breakdown of law and order on the reservations is symptomatic of the cultural destruction created by the government's attempts to force Indians into the melting pot. By replacing a system that worked with one that didn't, the government has made itself contemptible in the eyes of Indian people. Only the Indian's own self-discipline, reinforced by his culture and his beliefs, has saved him from total breakdown.

# 7

# The BIA: Big Brother Is Watching

> Will we let ourselves be destroyed in our turn without a struggle, give up our homes, our country bequeathed to us by the Great Spirit, the graves of our dead, and everything that is dear and sacred to us? I know you will cry with me, "Never! Never!"
>
> —Tecumtha (Tecumseh), 1800

Until a faction of the Trail of Broken Treaties caravan took over the Bureau of Indian Affairs central office in Washington, D.C., and held it in a state of siege during election week, 1972, most Americans were unfamiliar with the very name BIA. To Indians, however, it was all too familiar. To the activists, it was the Burro of Indian Affairs or Boone's Apple Farm—an apple, in this case, meaning an Indian who was red on the outside and white on the inside. But behind the bitter wit ran an underlying hatred so deep that, during the siege, all discipline broke down, and some militants, including old women and small children, literally tried to tear the building apart with their bare hands.

The Department of the Interior seized on this act of rage to characterize the whole Trail of Broken Treaties as an orgy of vandalism. Wild-eyed estimates of $2.5 million worth of damage were played up in the press, along with ugly photos of paint-smeared walls and shattered toilet bowls. When things calmed down, the damage estimates were revised into figures of thousands, but the image of cataclysmic violence had already been hammered into the public mind.

What could inspire such hatred in warmhearted Indian grandmothers and teen-aged girls? To understand the outburst, it is instructive to trace the history of the BIA back to its earliest beginnings.

On 12 July 1775 the Continental Congress first asserted its jurisdiction over the free Indian tribes by creating three Indian departments. Men of the caliber of Patrick Henry, Benjamin Franklin, and James Wilson were selected as the commissioners of the middle department. Henry—"Give me liberty or give me death"—was selected despite the fact that he was an active speculator in Indian lands and a stockholder in the Ohio Company, which was involved in Indian land schemes.

Ben Franklin was also involved in land speculation while he represented the American colonies to the English crown. He managed to secure twenty million acres of Indian land on behalf of the infamous Walpole Company, a scheme that endangered the financial interests of both Patrick Henry and George Washington who were active in the Ohio and Mississippi companies. Franklin gained seventy-two shares in exchange for his power with the British. He connived with and bribed other British officials with offers of company shares, and he overcame the steadfast opposition of the king's minister of American affairs who firmly protested that the land-grabbing schemes would break the Proclamation of 1763, which had promised to protect the Indians.

Proclaiming freedom with a forked tongue and stealing Indian property with both hands, the three departments worked overtime at relieving Indians of their land, and, very often, their lives. The benign Franklin, though opposed to outright murder of friendly Indians, once said that he thought the "savages" should be "extirpated with rum." With the Declaration of Independence came an all-out effort to bribe the tribes into neutrality or friendship while the fledgling government devised a strategy to rid themselves of the original Americans. Contrary to the florid and grisly accounts in history books, many Indians remained neutral or friendly to the new nation. The majority of the Six Nations of the Iroquois, a third force on the continent, kept a rigid neutrality. Some Mohawks and Senecas fought for the British under Joseph Brant and some Oneidas took the side of the colonists. Had the Six Nations and their allies come into the war wholeheartedly on the British side, it is not outside the realm of possibility that the colonies would have lost the Revolution, for a majority of whites were either neutral or Tories. The Six Nations and friends, even at that late date in their history of empire, could have probably fielded an army almost as big as Washington's, and this, added to the British and Tory forces, might have ended the war during the first precarious years of privations and desertions at Valley Forge and Morristown.

With the Revolution over, the Indians had lost their last chance to throw the invaders back into the sea, although, lulled by treaties, they didn't realize it for some years to come.

The white tide moved westward, isolating and destroying the tribes. Whole tribes vanished.

The story of how the West was lost has been told elsewhere. Corrupt since its inception, the BIA became notorious even among cavalry officers. Jobs in the bureau were political rewards, and most agents managed to save several times more than they legally earned. When the Indians revolted against mistreatment, the agents ran to the army. Between wars, the agents kept the Indians supplied with rifles and ammunition.

Lest anyone believe that BIA corruption occurred because the field agents were too far from Washington to be supervised, the statements of some of the commissioners of Indian affairs should be consulted to show that corruption, bigotry, and callousness flowed from the top down. With one or two possible exceptions, there was not a single sympathetic or respectable character in the office of commissioner from the time of Elbert Herring, the first commissioner, in 1832 to the administration of Charles J. Rhoads, appointed by Herbert Hoover in 1932.

Commissioner Elbert Herring, commenting on the Indian Removal Act that sent thousands of Cherokees and Choctaws to their deaths, said: "In the consummation of this grand and sacred object rests the sole chance of averting Indian annihilation. Founded in pure and disinterested motives, may it meet the approval of Heaven, by the complete attainment of its beneficent ends."

In 1838, while the literate, hard-working Cherokees were dying by the thousands, being evicted from their comfortable homes, and suffering rape, murder, and wholesale theft, Commissioner T. Hartley Crawford reported: "The principal lever by which Indians are to be lifted out of the mire of folly and vice in which they have sunk is education. . . . To teach a savage man to read, while he continues a savage in all else, is to throw seed on a rock . . . manual labor schools are what the Indian condition calls for."

While the gold-seekers in California were shooting Indians for sport and gang-raping their women, Commissioner Alfred B. Greenwood recommended that the new reservation policy aimed at protecting the California tribes be abandoned: "Neither the government nor California recognizes any right in the Indians of that state to one foot of land within her borders. An unnecessary number of reservations and separate farms have been established. The locations of many of them have proven unsuitable, and have not been sufficiently isolated. Should Congress authorize a change in the present system, and new reservations be established, great care should be taken so as to isolate the Indians from contact with the whites."

During Abraham Lincoln's administration, the Santee Sioux, pushed beyond endurance, were insulted by their agent, Andrew Myrick, who, when asked if the Indians should receive their rations according to treaties, said, "Let them eat grass, or their own dung." The desperate, half-starved Santees went wild. Myrick was caught and riddled with arrows and his mouth stuffed with wads of grass. The Indians burned several towns and killed many whites against whom they nurtured grievances, as well as a number of innocent bystanders who just happened to be encroaching on Indian land.

Troops and artillery were diverted from Civil War battlefields, and the Santees were put down, but not until eight hundred warriors had chased some thirty thousand whites out of Minnesota. The local courts sentenced every male Indian they could lay their hands on, including some who had been neutral or friendly, to death by hanging. Lincoln, reading the sentences, reversed decisions so that only those Indians convicted of murder or rape would be hanged. Those who merely took part in the fighting were given jail sentences or deported, along with most of the other Sioux in Minnesota, including friendlies and neutrals. At Mankato, Minnesota, the thirty-eight Sioux sentenced to die danced on the scaffold, insulted the white onlookers, and were hanged all at once from a giant gallows. Until very recently, the site was proudly commemorated by a stone marking Mankato as the scene of the greatest mass execution in American history. Subsequent investigation indicates that several Indians were hanged by mistake, including at least one man who saved a white woman from rape.

Speaking of the causes of the outbreak, BIA commissioner Dade wrote of the Indians: "They find themselves answerable to a system of local and federal laws, as well as their treaty stipulations, all of which are to the vast majority of them wholly unintelligible. If a white man does them an injury, redress is often beyond their reach. Or, if obtainable, is only had after delays and vexations which are themselves cruel injustice. If one of their number commits a crime, punishment is sure and swift, and oftentimes is visited upon the whole tribe."

By 1867, the Indian service had become so notoriously corrupt that most of their field agents probably could have fitted nicely into a statement by Acting Commissioner Mix. Blocking the Indian's road to civilization, he said, were several obstacles, "mainly, his almost constant contact with the vicious, unscrupulous whites, who not only teach him their base ways, but defraud and rob him, and, often without cause, with as little compunction as they would experience in killing a dog, take even his life."

In 1869, a new commissioner of Indian affairs took office at the behest of President Ulysses S. Grant. Ely Samuel Parker, a Seneca Indian himself, made a strong attempt to clean out the BIA.

Parker, whose Seneca name was Donehogawa, was a remarkable man, even for an Iroquois tribesman. Largely self-educated, he passed a bar examination for the state of New York, only to be barred from practicing law because of his race. Angered but undaunted, he found that nonwhites were not barred from the engineering profession, and he worked his way through Rensselaer Polytechnic Institute. While working as an engineer on canals in Illinois, Parker met Ulysses S. Grant and the two became friends. When the Civil War broke out, Grant helped get Parker into the army and appointed him as an aide. It was Lt. Col. Ely Parker, the self-educated Seneca, who, because of his fine penmanship, was chosen to write the articles of surrender at Appomattox Court House.

After the war, Parker rose to the rank of brigadier general. When Grant was elected to the presidency, he appointed Parker commissioner of Indian affairs.

Parker tried valiantly to reform the BIA, an operation somewhat on the scale of cleaning up the Augean stables. With Grant's support, he began to replace the politically appointed hacks and leeches with men recommended by religious denominations, a policy that was to have mixed and not altogether happy results for traditional believers on the reservations. He also tried to see that treaties were honored, that Indians on reservations received decent rations, and that schemes to defraud the tribes were thwarted. His honesty won him the hatred of the "Indian ring," the politicians who stood to profit from Indian warfare and exploitation, and their flunkies in Congress held up food appropriations for the Indians on reservations. In order to prevent another outbreak of warfare or starvation on the reservations, Parker violated some minor contract-bid rules to rush food to the West. Considering the bureau's outstanding record of crime, this was a pretty minor infraction, but it was enough. Parker was brought up on charges, of which he cleared himself, and was slandered as a "heathen" and a "remove from barbarism." Faced with insults and backbiting at every turn, and unwilling to cause his friend Grant further embarrassment, he resigned in the summer of 1871.

After the Indian ring crushed Parker, all the stops were out. The Indians were stripped of all legal rights except for treaty provisions, which nobody paid any attention to anyway. In 1872, surveying the rights of the Indian, Commissioner Walker wrote: "No one certainly will rejoice more heartily than the present Commissioner when the Indians of this country cease to be in a position to dictate, in any form or degree, to the government, when in fact, the last hostile tribe becomes reduced to the condition of suppliants for charity."

When the Indians finally were subjugated, the men in the BIA began to find new ways of enriching themselves. In Commissioner Atkins's 1886 report to the secretary of the interior, he outlined the unsuccessful leasing of Cheyenne and Arapaho lands to white cattle interests. These leases were declared null and void by presidential proclamation, and the cattle and cattlemen were removed from Indian land. Atkins said: "The Indians . . . no longer contemplate the monopoly of nine-tenths of their reservation by outsiders, but in place thereof they view with satisfaction their own fields of corn, and farms enclosed with fences, put up by their own labor." This satisfaction was rare indeed in Indian country. More typical was the horrible story told to a congressional investigating committee in which Martin Mitchell, an Assiniboin, remembered a winter at Fort Peck, Montana, after the buffalo were gone.

> Before the buffalo were killed the Indians were all strong and healthy and no disease among them. After the buffalo were all killed I remember the Indian agent told the Indians, "Now your buffaloes are all killed and gone, and now you have to stay here on the reservation and we are going to feed you." And that winter it was a hard winter, the Indians were starving. They gave us rations once a week, just enough to last one day, and the Indians they started to eat their pet dogs. After they ate all their dogs up, they started to eat their ponies. All this time the Indian Bureau had a

> warehouse full of grub. They stationed seven Indian policemen at the door so the Indians could not get at the food. This all happened in the winter of 1883 and 1884. Some of the Indians, their whole families starved to death. Early that spring, in 1884, I saw the dead bodies of the Indians wrapped in blankets and piled up like cordwood in the village of Wolf Point and the other Indians were so weak they could not bury their dead. What were left were nothing but skeletons. I think the Indian Bureau should have been prosecuted for murder or manslaughter at that time.

In other places, the story was much the same. On the Blackfoot reservation, over five hundred Indians starved to death while their agent meticulously fed his chickens with food from the BIA warehouse. Moved from Montana to Oklahoma, the Northern Cheyenne lost most of their children and old people to disease, aggravated by malnutrition, while their agent gave food to Christian Indians in preference to traditionals. "Our people kept dying, dying, dying, following one another out of this world," said one Cheyenne.

On 1 July 1889 Commissioner Thomas J. Morgan reported: "The settled policy of the government is to break up reservations, destroy tribal relations, settle Indians upon their own homesteads, incorporate them into the national life, and deal with them not as nations and tribes or bands, but as individual citizens. The American Indian is to become the Indian American. . . ."

The politics of hunger played its part in all this. The Sioux were promised that their rations would remain the same after the Allotment Act cut up their reservation. Immediately after the agreement was concluded, Congress cut the beef ration by two million pounds at Rosebud reservation, by one million pounds at Pine Ridge, and by lesser amounts at three other Sioux reservations. When their agent complained that his Indians were on half rations, he was told that it was better for them to be on half rations all year than on full rations for a few months and nothing for the rest of the year. To the proverb that it was cheaper to feed the Indians than to fight them, a heartless Congress added the postscript that it was cheapest of all to starve them and be done with it.

In these years of starvation and disease the Ghost Dance was born. A Paiute Indian, Wovoka, had a vision during a solar eclipse; in his vision he was transported to heaven and met his ancestors. He was told that a new dawn was coming for the Indians, soon dirt would fall from the sky and bury the white man and his railroads and mines, the buffalo and antelope would return, and the Indians' beloved dead would walk the earth again. All this was to happen, he was told, because Jesus, whom the white men had rejected and tortured, would return as an Indian.

If the Indians wanted to see their beloved dead again, Wovoka was told, they had only to dance to exhaustion and sing certain chants. Many Indians who did this had visions in which they saw their fathers, mothers, husbands, or friends. Others spoke of flying out of their bodies. The tendency today is to ascribe these visions to suggestion or hallucination, although they may have been psychical experiences. At any rate, the Ghost Dance was peaceful. Wovoka told his followers explicitly to abstain from violence and to wait for the Second Coming.

The Ghost Dance was feared by BIA agents as a religious revival and—paranoiacally—as the harbinger of a new Indian war. They wrongly attributed the Ghost Dance to Sitting Bull who was actually somewhat reticent about becoming involved in the ceremonies. The agent at Standing Rock reservation, James McLaughlin, harbored a long-standing grudge against the Hunkpapa medicine man. McLaughlin resented Sitting Bull's steadfast opposition to the Dawes Allotment Act as well as his refusal to give up one of his two wives, Seen-By-Her-Nation and Four Times, when McLaughlin attempted to break up the Sioux families that included plural wives. Sitting Bull, with his usual sagacity, asked McLaughlin which wife he should give up, and who would be a father to his children if he gave up either of them. When McLaughlin refused to choose, Sitting Bull indulged in a dry joke, telling the agent that if McLaughlin found him a white wife he'd give up both

Indian wives. Sitting Bull, of course, disliked white women and was sharp enough to know that the prejudice was mutual. But McLaughlin, who obviously had no sense of humor, wrote the conversation verbatim in his memoirs as proof that Sitting Bull was a vile, lecherous old savage. His book was titled, with superb irony, *My Friend, the Indian.*

In December 1890, with the Ghost Dance going on at all Sioux reservations, James McLaughlin decided to arrest his old enemy.

On the night of 14 December 1890, forty-three Indian police assembled at McLaughlin's house and prepared to go after Sitting Bull. The police, most of them Catholic converts of McLaughlin's, held a prayer vigil around a crucifix. McLaughlin's half-breed Santee wife tore some white cloth into strips to make bandanas that would enable them to recognize one another in the darkness. When the police set off to arrest Sitting Bull, their leader, Bullhead, carried in his pocket a letter, in English and Sioux, consisting of arrest orders; it concluded, "PS. You must not let him escape under any circumstances."

The police did their duty. During a scuffle, they shot the chief in the head and stomach, and, for good measure, killed his teen-aged son, Crowfoot. Sitting Bull's followers then killed six Sioux policemen, and the white cavalry troops had to be sent in to rescue the survivors. Eight other Indians were killed. It was a triumph of BIA diplomacy. At the very least, McLaughlin wanted to humiliate Sitting Bull, for he squelched plans to have Buffalo Bill Cody go in and extricate the chief, by getting Cody too drunk to walk. Sending Cody, a friend of Sitting Bull, would have made more sense than sending a bunch of sold-out Indians, whom Sitting Bull despised, to bring him in under guard. The great Sioux leader, like Crazy Horse before him, literally was offered a choice of death or dishonor, and, predictably, he chose death. In the parlance of organized crime, he was set up.

To the soldiers at Standing Rock Agency, the chief's funeral was a day of ghoulish amusement. They vied for the honor of driving a nail into his coffin, while a fat soldier sat on the lid of the crude box. The coffin was lowered into a hole filled with quicklime, like the grave of a common felon. McLaughlin was later honored by promotion to inspector of Indian affairs.

After Wounded Knee, the Ghost Dance faded out and the Indians sunk back to near despair.

In 1905, a commissioner of great intelligence and compassion came to office and said what many an Indian had been hoping to hear. Commissioner Francis E. Leupp wrote: "The Indian will never be judged aright till we learn to measure him by his own standards, as we whites would want to be measured if some more powerful race were to usurp dominion over us."

On 4 March 1909, in an effort to eliminate the criminal elements from the Indian service, Congress enacted a law establishing Indian *inspectors*. The inspectors were authorized to travel to reservations, ferret out corruption on the spot, and take whatever action they deemed necessary. They were to report directly to the commissioner of Indian affairs.

In case after case, these inspectors exposed Indian agents using their positions to enrich themselves. At the Rosebud reservation in the early 1930s, one agent was caught using his job as a front for a hot-car ring. More common were contracts beneficial to white ranchers. Another favorite trick was juggling the books so that the Indians only received a fraction of the food or other supplies intended for them, and the agent and contractors split the difference. In other cases, politically appointed agents were found grossly incompetent. In all such cases the inspectors relieved the Indian agents of their jobs within forty-eight hours.

But the corruption that flourished, more subtly, at higher levels, was left intact. The BIA had always been a political football for politicians from western states, and the commissioner became increasingly powerless under the pressures of special interest groups in Washington, D.C.

Congress had enacted the infamous Dawes Allotment Act in 1887, but the BIA had not forced the Indians to choose their allotments until Indian resistence reached a record low and pressures from homesteaders mounted. At about the same time that they were forced to choose their allotments, the Indians were forced to choose between their wives. The custom of plural wives was a necessity in many plains tribes because of the heavy losses of young men in warfare and the hunt, and the custom gained a kind of nobility, in that a man who provided for more than one wife was considered especially generous. Most plural wives were sisters, because this prevented jealousy and kept the bloodlines straight. But agents and preachers united to split up plural families, telling the husbands to choose one wife. Some Indian husbands cleverly turned the tables by urging the preachers to pick which wives were to be cast off and then tell the wives. The preachers were usually deathly afraid of Indian women, and many marriages were saved.

The churches had gotten a foothold on most reservations during the Grant-Parker bid to clean out the BIA. In order to placate the BIA and the army, the tribes had given each religious denomination land for their churches and preachers' homes, with deed provisions that church lands would revert to the tribe when no longer used for church purposes. True to the (white) American way, the churches caused Congress to enact legislation that gave them patent-in-fee deeds to this Indian land, thus freeing themselves from their agreements with the tribes. Thousands of acres were sold out from under the tribes by this trickery.

Missionaries and agents together began to work out ways of pitting Indians against Indians. The Indian service began recruiting Indians who were known sympathizers with the churches and the government—the sort of collaborators, one might observe, that one finds in any occupied country. These sellouts were given secondary jobs that directly affected the daily lives of other Indians.

In the commissary where rations were issued, Indians were hired to weigh the items that made up the staple diet of the reservation Indians. They also doled out surplus army blankets, gloves, overcoats, overshoes, and shoes. This placed the chosen Indians in a position to control the starving people who had to exist on government handouts because they could not hunt or leave the reservation to work.

Another method agents used to control a tribe's economy was to issue a relative or friend a trader's license. On 15 August 1876, two months after Custer's Last Stand, Congress enacted the Trader's Act, giving the commissioner of Indian affairs sole power and authority to appoint traders with the Indian tribes and to make such rules and regulations as the commissioner deemed proper, specifying the kind and quality of goods and the prices at which such goods should be sold to the Indians.

To prevent the hostile tribes from obtaining firearms, Congress gave the president the power to prohibit the importation of any particular article to reservations. Thus, by presidential order, a total prohibition could be placed on any trade with Indians. This law could be used as a weapon to bring about starvation among Indians who resisted government efforts to change their lives. Or it could be used to protect Indian interests.

In utter defiance of the Trader's Act, the agents conspired with the traders to create a monopoly within their reservations. For many years every Indian reservation was fenced in by three strands of barbed wire, and the Indians were not allowed to leave without a pass. The trading post, the only source of supply for vital necessities, was able to keep prices ridiculously high by maintaining a monopoly. Shoddy goods were sold for many times their regular price.

As with most aspects of Indian affairs, this situation has persisted. A report issued by the Federal Trade Commission (FTC) on 14 June 1973 declares that trading posts on the Navajo reservation are keeping the Indians in a state of economic slavery. The Navajos, the FTC said, were being victimized by language barriers, limited competition, and corrupt sales practices used for decades. Social security and welfare checks are often intercepted by trading post owners who get the Indians to sign the checks over under threat of losing credit. Often, the report said, the customer is not even sure of the amount of the check, because the trader sometimes obscures the dollar amount. The report also said that prices at Navajo trading posts exceed the national average by 27 percent, that the traders sometimes charge the equivalent of a 60 percent annual interest for loans made when the Indians pawn their silver and turquoise jewelry, and that some store owners employ questionable math to figure bills; other complaints point to the traders cheating Navajos outright.

This report—issued after Wounded Knee II—doesn't surprise anyone who knows the trading post business. Yet trading posts are the main source of food and clothing for many Indians who lack cars or transportation off-reservation. They are also a source of meager income to many older people who manufacture crafts and sell or pawn them at trading posts. Some traders regard themselves as morally pure, even saintly, because they sometimes help hungry Indians through the winter. But no one on the reservation believes that the essence of their business is charity. It's safe to say that an examination of trading practices on almost any reservation would disclose the same facts that the FTC found in Navajo country.

The predominant white impression is that trading posts sell a lot of souvenirs made in Hong Kong or Taiwan. This is largely true, even though there are federal laws against passing off imported handicrafts as Indian-made, since the Indians have to buy food and clothing at standard or inflated prices and can't compete in volume with the industrialized Orient. It is the Indian, far more than the white tourist, who gets ripped off by trading posts, even when the case in point is Hong Kong souvenirs. At one trading post in Arizona, old Indian people who go there to pick up their social security checks are forced to either spend their whole check at the trading post or shop elsewhere. Any amount left over from food expenditure is taken by forcing people to accept cheap foreign-made souvenirs. Some Indians don't even know how much their social security checks amount to, for the trading post is also the area's post office, and the traders open the checks.

The only bright spot is that retribution, so long awaited, seems to be coming, but not from the BIA. The recent popularity of Indian jewelry has created a wave of thefts from Indian traders, some of whom now live in constant fear of being robbed. Most of the thieves seem to be other whites, although young Indians also take off an unwary trader now and again.

Prejudice was no stranger on Indian reservations. BIA employees resided at the agency in government housing while Indians, particularly the full bloods, lived in tents, hogans, shacks, log cabins, abandoned cars, or caves. It was an unwritten law that the BIA employees refrain from socializing with Indians. They had their own clubs and church and civic organizations separated entirely from the Indians they supposedly served. This invisible curtain still exists in many places throughout the West. A white woman who taught school at Pine Ridge for years could only name one Indian girl as a friend, and a very distant friend at that. Many nurses who worked in Indian hospitals never spoke to their patients.

Under IRA, a sort of kangaroo court system was set up on the reservations which could exist nowhere else in the United States, although some justice-of-the-peace courts in the Deep South come close. The court consisted of a judge, who acted as judge, jury, prosecutor, and defense attorney. Although tribal courts handled only relatively minor offenses, they could hand out jail sentences of up to six months, not to mention fines much too heavy for the average Indian.

The main criterion for the office of tribal judge was neither intelligence, integrity, nor knowledge of the law, but, as one might expect, blind loyalty to the BIA. In fact, some tribes had laws barring anyone with a law degree from being a judge. Some tribal judges were so silly that they provided the Indians with a little comic relief in these grim years.

In one court, the judge was an Indian janitor who prided himself on his ability to speak English as he served the white man. A girl known for her sexual escapades, brought before him on charges of public intoxication, was pronounced guilty with the following extraordinary legal opinion:

"I hear about you all the time, so this time I give you soft one. Next time you come here, I give you long hard one!"

This judge did so well at his benchwork that he was promoted in his regular job when another janitor was killed in an accident. As he emerged from hearing the good news from the chief of the BIA education branch, he met the hated social worker in the hall and exclaimed proudly, "Miss Heinsmann, Mister Newport, he just knocked me up, I am generator like the stud now and I have two job now for my family." He was telling her that he had just gotten a raise which gave him responsibility over two buildings and that he could take better care of his family with the added income.

Time brought another war and another generation of Indian veterans. As the World War II veterans returned to their reservations after two or three years overseas, they ran into a profound reentry shock after years of heady freedom and equality, even admiration from their white buddies. Trying to apply their GI benefits toward bettering their lives, they learned that nothing had changed on the reservations.

Veteran after veteran ran into the same obstacles. When they went to banks off the reservations to borrow money on guaranteed GI loans, the bankers told them to go back to the reservation, that the white bankers couldn't deal with Indians. Hatred replaced the pride that many veterans had felt in serving their country.

When they turned to the tribe for loans, they were sent to the BIA Revolving Credit Fund, controlled by newly established area offices far from the reservations. Here they were given a new version of the old runaround. When they began to protest to their congressmen, the BIA credit personnel generally approved a starvation loan of less than five thousand dollars, with which the veterans could enter the cattle business. Approval of the loan came only after the veterans submitted to subsistence budgets of forty-five dollars per month. Angered by such indignities, many veterans entered the tribal council races and were elected. By

1952, Indian veterans were beginning to make their marks politically, and the BIA was confronted with a new breed of Indian.

At the same time, the BIA came under fire from Congress. In 1946, Congress had ordered the Department of the Interior to make a full report on each tribe under its jurisdiction, with emphasis on the tribe's ability to manage its own business. Word began to circulate that the BIA was beginning plans for what was termed the "Withdrawal Program." In plain English, plans were taking shape to abrogate the nation's sacred treaties and to sever all federal programs for Indian tribes.

The department made its report and Congress reacted by enacting the infamous House Concurrent Resolution 108, which stated: "It is the sense of Congress that Indian tribes shall be terminated as rapidly as possible." On 8 August 1953 this resolution was enacted by Congress without one single representative or senator objecting. It was slated to ring down the final curtain on the American Indian by withdrawing all federal assistance from the tribes, abolishing the BIA, and issuing title to well over fifty million acres of trust land. In a word, it was to be the long-awaited final solution to the Indian problem.

Seven days after enacting House Concurrent Resolution 108, Congress took another step toward destroying the Indians by enacting Public Law 280, giving the states of Washington, Oregon, Nebraska, Minnesota, and Wisconsin civil and criminal jurisdiction over Indian tribes, with some exceptions. In another provision, Congress granted all other states the right to change their enabling acts to take civil and criminal jurisdiction over all tribes. This meant that every white hustler who ever robbed an Indian in a fraudulent credit deal could now pursue him onto the sanctuary of the reservation, and it made further mockery of the tribal governments.

With the threat of termination looming over every reservation in the country, the battle lines were quickly drawn, incongruously enough, with the Indians rallying to fight to keep the hated BIA, rather than face total oblivion as tribes. Indian identity, so long suppressed, suddenly exploded, and Indians began dancing in full regalia again. Tribal council after tribal council instituted programs that showed they were not progressing and didn't want to be terminated. Meanwhile, government officials began to publicize termination as a boon to the Indians. Few media people took an interest in the battle against termination, and the general public never realized what was going on because the Indians had no way of reaching them.

Many of the Indians opposed to termination rallied around the National Congress of American Indians, an organization that originated inside the BIA in 1944 with the approval of John Collier, who hoped to use it as a means of controlling the tribes. In 1946, in Rapid City, South Dakota, the Sioux delegates surprised the NCAI's BIA members by making a motion that barred federal employees from being officers in the NCAI. The surprise motion passed by a wide margin and the BIA Indians were left without control of their own organization.

Several attempts were made to organize the nation's tribes within the NCAI between 1944 and 1953, the year that the Eisenhower administration began its determined effort to force termination on the tribes. The most feared senator behind the termination policy was Arthur Watkins, a Republican from Utah, who was the chairman of the Indian Affairs Subcommittee. Running Watkins a close second was Senator Clinton Anderson, a Democrat from New Mexico. Watkins repeatedly attacked the Indians as though each one had personally killed his mother. It was his committee that enacted House Concurrent Resolution 108 and Public Law 280, all within fifteen days and with no prior warning to the Indian tribes. President Eisenhower remarked that the act was "un-Christianlike" but signed it into law anyway.

When a tribe was terminated, it lost all the federal services its treaties entitled it to. The classic case is the disaster that overtook the Menominee tribe of Wisconsin. Within a short time of their termination, millions of dollars in tribal assets disappeared as the

Menominees tried to turn their reservation into a self-supporting county. Financing the hospital, police force, and other services formerly provided by federal funds endangered the tribe's forest holdings and community-owned sawmill. The result was to wreck the economy of the tribe and to saddle Wisconsin with a massive welfare problem, which the state could not handle. Wisconsin appealed to the federal government for help.

Thus the Indians and the taxpayers both lost. The only winners were the vultures who hovered around ready to buy up land from frightened, confused people who, after a hundred years and more of total paternalism, were turned out to manage their own affairs because of the whims of a handful of politicians and the desires of a handful of exploiters.

The tribes seemed headed for Indian doomsday. Congress was considering termination bills for any tribe that seemed anywhere near self-sufficient. The half-breeds of the Ute tribe of Utah fell into Watkins's trap when they were promised a large sum of money if they voted to terminate. The Menominees were terminated on 17 June 1954, and the Wyandotte tribe of Oklahoma was terminated on 1 August of the same year. The Indian-haters in Congress had a field day as the Ottawa tribe of Oklahoma was terminated on 3 August, and the Klamath tribe, including the Modoc and Yahooskin bands of Snake Indians received the congressional ax on Friday, 13 August. Some sixty-seven small bands that made up the Indian population of western Oregon were terminated on the same day.

Ten days later, the Alabama and Conshatta tribes were signed into oblivion by President Eisenhower. On 1 September the Paiute Indians of Utah ceased to exist as a recognized tribe. By this time, every Indian tribe in the country was quaking in fear of the seemingly heartless Congress and the president who was jamming legislation through as if he were firing a Gatling gun at the Indians.

The BIA during this dark era was headed by Glen L. Emmons, a New Mexico banker who believed Indians could be run like a bank. As commissioner he had impounded seven million dollars in the BIA Revolving Credit Fund, the Indians' sole credit source.

The tribes not yet destroyed by the termination policy began to feel its shock waves. Indian business came to a standstill except for land sales.

For all its faults, Collier's Indian Reorganization Act had stopped the loss of Indian land by declaring a moratorium on the sale of Indian holdings. But in 1948, after Collier had left his post as commissioner, Senator Francis Case, Republican of South Dakota, pushed through an amendment that gave the secretary of the interior the authority to approve Indian land sales.

The wildfire graft and corruption that had been part of the Indian service since 1849 had largely disappeared during Collier's regime and the moratorium on land sale. After the brief respite of Collier's twelve-year term, Case's amendment brought it all back with a vengeance as the land-grabbers moved back in to try to pry allotted land away from Indian owners. Since the IRA had provided for exchange of lands, this type of transaction became commonplace. Tribes and individual Indians would trade parcels of land with whites. The Indians, however, generally received one acre while the white man received two. The white man, of course, generously greased the palm of federal and tribal officials who processed the windfall. Complaints to Washington fell on deaf ears. BIA officials were getting rich by arranging land sales and land exchanges, and the BIA, the Indians' supposed protector, couldn't approve the sales fast enough. The Indian reservations became checkerboarded as the whites traded for or purchased Indian land. Most of the allotted reservations today are at least partly owned by whites.

BIA land appraisers, who were supposed to rule on the value of land being sold or traded, sat in their offices and appraised the land without seeing it, by the use of standard figures. Generally, a set price was used, such as $480 per quarter section (160 acres) of grassland and $960 per quarter section of farmland.

These appraisers and real estate employees of the reservations maintained another racket. They sold secret appraised prices of land that was to be sold in advertised public sales. Neighbors interested in securing Indian land were willing to pay a good price for the information, which enabled them to bid uncannily near the appraisal price instead of utilizing the market value level that controlled the sale of all non-Indian land.

Indian people didn't sell their land because they wanted to. Most needed the money for bare necessities. Land sale was often the only source of income, with the unemployment rate for reservation Indians between 1946 and 1963 averaging 85 percent. When tribes asked for poverty programs enabling them to create jobs for their hungry, ragged people, the BIA thumped them over the head, warning that any tribe nearing self-sufficiency would be terminated. The Indians had the choice of dire poverty on the reservations or termination and dire poverty without a land base. About the only bright spot for Indians in the 1950s was the transfer of the responsibility for Indian health from the BIA to HEW.

While termination raged, the NCAI seemed paralyzed. Instead of rallying the Indians to fight termination, NCAI leader Helen Peterson went on a round of speaking engagements to meet her office expenses in Washington. Miss Peterson, an Oglala Sioux, had no confidence in the reservation leadership, so she turned to the support of the so-called professional Indians who capitalized on their Indian blood while living among whites. In June 1961 Peterson and her cohorts, including Sol Tax, an anthropologist at the University of Chicago, tried to gain control over the nation's Indians by placing themselves in the position to nominate a new Indian commissioner if the Democrats won the election. They were defeated by a coalition of tribal Indians, headed by the well-organized Sioux operating under the title Mid-west Inter-tribal Council.

The strategy of the Peterson element was to force delegates at a Chicago conference to accept a prewritten statement of Indian policy. The tribes defeated this move and began to write their own statement. The final draft was read and approved on 16 June 1961 and submitted to William Keeler, chief of the Cherokee

# THE ROAD TO WOUNDED KNEE II

WIDE WORLD

*Overleaf:*

*Dennis Banks, Chippewa AIM co-founder, at Wounded Knee, South Dakota, 1973. Church where hostages were held is in the background.*

*Indians who had seized Alcatraz Island celebrate Thanksgiving 1969, in the exercise yard of the former prison.*

*Commissioner of the BIA, Louis R. Bruce, meets with Indian protest group in his office in 1971. AIM leader Russell Means, 1st row, right.*

WIDE WORLD

WIDE WORLD

JOHN KOSTER

*Indians at an East Coast powwow, the only contact many urban Indians have with their own culture.*

*Thanksgiving 1972: Indian protesters climb the* Mayflower *for "a day of mourning."*

*Indians guard the BIA building in Washington, which they occupied and refused to leave, November 1972.*

WIDE WORLD

*BIA Commissioner Bruce showing support for the Indians who had taken over the BIA the night before.*

WIDE WORLD

*Indians inside the federal BIA building. Plans to evict the protesters forcibly were abandoned.*

WIDE WORLD

*An outside view of a BIA building door barricaded by Indians during their takeover in fall 1972.*

*A woman who succumbed to insulin shock is evacuated from the BIA during the siege.*

RICHARD RAINEY

RICHARD RAINEY

JOHN KOSTER

CAROL BENNETT

RICHARD RAINEY

*Far left, Russell Means addresses Indians besieged at the BIA. At left, George Mitchell, a founder of AIM, who dropped out shortly after this.*

*Below, an elderly woman speaks her piece to newsmen at the BIA siege.*

RICHARD RAINEY

*An Indian woman arrives in Washington on a tribal bus for the Trail of Broken Treaties demonstration, 1972.*

*February 1973: Indians being arrested in Custer, South Dakota, as the Chamber of Commerce burns.*

WIDE WORLD

WIDE WORLD

WIDE WORLD

**T***op left, Attorney William Kunstler talks with AIM leaders Russell Means, center, and Dennis Banks at Wounded Knee, South Dakota, March 1973.*

**B***elow left, an AIM woman on the steps of a building in Wounded Knee, 1973.*

**B***elow, state troopers in Custer, South Dakota, while Indians are being arraigned inside for rioting.*

WIDE WORLD

WIDE WORLD

*Teen-age AIM Indians use a trading post roof for an armed command post at Wounded Knee on Pine Ridge Reservation.*

*An AIM member in a bunker in front of a church at Wounded Knee which was occupied by Indians in 1973.*

WIDE WORLD

*Oscar Bear Runner guards an area at Wounded Knee being set up for negotiations with the Justice Department.*

WIDE WORLD

*Government agents maintain a watch on the AIM members who control village of Wounded Knee in March 1973.*

WIDE WORLD

*Russell Means, left, and assistant U.S. Attorney General Kent Frizzell sign a settlement on Wounded Knee problem.*

WIDE WORLD

*Roadblock which barred food and medicine to militant Indians but gave access to federal officers.*

*AIM leader Clyde Bellecourt, at left, and AIM attorney Ramon Roubideaux while treaty discussions go on between White House aides and Sioux chiefs.*

WIDE WORLD

WIDE WORLD

JOHN KOSTER

*Mrs. Susie Yellowtail and husband Tom, a Crow medicine man, speak about Indian health problems at a white public school.*

*After Wounded Knee II, people gather in a tribal chairman's office, seeking to fulfill their desperate needs and desires.*

AYNE MOORE

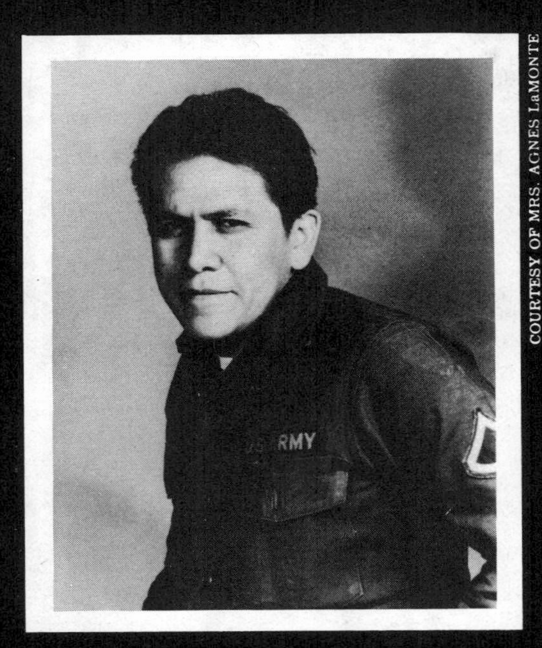


COURTESY OF MRS. AGNES LaMONTE

*Buddy LaMonte photographed while on active duty in the U.S. Army. At Wounded Knee, April 1973, he was machine-gunned to death when he emerged from an AIM bunker. Earlier, he had told relatives, "If anything happens to me, I want to be buried at Wounded Knee."*

Nation, who was also a member of the special task force appointed by John F. Kennedy.

Kennedy's administration was not perfect. The Senecas and other Iroquois tribesmen still blame him for selling them out to the steel industry over Kinzua Dam, which inundated part of their reservation. But the Kennedy years were a respite from persecution. There was no termination while he held office. And if he never did another thing, all reservation Indians would owe him eternal gratitude for his crushing of the heirship bill, which could have led to the total breakup of the Indian land base. This act, introduced by some misguided would-be Indian leaders and fervently endorsed by land-hungry western politicians, would have simplified the heirship problem by giving the Indians title to land and allowing them to sell it. Only a bad administration would have been necessary to reduce the tribal people to dire poverty and force them to sell land for food. When Kennedy let it be known that he was opposed to this act—after a briefing by Indian leaders—it died in Congress. BIA Commissioner Philleo Nash, appointed by Kennedy, began to institute policies that reflected the president's compassion. When Kennedy met with 102 Indian delegates in the White House rose garden, it looked like a new dawn in Indian-U.S. relations. Just as the White House was gearing itself toward instituting radical changes in Indian policy and preparing legislation that would be in tune with the times, the president was assassinated.

President Johnson removed Philleo Nash and replaced him with Robert Bennett, an old-time bureaucrat who had been through the BIA mill. Bennett was a man of considerable charm—he played the piano very well and was always a genial host—but the general consensus of his term as commissioner was that he was too nice a guy to rock the boat or bring about any meaningful change. Bennett, himself an Oneida Indian, had been an area director of the BIA at Aberdeen, South Dakota, where he supervised several tribal programs involving millions of dollars. The Cheyenne River Sioux tribe received $10.6 million for the loss of land to the Army Corps of Engineers' Oahe Dam project, only to squander it on a program authorized by Bennett. The Lower Brulé Sioux tribe and the Fort Thompson Sioux tribe ended up with the same type of program, which caused an internal struggle so virulent that the BIA had to finally take over the Fort Thompson tribal council.

Whatever friendly wishes President Johnson had for other minorities, his treatment of the Indians will never win his memory any laurel wreaths. His so-called self-determination policy unleashed a tidal wave of theft, embezzlement, graft, and corruption. The new Anti-Poverty Act, the newly founded Tribal Housing Authorities, and the so-called Buy Indian Act bypassed the two most important needs of the tribes—decent food and the end of land sales—and poured millions of tax dollars into a few highly salaried jobs in the Office of Economic Opportunity (OEO), multimillion-dollar housing contracts, and BIA "buy Indian" contracts.

These buy Indian contracts were the unnatural offspring of the Buy Indian Act by which Congress permitted the secretary of the interior to make direct purchases of Indian goods or service. Contracts, as such, were never mentioned in the law. The act may have been intended as a stimulus to Indian enterprise, but it quickly pried open the door to a new wave of corruption.

The Johnson administration disregarded all the danger signals pouring back to Washington that protested crimes committed by Indian leaders against their own people. Simple Indians inured to poverty as a life-style suddenly found their tribal governments floundering around in millions of dollars, with no controls over them other than inept, venal, and stupid BIA officials.

Indians had seen corruption, but the Johnson administration programs overshadowed anything in the past, if only because the scale was so much larger. Commissioner Bennett spent most of his time trying to cover up scandals, but he admitted to the Episcopal Church's Indian Committee that the tribes were running away uncontrollably and that politics prevented anyone from stopping it. Tribal chairmen all too often followed their only example of leadership—the BIA—and got rich on everything that crossed their desks. Corrupt white businessmen had a field day securing Indian fronts through which they could win multimillion-dollar contracts under the Buy Indian Act. The Indian on the board of directors became the western equivalent of the black man whose desk was close to the door.

The architect of this self-determination policy was none other than George McGovern, who had introduced the basic legislation—Senate Concurrent Resolution 114—in 1966. The senator from South Dakota had his eye on the presidency and couldn't look back home to see that his self-determination had a number of lethal flaws, most of them based on the fact that the 2,600 laws already affecting Indians were not geared to self-determination. There are, for instance, no conflict-of-interest laws to control tribal officials who are suddenly dealing in millions of dollars. There were no accountability laws to hold elected officials accountable to the federal government or to their own tribal brothers. There are no election laws to keep tribal elections honest and no laws to prohibit elected tribal officials from using federal funds to reelect themselves. There are no laws to provide for the jurisdiction of federal courts over tribal chairmen who had exceeded their authority.

The Indian Self-Determination Act was a license to steal.

The total lack of protective laws placed every Indian at the mercy of men unscrupulous enough to take advantage of their own people. Once in office, tribal officials who lacked any semblance of honor could corrupt elections, bribe voters, or rig the poll watchers, as well as coerce people dependent on them for jobs into voting them into office again and again. As people in America are finally beginning to realize, it is nearly impossible to defeat an incumbent who has unlimited money. This is as true of an Indian official as it is of other Americans.

BIA personnel like to praise themselves on the training programs they make available to Indians. Thus it is strange that not one hundred Indians of the million or so living today have any knowledge of the internal functioning of the BIA itself.

BIA officials do not even advise their closest puppet chairmen of their legal rights. Few Indians know that the decisions of the BIA and tribal councils are subject to appeal to the secretary of the interior. This procedure is clearly set down in the little-known federally printed *Code of Federal Regulations: Title 25—Indians.*

This code states that the actions of a tribal council that affect the tribe as a whole are subject to appeal. Although the system is anything but due process, it does allow an Indian the right to administrative appeal, a fact not generally known to Indians themselves.

The Indian who wants to appeal had better take pains to secure a copy of this arcane *Code of Federal Regulations,* for many of those concerned would prefer to pretend it doesn't exist.

The first level of appeal is to the superintendent of the reservation. This clearly shows who really has the power in the tribal administration. Failing in his appeal to the superintendent, the Indian can then appeal to the area office, usually located far from his reservation. The next appeal is to the commissioner of Indian affairs, and a final appeal can be made to the secretary of the interior. If the secretary rules on a decision, it can only be taken into federal court if fraud can be shown.

In actual operation this system of appeal is a total failure, of course, and probably intentionally so. The federal officials have left the time element out of the applicable regulations controlling such an action. In the few instances where this type of appeal is pursued, BIA officials let the matter die a natural death. If an Indian presses an appeal—assuming he has the time, money, and education to do so—it can easily take three years before a final decision is reached.

Another weakness in this system is that the secretary of the interior will not enforce a decision even if there has been a crime committed.

The *Farmer's Almanac* of white tape is the *Indian Affairs Manual* (IAM), which consists of instructions on how a BIA official is to carry out his responsibilities.

In practical terms, it is a jungle of terminology utilized to confound the Indian who desires to take any constructive action. The BIA manual is usually thrown in the path of an uncontrollable tribal council like a roadblock.

The Indian people were thus saddled with corruption because Congress could not take time to investigate outmoded federal statutes. Laws that were written for the age of Crazy Horse were incapable of bearing the strain of the age of Capone.

Richard M. Nixon was elected and sworn in as president, and in a highly publicized gesture, he selected Louis Rooks Bruce, a Sioux-Mohawk dairy farmer from New York State, as his commissioner of Indian affairs. Reams of publicity were churned up about finally having an Indian in the job. Reporters who took these stories down probably never heard of Robert Bennett, let alone Ely S. Parker.

On 8 July 1970 President Nixon delivered his Indian legislative program with a message that seemed like a landmark in Indian rights. The speech recognized Indians as the most deprived and isolated minority group in America by virtually every scale—employment, income, education, and health—and stated bluntly that this condition was the heritage of centuries of injustice. It recognized that termination was a violation of sacred treaties, that it had a disastrous effect on the tribes terminated, and that it had caused other tribes to deliberately hesitate and remain backward and poor rather than risk termination and the loss of their lands. Nixon, in his speech, flatly rejected termination. He advocated Indian control of federal programs. Indian schools would be brought under Indian control, and more credit would be made available to Indian people.

The BIA's main hang-up has always been their trust responsibility over the Indian land base and moneys. The bureau is, in effect, the caretaker and guardian of Indian land, Indian moneys, and almost everything else. Yet the Department of the Interior is responsible for the use of national resources. This is an inevitable conflict of interest, for the secretary of the interior is forced to choose between the best interests of the Indians and the best interest of the nation as a whole. A brief look at three hundred years of expropriation makes it obvious which interest has habitually won out.

Attempts to resolve this conflict of interest by patchwork legislation are doomed. The only real answer would be to remove Indian affairs from the Department of the Interior and either (at best) set it up as a separate department responsible only to the White House, or, at worst, to transfer Indian affairs to a department, such as HEW, where the conflict of interest is less inherent. But the Nixon administration's self-determination policy refused to recognize this obvious fact and chose to pursue the idea of creating a "Trust Council" inside the Department of the Interior, which would choose between white mainstream or corporate interests and Indian interest.

Perhaps best of all, Nixon said that efforts would be made to eliminate these inherent conflicts of interest between the Indian tribes and their supposed protector, the Department of the Interior. Amazingly enough, the speech actually implied what many Indians had been screaming for a generation and more—that in a choice between a big land or mineral corporate interest and the Indians, the Indians always lost.

Taken at face value, the 8 July message was probably the greatest set of promises ever made to the Indian Americans. The results remained to be seen.

With just a twinge of cynicism, one of the several white experts who helped prepare the speech described the motivation for it. The Nixon administration realized, he said, that they didn't have much of a sympathetic image with minority groups. Gallup polls, among other sources, had long indicated that the American Indian had the greatest quotient of popular sympathy with white American voters. Therefore, anything that looked like it helped the Indians would swing a huge white sympathy vote and give the Republicans something to be proud of, for a change, in their dealings with the underprivileged. An added dividend, which even the white cynic wasn't skeptical enough to mention, is that the ignorance of the general public about matters affecting Indians is so great that the actual results of all the promises would remain unknown. People in Shaker Heights or Larchmont or Upper Montclair didn't have Indian maids or chauffeurs, so they couldn't ask any firsthand source whether the programs were really reaching the people. To the movers and shakers of the white business and political world, Pine Ridge or Window Rock are farther away than the moon and not nearly as well represented on the covers of *Time* and *Newsweek*.

Shortly after the 8 July message, Nixon gave Commissioner Bruce fourteen select Indian advisers to assist him in the tremendous undertaking of formulating and executing new Indian policy, developing necessary legislation, and building a Bureau of Indian Affairs that would serve as adviser, partner, and resource agency to the tribes.

For the first time in 194 years, the congressional climate was nearly perfect for such reform, the president had gone on record supporting it, and Indians were largely in control of the BIA.

The new team of Indian appointees studied conditions for a while. Shortly, they startled the Indian world with the announcement of a new alignment for the BIA. The all-powerful reservation superintendents were to become known as *field representatives,* and the area directors over them would be stripped of their powers and would henceforth serve as a resource agency for the tribes in their sectors. The entire BIA would become an adviser instead of a dictator, supporting the tribes with contractual services. Gradually, the tribes would assume the right to control and operate their own federal programs.

Promising as this announcement was, it was in direct legal conflict with existing congressional acts that held sway over Indian lives. Under title 25, section 33 of the *United States Code,* a superintendent in charge of a reservation is a position titled and created by Congress. The position cannot be changed or abolished without an act of Congress.

Similarly, the new alignment would have arbitrarily instituted a totally different legal status than that which was intended by the law of the land. Specifically, the law requires that the commissioner of Indian affairs, under the direction of the secretary of the interior and agreeably to such regulations as the president may prescribe, manage all Indian affairs and all matters arising out of Indian relations. Thus these three federal officials—the president, the secretary of the interior, and the commissioner of Indian affairs—have complete control over Indian affairs and relations and must exercise that lawful authority until Congress amends, rescinds, or repeals all or a portion of the authorization.

On the other hand, Congress secures its power from the Constitution, which provides in article 1, section 8, that "The Congress shall have power . . . to regulate commerce with foreign nations, and among the several states, and with the Indian tribes."

Thus the Department of the Interior's realignment policy was a violation of the law of the land, in that it tried to bypass the legal authorities. The realignment policy not only violated the spirit and letter of the law, but it broke faith with all the tribes that had organized under the Indian Reorganization Act of 1934 and the Oklahoma Welfare Act of 1936. Each tribe's constitution contains a provision specifically stating that the "superintendent shall approve any ordinance or resolution. . . ." Moreover, all tribes that have constitutions approved by the secretary of the interior have the following attachment:

> I Harold L. Ickes, the Secretary of the Interior of the United States of America, by virtue of the authority granted me by the act of June 18, 1934 [48 Stat. 984, the Indian Reorganization Act] as amended, do hereby approve the attached constitution and by-laws of the ——— tribe of ———.
>
> All rules and regulations heretofore promulgated by the Interior Department or by the Office of Indian Affairs, so far as they may be incompatible with any of the provisions of the said constitution and by-laws are declared to be inapplicable to the ——— tribe.

All officers and employees of the Interior Department are ordered to abide by the provisions of the said constitution and by-laws.
Signed, John Collier
Signed, Harold L. Ickes
Secretary of the Interior
Washington, D.C. December 20, 1935.

This order would seem to state, clearly enough, that anything affecting Indians that disagrees with the tribal constitution is null and void, yet Commissioner Bruce and his troops deliberately made a nationwide effort to violate it with the Realignment Act. Indians across the country protested. The Senate subcommittee called a hearing on the act, but everybody in the Senate sat on their hands while Bruce and his team blundered again and again. Although their efforts were not all wrong and their ideas about reducing BIA paternalism were well intentioned, their confused efforts could only lead to confrontation between the government and the tribes. Which is just what happened.

Nixon's first secretary of the interior was Walter Hickel, a self-made millionaire who rose from being a dishwasher to become the first Republican governor of Alaska. Conservationists who learned of Hickel's appointment hit the ceiling when they recalled statements he had made about not agreeing with "conservation for conservation's sake." Indians who knew his reputation in Alaska coined a maxim: "If you liked Custer, you'll love Hickel."

Nevertheless, Hickel was confirmed and began his reign, adopting some of the trappings, at least in terms of the Indian paintings on the wall, left over from the Ickes-Collier years.

Contrary to many people's expectations, Hickel got himself in trouble not by his disregard for conservationists but for being too zealous in the direction of ecology, a movement that was belatedly but frantically publicized in 1970. Conservationists gave Hickel points for his protection of the environment, but he didn't find much favor in the White House, either for his ecology interest or for his criticism of Nixon's remoteness and his cavalier treatment of young peace protesters.

In November 1970 Hickel was invited to confer with the president for what he thought was a budget meeting. Half an hour later, he was out of a job. The reason given was "lack of mutual confidence."

Nixon promptly eliminated inconsistencies in his cabinet by appointing Rogers C. B. Morton as secretary of the interior. Morton, the Republican national chairman, was the younger brother of Thurston Morton, a former Republican national chairman and a major backer of Nixon's unsuccessful 1960 campaign against Kennedy. Big brother Thurston, a banker, had had affiliations with several large corporations, including Pittsfield Coal, an outfit that manufactures strip-mining equipment. Although some questions were raised about Rogers Morton's own investments, he cleared the Senate confirmation hearing much more easily than Hickel had.

When Morton was still Republican national chairman, he had stated that he was opposed to some of the leftovers of the Kennedy-Johnson years. "People," he said, "did not like food stamps because they made the users feel uncomfortable." And, he added, "Programs for old people were not doing well because the old people didn't like to feel like a burden on the younger generation."

Shortly after taking over as secretary of the interior, Morton let it be known, as one newspaper said, that if it was a choice between trees and coal mines, he wasn't likely to pick trees. "Those who would stop the extraction of oil or coal, those who would not permit development of nuclear energy, are not realistic," he said.

Not long after Morton came to power, John O. Crow was promoted to the position of deputy commissioner of Indian affairs. Crow was an old-line BIA bureaucrat, supposedly one-quarter Cherokee, with almost thirty years of service under his belt. He had served as a reservation superintendent from 1942 to 1957 at four different reservations in the Southwest and then had taken on a variety of jobs at the central office in Washington.

Crow hadn't been in office very long when the word leaked out from the younger Indians recently appointed by the Nixon administration that he had been put in his job to keep the lid on the activist BIA faction. Rumors of internal conflict began to come from the once monolithic BIA, dimly perceived on most reservations, as if two monsters were battling to the death at the bottom of some murky pond. The clash was said to be a power struggle between the young activists (called Bruce's Troops or the Dirty Dozen) and the Crow faction of old-line bureaucrats (dubbed the Green Eyeshade Gang or the Haskell Mafia, a reference to Crow's alma mater, an Indian school that was a slight remove from Pratt's Indian-feeding station at Carlisle).

By the early fall of 1971, this infighting and Crow's tactics of roadblocking Indian progress and reform had gotten so bad that Peter MacDonald, a Nixon Republican and tribal chairman of the Navajos, the nation's largest tribe, sent a protest to Washington. This attracted little notice, especially because a few days later a more tangible protest arrived in the form of sixty AIM and NIYC activists led by Russell Means. On 22 September 1971 the Means gang issued forth from their command post, the Tom Jones Pub, and seized control of the BIA's information office, announcing that they had come to put a citizen's arrest on John O. Crow and Wilma Victor, former headmistress of the notorious Intermountain Boarding School. Owing to astute advance publicity, the network TV cameras arrived ahead of the Means war party and got to film Russell and Ted Means almost making it up the BIA's central staircase before they were attacked and dragged off by the highly trained cops of Washington, D.C.

As if to strengthen the rumors of factional fighting, Bruce saw to it that all charges were dropped and went so far as to thank Means for saving his job, all of which raised some interesting questions about who was really running the show.

Not long after the deplorable incident and the MacDonald protest, a reporter asked Rogers Morton if he had given any thought to removing John Crow. Morton praised Crow as "a good, tough administrator" and said that he wouldn't remove him.

"He's not a good administrator, but he is tough on

Indian people," said Herb Johnson, a Seminole and moderate AIM partisan. He also laughed at Crow's claims to be one-quarter Cherokee. The Cherokees are the tribe that the vast majority of non-Indians claim relationship to, a fact that annoys the genuine Cherokees even more than it bothers other Indians.

Despite protests flowing in from the reservations, the Nixon administration, in its haste to institute its self-determination policy, forged ahead, making all the same mistakes that had marked the disastrous Johnson administration. The elected Indian officials were being allowed to enter contracts, borrow money, sell tribal property, and mortgage tribal lands without consulting the governing bodies of their own tribes. Tribal councilmen were bought off with high-salaried jobs paid for by federal grant money, and their relatives were hired as well. Government-created tribal housing authorities were breaking every regulation and policy ever set up and catering to relatives and political cronies. One tribe reported $146,000 due in unpaid rentals on the low-cost, low-rent housing units on their reservation. The Department of Housing and Urban Development looked the other way until the tribal housing authority declared insolvency and bankruptcy.

In another case, the Department of Housing and Urban Development sponsored construction of four hundred plywood houses that have been known to burn to cinders in less than fifteen minutes. One expert appraiser, a white trailer builder named Henry Moore, set the value of these low-cost houses at $4,600 each. They cost the government and the tribal debt $14,000 apiece, and every tribal or federal official on the reservation refuses to show investigators the contract under which they were built. Three people have already been burned to death in these expensive firetraps.

The same tribe has a $94,000 Economic Development Administration loan that paid for purchase of a 1½-acre tract of land and for construction of roads and underground conduits on it. Since land all around this 1½-acre plot sells for $45 to $65 per acre, this must easily be the most expensive patch of weeds in South Dakota, if not the world.

On one reservation, the tribe borrowed $1,502,000 for a term of forty-one years in spite of the fact that the tribal charter and the Indian Reorganization Act prohibit the mortagaging of tribal lands for more than ten years.

A few figures reveal the fantastic inefficiency of the BIA. In 1970, federal funds allocated to Indians living on reservations from all sources (mostly BIA. OEO, and HEW) totaled $460 million. If this money were to be directly distributed to the Indians, each family would have had a yearly income of $5,600. Instead, the average yearly income for an Indian family living on a reservation from all sources (including land leases, work, and pensions) was $1,500. The rest of money vanishes somewhere between the taxpayers and the Indians. Most of it goes for bureaucrats' salaries, cars, office space and equipment, and public relations instead of for food, job training, and medical care.

All sources spent $460,000,000 in 1970. By 1973, the BIA alone was asking for $544,749,000. If the system of distributing the wealth has improved much since 1970, the people on the reservations haven't noticed.

This sort of corruption horrifies Indian people, not only because of the terrible impression it creates of all Indians when a few leaders indulge in it, but because thousands of Indians still go hungry and ill-clad despite huge expenditures of taxpayers' money on graft-laden and ridiculous projects. The most dreadful prospect is that Indian land is the collateral for most of these loans, and many Indians fear that the land will be confiscated for nonpayment of debts when the loans are not paid off. Having resisted termination from the outside, the tribes face the threat of being terminated by the greed and stupidity of a few of their own elected officials. Thus Nixon's self-determination policy has been dubbed the "self-termination policy" by those who feel they have good reason to distrust the government and the BIA.

While responsible people on the reservations were feverishly protesting this apparent self-termination policy, Commissioner Bruce was feverishly organizing the

National Tribal Chairman's Association (NTCA). This seemed illogical, for the Indians scarcely needed another national organization. They already had the following: (1) the NCAI, which had become uncomfortably independent of the BIA and had formed the strongest voice against termination; (2) the NIYC, formed in 1961, which represented a great many Indian college and high school students; (3) the AIM, founded in 1968, the most radical group of all, which at this time was largely composed of urban Indians, a group that the BIA preferred to ignore completely; and (4) the Association on American Indian Affairs, a white-dominated group that had been around since the 1920s and annoyed many Indians by trying to formulate policy on their behalf without consulting their wishes. There are a host of smaller groups, many of them oriented around various church groups. Indian people often joke that soon every Indian will have his own organization.

The National Tribal Chairman's Association, however, was a political necessity, because the administration wanted not a sounding board but an echo board, a puppet group that would agree with the government instead of opposing them, as all the above groups did most of the time.

Once established as an organization under the laws of the District of Columbia, the thirty-six chairmen in the charter membership of the NTCA elected the Reverend Webster Two Hawk, an Episcopalian minister, as the chairman of all the nation's tribal chairmen.

They couldn't have made a better choice. Two Hawk was agreeable to anything the administration wanted to do, and for a number of reasons. He was in trouble at home on the Rosebud reservation where he had consistently refused to show his tribe's financial records to tribal members. Among the other highlights of his political carrer, Two Hawk was the godfather of Cannon Production's filming of *Journey through Rosebud,* described with only mild exaggeration as the first Indian porno flick. The movie company had sold Two Hawk on the idea of filming an Indian movie on the Rosebud reservation, using Indian actors. But when the time came for casting, the leads were played by two white men and a Eurasian girl.

When the film crew got to the reservation they gave the local Indians a few brief speaking parts. An Indian cultural group called Unity showed up and demanded to see a copy of the shooting script, implying that it might be demeaning to Indian culture. They were curtly rebuffed, and when they staged a protest, Two Hawk called them outsiders and Communists and threatened them with his tribal police.

The most interesting thing about the film was its regional editing. The version shown in New York City contained some steamy bedroom scenes that were cut out of the version shown to people on the reservation. Fortunately for the film makers, the picture was so intrinsically bad that it bombed out at the box office before any of the Indian groups had a chance to organize a massive protest campaign.

Under Two Hawk's leadership, the National Tribal Chairman's Association became everything the administration could have hoped for.

To further complicate life for the reservation Indians, the Nixon administration advised the chairmen to incorporate under state laws in the various states so that they could serve as the grantees for all federal grants. The tribal chairmen swiftly did so, under the laws of their respective states. The administration completely overlooked the fact that this represented a direct conflict of interest. How could a tribal chairman properly serve his people if he was busy protecting his own corporation? How could a tribal member sue for an accounting of federal funds that were intended for his reservation?

But why think about it, the tribal chairmen must have reasoned. More important things were afoot, namely the presidential campaign of 1972. On 10 and 11 August the NTCA met in the delightfully cool city of Eugene, Oregon, to publicize the Indians' progress. Secretary of the interior Rogers Morton praised President Nixon in a lengthy speech as the NTCA members brooded over the fact that only 144 chairmen were in attendance, even though the tab for this junket was being picked up by the Nixon administration. The 144 chairmen realized, even if Morton didn't, that they represented far less than half of the nation's tribal chairmen. Some may have felt a twinge of guilt, for 65 percent of the nation's chairmen had refused to sell out their people for a free vacation and pocket money.

As the Republican National Convention in Miami drew near, rumors began to circulate that orders had been given in Washington to issue United States Treasury checks to certain tribal chairmen. The cover story about this dole was that the NTCA was meeting in Georgia at the same time that the convention was going on in Miami. However, at least six tribal chairmen were in attendance for the entire convention. One of them was none other than the Reverend Webster Two Hawk.

At the Democratic convention, on the other hand, Indians were visually represented by a man in full warbonnet and buckskin shirt with red, white, and blue beadwork. He was photographed shaking hands with somebody in an Uncle Sam costume. This shows the role that his Indian neighbors played in the mind of the senator from South Dakota.

The frustration of the reservation people was growing, for, despite grants of millions of dollars, little or nothing had changed. Old women still pondered whether they should sell their land for food to get through the winter, while the tribal chairmen and superintendent spent ninety-four thousand dollars on an acre and a half of weeds. Children still went to school in ragged hand-me-downs and read from tattered, outmoded, racist textbooks, while tribal chairmen and their relatives sported three-hundred-dollar suits and drove new limousines. The ambulances to take the sick and injured to faraway Public Health Service hospitals operated on depleted funds, while the tribal chairmen flew around the country by jet to agree with the Nixon administration that things were really looking up out there in Indian country.

The self-determination policy and incorporation may have freed the tribal chairmen, but the individual Indian still lived under bureaucratic oppression. The landowner could not collect his lease money for more than one year at a time. His lease income went to the U.S. Treasury to be doled out. The unemployment or underemployment rate on most reservations still hovers around 80 percent. U.S. Public Health Service doctors continued to scream at any Indian rash enough to get sick at night or over the weekend. Social workers still controlled the individual Indian's money as if it came out of their own pockets.

Anesthetized by the somnolent noddings of the NTCA, neither the BIA, the Department of the Interior, nor the Nixon administration saw any reason to expect trouble from Indian country as they geared down for the last months of the presidential campaign. But as history proved, they were wrong.

# 8

# Tribal Government: Blueprint for Corruption

> The white man will never be alone. Let him be just and deal kindly with my people, for the dead are not altogether powerless. Dead, did I say? There is no death, only a change of worlds.
>
> —Chief Seathe Seattle, 1855

The principle that Indian tribes are political bodies with powers of self-government was first clearly enunciated by Chief Justice John Marshall in 1832 in the case of *Worcester* v. *Georgia,* involving the Cherokee troubles. Indian tribes or nations, Marshall declared, had always been considered distinct, independent political communities, retaining their original natural rights.

The Supreme Court also held that the accepted rules of international law applied to Indians: "The settled doctrine of the law of nations is, that a weaker power does not surrender its independence—its right to self-government—by association with a stronger nation and taking its protection."

Thus the United States committed itself to the legal concept of Indian tribes as self-governing entities. The attempt of the Indians to preserve this self-government has been a long, bitter struggle.

Under the protection of the First, Fifth, Fourteenth, and Fifteenth amendments, Indian people are supposedly protected from racial discrimination by governmental agencies. And despite widely prevalent impressions to the contrary, Indians born in the United States are automatically citizens of the United States and of the states in which they reside. As such, they are entitled to vote, hold office, sue, make contracts, and enjoy the same liberties as their fellow citizens. These rights take on special significance against the background of a highly organized administrative control exercised by the federal government.

The doctrine that Indian affairs are subject to federal rather than state control derives from the U.S. Constitution, which specifically states that Congress shall have the power to regulate commerce with Indian tribes. And, with certain exceptions, Indians on a reservation are not subject to state laws. The exceptions are in the fields of criminal law and of taxation. Congress has seen fit to enact laws providing that individual Indian allotments are probated in accordance with state statutes, creating great confusion and untold opportunities for unscrupulous lawyers. Also, in Oklahoma, Indians are subject to state laws. But in both cases, as well as in various other matters, the power of the state is defined by federal legislation.

Although Indian treaties are absolutely silent on the matter of tribal government, the effect of government policies has been to destroy traditional tribal government by instituting regulations that prohibited Indian leaders from exercising their authority. At the same time, the tribes' religious leaders were kept in a virtual state of slavery and were forbidden to practice their religions. This was important because Indian religion and traditional government went hand in hand. Beneath the facade of benevolence spouted by the Supreme Court, the federal government did all in its power to destroy both.

In 1926, the Senate ordered a survey of conditions in answer to the complaints of Indians across the nation about the terrible living conditions and the graft and corruption on the part of the Indian agents. The famous Merriam Report, *Problems of Indian Administration,* was the result.

In evaluating this report, the American Indian Defense Association said, in part:

> The report of the Institute for Government Research is the most important single document in Indian affairs since Helen Hunt Jackson's "A Century of Dishonor,"

> published 45 years ago. It contains three sections which intrinsically are very fine. (Health, Education, and Women and Family and Community Life). Its 847 pages of text are a result of team-work between ten specialists. The studied moderation of its language; the avoidance of a suggestion even as to where responsibility shall be placed; the omission (save in regard to health and education) of most facts which give a quality of sinister deliberateness to the wrongs suffered by Indians; its nearly total avoidance of those skeleton closets, the handling of individual Indian trust monies and reimbursable indebtedness; these qualities of the report increase its convincingness and usefulness.

The Merriam Report stirred the general public into action that was transformed into congressional reaction, and the result of the maze of complaints and corruption was the Howard-Wheeler bill. After a series of hearings in Congress, the bill was enacted into law on 18 June as the Indian Reorganization Act of 1934.

Before the IRA, there were almost as many tribal governing bodies as there were tribes. Owing to restrictive federal policies, some tribes were actually without a government. The actual power on the reservations, as far as the government was concerned, was the Indian agent, acting on behalf of the secretary of the interior. The tribes themselves sometimes managed to maintain a link with their past in the form of traditional governing bodies. The form differed tribe by tribe. The Red Lake Chippewas of Minnesota maintained their traditional chief system, in which chieftainship was hereditary. The Sioux across South Dakota were operating under the three-quarters-majority council system that stemmed from the Sioux Treaty of 1868. This required that three-fourths of all adult males sign any legislation affecting the tribe. The Pueblo tribes of the Southwest operated their traditional Kiva system, which was strongly linked to their religion. The Crow tribe of Montana kept their general council system, a forum of one hundred people empowered to represent the rest of the tribe.

On their own, the Indian peoples had developed the checks and balances that were needed to keep a brake on ambition. Most plains tribes originally had at least two governing bodies that kept the power decentralized. Among the Cheyenne, for example, four old man chiefs served as advisers and executives, and a council of forty chiefs made up the legislative body. The police duties were assumed by three or more warrior societies, which were rotated to prevent any group from gaining power. Each warrior society was headed by a big war chief, assisted by nine little war chiefs. The various council chiefs expressed the will of the people, and the government had no right to compel anyone to take any action unless to do otherwise would threaten the whole tribe.

Whites who knew anything about traditional Indian tribal government were usually impressed. "The government of the Indian tribe is in the hands of the chiefs, who attain that office by merit or by exploits," Father Jean De Smet wrote in a letter to European friends in 1857.

> Their power consists solely in their influence; it is great or little in proportion to the wisdom, benevolence, and courage that they have displayed. The Chief does not exercise his authority by command but by persuasion. He never levies taxes: On the contrary, he is so much in the habit of giving away his own property, as well to aid a needy individual as to further the public good, that he is ordinarily one of the poorest in the village. I know of no government that allows so great personal liberty, and in which there is at the same time so little of anarchy and so much subordination and devotion . . . is it these people whom the civilized nations dare to call by the name of "savages"?*

De Smet had lived with Indians for half his life, and familiarity bred respect. A more generally accepted view of the era was that of Horace Greeley, the New York editor who became an instant Indian expert on a quick tour of the continent in 1859. He said:

> The Indians are children. Their arts, wars, treaties, habitations, alliances, crafts, properties, commerce,

---

*Quoted in *Wind River Rendezvous*, a mission newspaper published by St. Stephen's Indian School, Wind River, Wyoming.

> comforts all belong to the very lowest and rudest ages of human existence. . . . Any band of schoolboys, from ten to fifteen years of age, are quite as capable of ruling their appetites, devising and upholding a public policy, constituting a state or community, as the average Indian tribe. And unless they shall be treated as a truly Christian community would treat a band of orphan children providentially thrown on its hands, the aborigines of this country will be practically extinct within the next fifty years.

When they terminated treaty making in 1871, racist politicians, as ignorant but far less sympathetic than Greeley, used similarly contemptuous views to decide that all those treaties had been children's games after all.

The New Deal's Indian Reorganization Act of 1934 carried the promise of constitutional guarantees of liberty; finances for economic growth; an end to the steady loss of Indian lands; legal counsel needed by the tribes in order to cope with modern society; and lastly, the right to self-government to those who chose to adopt it.

Despite the golden promises, many traditional leaders were wary of anything that would disrupt the forms of government the Indians had created for themselves. The bitterly fought battle of the traditionals against the Indian Reorganization Act raged from 1934 until 1940. In the end, the Indian opposition was the victim of a provision of the act that allowed it to be adopted by 30 percent of the voting-age population of the reservation. This was a deviation both from Indian tradition and American democracy, since it allowed less than a majority to rule. The same provision that sets 30 percent as a quorum supposedly allows the Indians to petition for a referendum to recall the tribal constitution by securing at least 30 percent of the voting-age population's signatures. Yet the secretary of the interior has invariably ignored this and has categorically refused to hold referendums to repeal the tribal government system set up by the IRA. Thus the government has twisted its own rules for its own convenience.

In actual practice, a tribal council is a strange vintage of constitutional government: the federal government is divided into the executive, legislative, and judicial branches; the tribal constitutions created by the federal government provide for one single governing body, which tends to operate under constant conflicts of interest.

Under the IRA, the tribal president, chairman, or chief is generally empowered only to carry out the resolutions, ordinances, or directives of the tribal council. Thus, Indians have a government executive who can only function whenever the tribal council orders him to act. Likewise, the vice-president, vice-chairman, or vice-chief can only act in the absence of the president, chairman, or chief.

The tribal secretary, although he may be a constitutional officer, is the keeper of the tribal records and as such is subject to the powers of the tribal council. The tribal treasurer is the custodian of all tribal funds and can disburse such funds only by orders of the tribal council.

The size of the tribal council depends on the size of the tribe. Many have as few as six members; the Navajo tribe has seventy-two. The average number is around sixteen.

These councilmen are elected by various methods. On the Sioux reservations of Rosebud and Pine Ridge, among others, the tribe has an open nonpartisan primary, in which anyone with the required number of signatures on his nominating petition can get on the ballot. The primary narrows the field down to two candidates for each office. These two vie for office in the final election, usually about two months after the primary.

On other reservations, like the Crow reservation of Montana, there is no primary. The general election is open, with as many as a dozen candidates running as spoilers to take votes away from their friend's political opponents. Anyone who thinks that Indian people lack political sophistication would find some of the elections held by the north plains tribes, the Sioux in particular, to be very instructive. Not the least compelling reason for seeking office is that tribal chairmen receive a five-figure income—not easy to come by on a reservation—and can control a great deal of patronage, such as jobs for relatives.

Tribal constitutions specifically grant tribal councils the power to act for and in behalf of the entire tribe, without consulting the wishes of the people.

The tribal council has the power to negotiate with the federal, state, and local governments; to legislate the economic, social, educational, and domestic affairs of the tribe; to establish a tribal court, maintain a law-and-order code; to control domestic relations; to charter subordinate tribal enterprises; and to regulate the appointment of guardians for minors and mental incompetents.

In the area of land, the tribal council was empowered with restricting undesirable persons from the reservation; making assignments of tribal land to members; employing legal counsel for the advancement and protection of the tribe; purchasing lands through condemnation in courts of competent jurisdiction; governing the inheritance of real and personal property; and executing leases on tribal land. In addition, the council had the power to veto any action that would destroy tribal property.

The council also had the power to expend tribal funds; to levy taxes on tribal members or require the performance of labor in lieu of taxes; to regulate tribal elections; to advise the secretary of the interior on budget estimates prior to submission to Congress or the Bureau of the Budget; and to regulate their own procedure.

Despite this impressive list of powers, tribal self-government was a charade. The tribal constitution provides that the secretary of the interior approve the tribal council's actions, which means that the conflict of interest inherent in Interior's control over the Indian tribes is written right into their constitutions.

To add to the confusion, the Department of the Interior holds that the charters issued to the tribes are separate and distinct documents with no application or control over the tribal constitutions. This is an extremely contradictory position for the Department of the Interior to take, since the tribal constitutions, *Powers of the Tribal Council,* say bluntly:

"To manage economic affairs and enterprises of the tribe in accordance with the terms of the charter which may be issued to the tribe by the Secretary of the Interior . . ."

Thus the government set up for the Indians by Congress violates the Congress's own form of government. Indians hate this second-class form of government because their original, traditional tribal governments were invariably far superior.

Time and again, the Department of the Interior has interfered in tribal affairs against the Indians' best interests. For instance, a tribe may have a tremendous reserve of oil and gas on their reservation and have no desire to have some oil company exploit their wealth. They would prefer to form a tribally owned oil company employing their own people and profiting the tribe. But government officials will be bribed and the BIA will begin applying pressure to force the tribal council members to enact a resolution to advertise the oil and gas leases in their reservation for public bids.

A specific example of a resolution under BIA pressure that led to disaster is the one that allowed Peabody Coal to begin strip-mining operations on Black Mesa, the sacred mountain revered by traditional Navajos. Years ago, when the Navajo tribal council approved this resolution, they didn't realize that the strip mining would leave their land desolate and useless for grazing for generations, nor that the coal burned in the nearby Four Corners power plant would create the worst air pollution in America, pollution that ecology groups have predicted will be ten times worse than in New York City or Los Angeles. Today the Crow and Northern Cheyenne people of Montana are divided on the issue of strip mining following passage of a similar resolution by their tribal council, which will allow Peabody Coal to tear away the soil to reach the soft coal deposits underneath. Peabody Coal never bothered to mention the soil wastage, pollution, or the fact that their program will create a new city of over twenty thousand people on the Cheyenne reservation.

Instead, they gave the tribal council a full public relations treatment.

"They even flew some of our tribal officials to Germany to show them how they mine coal in the Saar," one Crow matriarch said. "They should have flown them to Appalachia and shown them that instead. If the strip mining gets in there, that land will be useless for a generation."

The Montana coal case is not an isolated instance. The BIA has habitually meddled in tribal business, usually to the tribe's detriment.

After the BIA had established blocks of land known as range units, they began making loans to the tribes to establish Indian credit corporations, under the tribal council's authority to charter subordinate organizations. The tribal credit corporation was totally controlled by the BIA's required secretarial-approval clause. This credit corporation was intended to advance money for Indians who desired to enter business. The funds were supposed to provide capital for opening filling stations and grocery stores, or buying livestock or farm machinery to be used in working the Indians' land. In actual practice, the BIA would only approve loans that led to Indian indebtedness.

Nearly every loan client was limited to a loan of five thousand dollars or less, when twelve thousand dollars would have ensured success. But despite the fact that the loans were failure-bound, the Indian Loan System had a national loss rate of less than 1 percent. The Indian—unlike the government—paid his debts.

This Indians' relations with the federal government began and usually ended with the BIA superintendent, and it was the superintendent, not the tribal council, who held the real power on most reservations. Except in rare cases, the balance of power has not changed since the days of the 1880s when the Indian agent ran his reservation like an army camp. Tribal government, as provided for by the Indian Reorganization Act and administered by the BIA, is now and always has been such a mess that those few tribes who escaped from the IRA government, like the Onondagas of upstate New York, feel that they are much better off under their traditional form of government.

In battles between the all-powerful superintendents and the Indian people, all too many elected officials washed their hands of the whole affair and let their constituents do their own fighting. Those elected officials who chose to try to defend their people were drawn into constant battles with the superintendents, but because of the pervasive apathy of reservation living and because of their lack of knowledge of how to appeal a decision, most individual Indians seemed to think that attempts to protect their people were hopeless. One could hardly expect the Indians to be informed on Indian law when 99.44 percent of the nation's lawyers know nothing of the matter either.

Another very special fact is that Indians or anyone else affected have the right to an administrative appeals system. This is a tiresome and almost endless process because the government on any level is not subject to time limitations. Most Indian appeals taken in this manner die a natural death for lack of persistence on the part of those who seek such adjudication.

Unlike the Indians, who felt strangled and frustrated by this morass of white tape, BIA officials seemed to thrive on it. But they took pains to stifle any challenge to their powers.

On the Rosebud reservation in the 1930s, Superintendent C. R. Whitlock had his tribal meetings down so pat that he first instructed his tribal councilmen how to vote and then made wax phonograph recordings of all their votes in case the record was called into question.

The superintendents guarded their dictatorial powers jealously. Indians who protested the superintendent's decisions found themselves penalized by the BIA men in a dozen different ways. Government rations and purchase orders for food would be cut off from whole families because of their opposition to the Indians' New Deal. This was a lethal weapon, for at this time the purchase orders were the only access Indians had to their land lease money deposited in individual Indian's accounts. These purchase orders were issued in lieu of cash and could be used only for staple foods.

Dick Mouse, a full-blood Sioux widely known for his singing voice and his wit, was one of those who registered complaints every time he was issued a purchase order because of the prohibition against buying fruit, sweets, tobacco, or receiving cash. He felt that the government was treating him like a simpleton or a child and he often said so. After joking bitterly about the purchase orders in Sioux, he would translate his feelings into rudimentary English for the benefit of the BIA staff.

"Sumabitch farm agent gimme purch' order. Can't buy orange! Can't even buy apple!"

The superintendents had other means of harassment. Land agents leased Indian land by permission of the "super"; the welfare workers issued rations with the approval of the "super"; the farm agent issued permits to sell I.D. cattle (those bearing the Interior Department's brand) with the approval of the "super." The superintendent was the judge, police chief, gardener, cowboy, banker, real estate agent, and secret head of state all wrapped up in one.

With the tutelage of the superintendents so readily available, election fraud became as common as campaign buttons and bumper stickers, and all sorts of manipulations became almost a fixed policy. On one Sioux reservation in the 1950s, BIA officials stood by while the incumbent tribal councilmen handed out fifty-dollar U.S. Treasury checks to those who voted for them. On another, the tribal chairman stated in no uncertain terms that a duly qualified candidate for the office of chairman would not be seated even if he were elected. The ballots printed for this election showed that one chairman had his own name printed larger than that of his opposition.

On the Turtle Mountain Chippewa reservation of North Dakota, the BIA actually approved a tribal constitution that ended all elections and allowed the tribal chairman to remain in office for life. When this chairman later created publicity that embarrassed the Department of the Interior by trying to sell tribal lands to the USSR, the BIA ordered a referendum to amend the situation. The people at Turtle Mountain wholeheartedly ousted their would-be king and restored elections.

One Rosebud reservation election of the 1960s shows how far the BIA will actually go. In this election, the secretary of the interior had appointed the reservation superintendent, Harold Schunk, as chairman of a referendum election on amendments of the tribal constitution, bylaws, and charter.

This meant simply that he was charged with the responsibility of seeing that the election committees of the twenty-one communities where polling places stood were honest and protected the tribal members' right to vote.

In October 1966 the tribal members went to the polls to approve nine important amendments to the tribal constitution and bylaws. At seven out of twenty-one communities, the tribal members were denied the right to vote.

In a sworn affidavit, a number of tribal members protested this illegal and fraudulent election to the secretary of the interior, only to have the appeal denied without the least concern. The Department of the Interior, which could tell Indians how to run the smallest aspects of their everyday lives, said that they could not interfere in intratribal affairs.

In October 1967 the first tribal election was held under the amendments. At stake were the tribe's twenty-two council seats, the vice-presidency, and the tribal presidency, the chairman's job. On the day before the election, all election members (three for each community) were briefed on procedures. During the briefing, the tribe's central election committee ordered that no tribal members could vote if they resided in the towns of Winner, Colome, Dallas, Gregory, Burke, Herrick, and Saint Charles. Hundreds of tribal members from these communities who went to the polls were turned away, for it was well known that these people were going to vote against the reigning administration.

This election too was protested, with a legally filed administrative appeal in compliance with the regulations set forth by the secretary of the interior. The appeal was again denied, and Interior again refused to interfere in intratribal affairs. Had their own picked candidates been defeated, one suspects that they would have been more sympathetic.

Reservation politicos have bought votes with jobs and promises of jobs, have used OEO money to pay for votes, and have had Legal Aid Service personnel and OEO employees haul voters pledged to back incumbents to the polls in federal vehicles. One OEO lawyer, supposedly bound to neutrality in tribal politics, went so far as to print campaign literature for the incumbent after tribal officials had helped him cover up charges that he raped a fifteen-year-old Indian girl.

Trouble with ambitious and greedy lawyers was nothing new on the reservations. When the Indian Reorganization Act first came onto the reservations, lawyers all over the country spotted a potentially lucrative practice in representing Indian tribes. A lawyer named James Curry was the first of many to capitalize on the new opportunity. Curry secured contracts with several tribes, then began to press for the necessary approval from the secretary of the interior. To comply with the law, Curry had the contracts executed before a federal district court judge and precisely fulfilled other legal requirements. Reluctantly, Secretary Harold Ickes approved several contracts for Curry.

But Curry was not satisfied. He set out to secure contracts from tribes across the county. Usually he contacted a tribal member who had influence with the tribe and got the Indian to set up a council meeting where he could make his pitch.

When a complaint was registered, an investigation disclosed that Curry had been selling his contracts to other attorneys without secretarial approval and without the consent of the tribes whose contracts were being sold. His contracts were set aside and several other firms moved in to try to take over where Curry left off.

Tribal attorneys cannot represent individual Indians but can only act on matters affecting the entire tribe.

Thus individual Indians are left entirely without counsel while they are actually paying handsome retainers for their tribal lawyers. For example, the Navajo pay a thirty-five-thousand-dollar annual retainer for their general counsel.

One threat that seemed to stir the BIA bureaucrats to action was fear of losing their jobs. In 1946, Indian reservations were suddenly advised that a Withdrawal Program was under way. Congress had gone on a budget-cutting spree at the end of the war and whacked away an enormous chunk of the BIA budget. But the BIA, like some species of vermin, proved harder to kill than Congress had expected. Picking up the ball for an end run around Congress, the BIA simply promulgated new regulations under the law and established the necessary tribal organizations to carry on business as usual. On most reservations, the BIA created Tribal Leasing Enterprises by advising their puppet tribal councils to enact resolutions setting up these organizations, with a schedule of fees that would be charged for doing business. Soil Conservation Enterprises were also set up at the BIA's behest, and business went on as usual.

The BIA had neatly evaded any damage to itself, but Indians suffered grievously because the tribal councils had failed them. They could have forced the secretary of the interior to inform them of all budgetary estimates prior to submission to the Bureau of the Budget and to Congress, as he was required to do by law. But no such action was taken, and Indians died of tuberculosis while the sanitoriums operated on reduced budgets and were unable to accommodate them.

The Indians who fought in World War II came back to the reservations with the determination that things would change. Although some of them sold out or fell by the wayside, there were enough men of courage and willpower to make some changes for the better, in spite of the system foisted off on the Indians by the Indian Reorganization Act. In 1951, they finally got rid of the hated purchase orders, so that Indians could be paid in cash for the value (however meager) of their leased land. In 1956, Indians in Arizona and New

Mexico finally got the right to vote in state elections after a long and protracted battle against the poll tax and literacy tests. Whites who wanted to keep Indians out of state politics countered the Navajos' new rights to vote by spreading the rumor that Indians who voted would also be taxed, even if they lived on tax-exempt reservation land. This tactic is used to thwart Indian attempts to enter into state politics to this very day.

Enraged at the conditions on the reservations, where land was being leased at sixteen cents per acre while their families lived in misery, Indian veterans were unwilling to endure any more degradation. They issued a challenge to the BIA to improve conditions, but their challenge went unanswered. The voices of Indian leaders who tried to bring the nation's attention to poverty on the reservations fell on deaf ears. After all, poverty program directors reasoned, the Indians had the BIA to take care of them. The media also largely ignored the struggle of the new breed of Indian leaders. The only Indians known to the nation at large were those gunned down by John Wayne.

Around 1959, younger leaders of the Sioux and other tribes began to get attention as they interested some prominent whites in their cause. Marlon Brando, Eugene Burdick, and Senator John F. Kennedy began to call attention to the national disgrace.

On the reservations, tribal councils began to assume the responsibility of protecting members of their tribes, regardless of their place of residence. And the Indians needed protection. In South Dakota, as in many other states, the state penitentiary population was at least one-third Indian, many of them jailed for crimes in which a white culprit would have been allowed to make restitution or serve a much shorter sentence. The Indian prisoners were segregated by cellblocks.

During the Johnson and Nixon administrations, tribal councils have degenerated to the point where the young and the old on reservations can no longer use the normal channels to communicate with the men that supposedly represent them. Many tribal chairmen, losing sight of the needs of their people, began to enrich themselves from the wildcat spending under Johnson and Nixon. Instead of trying to work through a system that had discredited itself in their eyes, the younger Indians of the 1960s rallied behind such organizations as the National Indian Youth Council, United Native Americans, and the American Indian Movement.

The apathy of the councilmen to the needs of their own people, the sneers and giggles of congressmen whose help was sought, and the growing tide of murders of Indians that seemed to mark 1972 as the year of renewed genocide brought the dissatisfaction and anger of the younger Indians, and of many of their elders, to the boiling point.

In January 1972 rumors began to spread through Indian country about the death of Raymond Yellow Thunder, a gentle fifty-one-year-old Sioux cowboy who had been found propped up in a truck cab in a used-car lot in Gordon, Nebraska. The case was too awful, too typical, to be ignored. The story that developed was that about a week before his body was found, Yellow Thunder had been kidnapped by five drunken whites—four men and a girl—stripped of his pants, and thrown naked from the waist down into the middle of a dance at the Gordon American Legion Hall. He complained to local police. A week later, when he was found dead, the police claimed that he must have fallen down, hit his head, and crawled into the truck cab to die. The obvious cover-up only expanded rumors made believable by the fact that Yellow Thunder's sister had been killed in the same town twenty years before. Some people said that Yellow Thunder had been tortured, burned with cigarettes, and castrated.

One bitter morning in February 1972, two thousand white residents of Gordon awoke to find their streets crowded with thirteen hundred angry Indians, some wearing traditional regalia and others clad in upside-down American flags. Led by AIM leaders Russell Means and Dennis Banks, the Indians had come to demand justice. After three days of noise and menace, local and state officials backed down and acceded to a number of AIM's demands. Two of the whites implicated in Yellow Thunder's death were jailed, a policeman alleged to have molested Indian women was suspended, and local and state officials promised to investigate charges of discrimination.

On the way back from Gordon to Pine Ridge, a splinter group from the caravan barged into the Wounded Knee Trading Post, where Pine Ridge's Indians claimed they had been cheated and insulted for decades. The raiding party slapped the trading post's management around and made off with antique costumes, regalia, and jewelry worth anywhere from $500,000 (the owner's estimate) to $50,000 (the FBI's estimate). That night, activists and rowdies staged a firelight war dance in full view of the trading post's frightened staff. When someone asked the tribal police what they intended to do about the looting, the police chief deadpanned: "We're investigating."

The AIM leaders, particularly Means, were warmly received on the Pine Ridge reservation. For AIM, the Gordon victory, though largely a paper conquest in terms of concrete results, was a major breakthrough. Not only had the racist whites of Nebraska been given a healthy scare, but the reservation people of Pine Ridge took the urban militants of AIM unto their bosom, at least temporarily.

# 9
# The Trail of Broken Treaties

> What white man can say I ever stole his land or a penny of his money? Yet they say I am a thief. What white woman, however lovely, was ever captive or insulted by me? Yet they say I am a bad Indian. What white man has ever seen me drunk? Who has ever come to me hungry and went away unfed? Who has ever seen me beat my wives or abuse my children? What law have I broken? Is it wrong for me to love my own? Is it wicked for me because my skin is red? Because I am a Sioux? Because I was born where my father lived? Because I would die for my people and my country?
>
> —Sitting Bull

The sacred Sun Dance had long been forbidden by white authorities because it was the central rite of the old Sioux religion. The Sun Dance began to be reborn in the early 1960s and by 1970 had become a focal point of Sioux traditionals. Russell Means was the first of the AIM activists to be pierced, and several others followed his example in 1971 and 1972.

But the traditional Sun Dance in 1972 concluded on a note of frustration and anger. The people at Rosebud reservation, where the ritual was held, had elected the Reverend Webster Two Hawk as their tribal president. Two Hawk was the bane of Indian activists, AIM and non-AIM alike, because he was the head of the NTCA and because he had swiftly broken most of his campaign promises as soon as he was in office. Two Hawk had promised to raise the full bloods to his level; instead, he hired his relatives and non-Indians for all the better jobs. He also broke his promise to purchase land by buying up all outstanding stock in the Tribal Land Enterprise, a subsidiary of the tribal government.

For years, I had dreamed of having a force of at least two hundred Indians in Washington, D.C., to demonstrate "Indian style" until the Congress and the president took notice. On 17 August 1972, with the AIM leadership gathered at the Sun Dance surrounded by the Sioux people, I saw a chance to make my dream a reality.

AIM had been founded in July 1968 by George Mitchell and Dennis Banks, two Chippewa Indians then living in Minneapolis. Mitchell, a sensitive and rather mild man, actually drew up the AIM charter, but he was subsequently pushed into the background by more flamboyant types. By 1972, AIM's principal leaders were Dennis Banks, Clyde and Vernon Bellecourt, and Russell Means.

Banks, the AIM cofounder, was about thirty-eight, a striking figure with considerable charm. The two Bellecourts, both of whom had done time for felonies—armed robbery for Vernon, burglary for Clyde—were, respectively, the directors of the Denver and Minneapolis chapters. Clyde Bellecourt, who had served fourteen years in prison, was one of the earlier members of AIM. Vernon, who had gone straight as a hairdresser after an impressive juvenile record, was a more recent addition.

Means, at thirty-two, was the youngest of the major AIM leaders and the most perplexing. He was an Oglala Sioux, born on the Pine Ridge reservation and raised there and in urban areas. After a year on skid row in Los Angeles, he made an effort to give up drinking and began to attend colleges—five of them—but didn't graduate. After a stint working for the tribal council on the Rosebud reservation he applied for relocation to Cleveland and shortly became director of the Cleveland American Indian Center.

At this post, he revealed his bizarre knack for staging demonstrations that attracted the sort of press coverage Indians had been looking for: the capture of the *Mayflower II* on Thanksgiving of 1970, a brief occupation of Mount Rushmore in June 1971, and an abortive attempt to seize the BIA central office on 22 September of the same year. His genius for public relations seemed to create a certain amount of envy in the older AIM leaders, but because he was the most Indian of the four by blood and by temperament, and because he had never been convicted of a felony, he usually served as the group's spokesman.

AIM's greatest victory had been at Gordon, Nebraska, where their take-over of the Nebraska whiskey town had lead to some concrete changes instead of the usual mass arrest with brutality. Their greatest fiasco was at Cass Lake in April 1972 where the organization moved in with guns to back up the Chippewa tribe, which was trying to enforce a federal court ruling that white men had to buy tribal fishing licenses. The reservation Chippewas asked the armed AIM detachment to leave, and an argument between the various factions almost turned into a gunfight as some AIM members voted to leave and others to stay in defiance of the tribe.

Shortly after the Cass Lake episode, AIM seemed sure to wither away. Means was harassed out of Cleveland by the press as well as by baseball fans because of his attempt to sue the Cleveland Indians team for nine million dollars. His suit was based on the fact that the team's cartoon mascot, Chief Wahoo, was demeaning. Banks was also terminated from any power in the national organization, and the AIM scene slumbered uneasily through the summer of 1972.

The Rosebud Sun Dance brought the various leaders together again, but they seemed at a loss to find any cause worthy of one of their demonstrations. One idea they kicked around was a protest of the treatment of three hundred Indian skeletons at the University of South Dakota at Vermillion, to demand their reburial. At this low ebb in their fortunes, I suggested a national demonstration.

A plan had been forming in my mind, but owing to fear of termination I had never taken measures to have it introduced as legislation. Now, with a number of Indian organizations available and the national elections approaching, the time seemed ripe.

After everyone else had run dry of suggestions, I called for my turn to speak.

> For years, it has been my dream to take 200 Indians into the capital of our nation and to stay there until the government takes action to correct the abuse, discrimination, and injustices committed against our people. I have dreamed that before my eyes close in death, all Indians would be able to walk this earth with pride and dignity instead of being ashamed of tribal government that will eventually lead our people to termination.
>
> As an Indian, I challenge all organizations on behalf of the American Indians and Friends Incorporated, to join together under the banner of the Trail of Broken Treaties and proceed to Washington, where we will show the world what Indians truly stand for.
>
> Should the Indian organizations accept this challenge, we should be on our very best behavior in executing a spiritual movement as predicted by our medicine men of old. There cannot be any liquor or drugs used by anyone, and our plan should consist of a schedule of peaceful negotiations and religious ceremonies that will make our fellow citizens realize the power bestowed upon the Indian so that Grandfather, God, will make all mankind realize that we are human beings who are guided by the Great Spirit. If you can accept these terms in the execution of a great effort to educate the general public, impress the president, and Congress, we shall have made the greatest advance ever on behalf of the people we represent. This shall be our finest hour if we are successful in maintaining discipline that shall bring fruit to our hungry people.

Vern Bellecourt, then serving as national coordinator for AIM, stood to accept the challenge.

"Many Indians have dreamed of reaching this goal and AIM will take the responsibility of coordinating the effort by calling a meeting in Denver, Colorado, where all Indian organizations can join in this vital and important event."

Others also approved the idea. Thus the Trail of Broken Treaties was born at Crow Dog's Paradise, the home of the Henry and Leonard Crow Dog families of medicine men. Beneath the pine boughs of the Sun

Dance shade, the leaders of the various groups discussed the plans and began to organize.

The Denver meeting took place between 30 September and 2 October. Russell Means and Dennis Banks were chosen to form caravans in San Francisco and Seattle and lead them across the country, gathering people and momentum until they converged on Washington at the end of October. The caravans were far from secret. Within days of the first meeting, the Department of the Interior had received word of the plans through their informers, and they were filled with apprehension.

Among the men at the top was Harrison Loesch, assistant secretary of the interior, Bureau of Land Management, the office that has charge of Indian affairs. When Loesch and I were on the Dick Cavett show, he admitted to a nationwide audience that he didn't know anything about Indians. He didn't seem to want to learn anything either, because by 11 October he had issued a memorandum to Louis Bruce, commissioner of Indian affairs, ordering that no aid be given to the people of the Trail of Broken Treaties caravans. Bruce followed through by sending telegrams to practically every BIA official advising them not to aid AIM directly or indirectly.

The caravans continued to rumble ominously in the ears of the Department of the Interior officials who must have realized that the phenomenon of Indians speaking for themselves boded them no good. The news media presented an oddly fragmented version of the whole buildup. Each area office of the Associated Press seemed to think that the caravan had originated in its own backyard. Reports flowed in from Oklahoma, Minnesota, and points west, so that it must have seemed to the bureaucrats at Interior that every Indian they'd ever wronged was about to descend on them.

I had been elected cochairman, along with Reuben Snake, a Winnebago Indian who lived in Albuquerque. It was my responsibility to organize the East Coast area Indians and friendly whites. My main duties were raising funds and making advance preparations in Washington.

On 20 October, at the headquarters of the Park Service on Haines Point in D.C., I got some idea of what I was up against at a meeting to negotiate for the permits covering our schedule of demonstrations. There was palpable tension as I entered the building, and uniformed policemen were everywhere. The conference room was full of men dressed as if they were expecting some dignitaries to arrive, but they themselves were the dignitaries. They represented the seven factions of police with jurisdiction in the District of Columbia, plus the Secret Service, the FBI, and the Military District of Columbia.

My cohorts at this meeting were Anita Collins and Ralph Ware of AIM and Terrence Sidley, an attorney. As the assistant solicitor from the Interior Department began to drone on about the schedules, my colleagues and I began to fidget. After about an hour I'd had enough, and I cut in.

"We didn't come here to haggle with you, and we didn't come to rape your women, scalp anyone, or raise hell in the streets, but if that's what you want, that's exactly what you'll get. Now, let's sit down like intelligent people and get to the point. I don't have all day to waste trying to get permits to go to places where anyone else can go without permits."

Everybody seemed relieved, and a frank discussion took place and ended on a friendly note. I was amazed at the importance that the federal government seemed to be placing on the Trail of Broken Treaties and all the more so when a policeman told me that we were wanted at the Department of the Interior after the meeting to confer with all federal agencies on the secretarial level.

When we arrived at the conference room to meet with Loesch, we found that representatives from every federal agency with responsibilities for Indians had arrived there and wanted to rehash the schedule. The atmosphere was one of mutual distrust. Loesch had heard that the Trail of Broken Treaties was planned as a violent showdown with federal officials rather than as a religious vigil. Conversely, a federal employee had informed us that every official we wanted to see would be "out of town" for the duration of the Trail. Again, we made it clear that our intentions were peaceful, but that if the government provoked trouble they could have a fight on their hands. The officials agreed to meet with us again on 27 October.

The AIM office for the Trail was set up at 1816 Jefferson Place NW, and manned by volunteers. As the countdown to election week grew shorter, tension began to build among almost everyone involved. The AIM caravans converged on Minneapolis and Saint Paul in the last week of October. The AIM leaders gathered some publicity with a take-over of the BIA area office in Minneapolis, an action that lasted about two hours. Some two hundred dollars worth of Indian relics apparently left the building with the AIM forces when they evacuated.

A conference call was set up between myself, Means, and Clyde and Vernon Bellecourt. I was disturbed by the Minneapolis take-over, by an unauthorized letter that Dennis Banks sent to Nixon, and by speeches about a nebulous twenty-point demand that the AIM leaders had apparently drawn up without consulting me or the other Indian leaders. After some hot words on both sides, we agreed to adhere to the original plans for a nonviolent religious vigil.

But inside AIM, other thoughts were being kicked around. Advance publicity had predicted huge numbers of Indian people rolling into Washington. Estimates ranged from thirty thousand to a hundred thousand, but suppression had cut the numbers of Indians in the caravans drastically. Many people who wanted to take part simply didn't have money to throw away driving around the country. Others feared to lose their jobs by taking part in anything that exposed the BIA to criticism. Even Reuben Snake, my fellow cochairman, was unable to participate because of job pressure.

Shortly after the seizure of the Minneapolis area office, radio broadcasts had thirty to forty thousand Indians moving on Washington. A reporter called Means in Minneapolis to confirm this. Means burst into hysterical laughter. "Maybe there are, but I don't know where the hell they're all coming from. All I've got here is eight hundred."

The AIM leaders had vowed to make the Trail of Broken Treaties the biggest event in the struggle for Indian rights since Alcatraz (the one recent protest in which AIM played no part), and probably they feared humiliation if only a handful of people turned out and were lost in the crowds of Washington during election week.

Their philosophy also differed from those of the more moderate Indian leaders. "In all our demonstrations we have yet to hurt anybody or destroy any property," Means said in a speech late in 1971. "However, because the white man is such a violent dude and because he digs violence so much, we have found that the only way the white man will listen to us is for us to create a disturbance in the world."

He put it even more succinctly to the only white newsman he ever confided in. "I've had dealing with AP, UPI, and all three major TV networks, and the only thing they ever want to know is how many people went to the hospital and how many people went to jail."

Ironically, while the AIM leaders mulled over the possibility of a fiasco, a thaw seemed to be setting in between the federal officials and the Trail's advance party in Washington. At our meeting on 27 October the federal officials met us at the Interior Department offices for a productive and rather friendly meeting. They asked us again to make sure that the caravan remained totally nonviolent and went so far as to offer us some minor help. John Crow, deputy chief of the BIA, was given clearance from Interior to furnish us with some bond and carbon paper and to pay two secretaries for the Trail office.

At the same time, the White House leaked word to Ralph Ware and myself that they'd feel more comfortable about the whole thing if NTCA president Rev. Webster Two Hawk was invited to take part in the Trail. Since the Trail of Broken Treaties was intended to reflect the needs and wishes of all the Indian people, even those who were under the government's thumb, I didn't raise any objections. I called Two Hawk and he agreed to be the opening speaker at the first assembly in Washington.

On the evening of 27 October, the National Congress of American Indians arranged a meeting with several Indian-interest groups at the BIA auditorium. Many Indian people who worked for various federal departments and in charity groups attended. During the meeting, Ramona Bennett, a member of Hank Adams's Survival of American Indians group, began passing out copies of a telegram, which, incredibly, ordered me to stop fighting and cooperate with Ramona Bennett. The thing was supposedly signed by Russ Means, Sid Mills, both Bellecourts, and Banks. This inexplicable telegram created pandemonium, and within minutes there was no one left in the auditorium but Miss Bennett's group and those of us who were manning the Trail office. I was outraged by this silly and disruptive power play and said so in no uncertain terms. George Mitchell, AIM's cofounder and their man in Washington joined me in telling Miss Bennett off.

No sooner had she been dispensed with—at least temporarily—than an even worse shock hit the Washington advance team. Most of the church groups who had offered housing for the demonstrators changed their minds at the last minute, broke their word, and withdrew their offers. Both the Catholic and the Jewish religious communities abruptly backed off from their commitments. Investigations on our part disclosed that Harrison Loesch's office had put out the word to stay away from the Trail of Broken Treaties.

The only housing left open to the caravan was Saint Stephen's Episcopal Church on Sixteenth Street. A small contingent of Indians from Des Moines, Iowa, had been staying there for a week, sharing the dinner tables with the elderly poor who came there for the two meals a day the church offered.

The Trail caravan rumbled into Washington at 6:00 A.M. 1 November and were directed to Saint Stephen's. All hell promptly broke loose as the AIM elements began to condemn the accommodations. AIM leaders shouted that they had just come from slum conditions in Minneapolis and weren't about to put up with rats and broken toilets in Washington. The AIM faction, followed by many other caravan members, boiled out of Saint Stephen's and staged a brief, abortive march on the White House. The march was heavily shadowed by police who tried to turn the hordes of protestors toward West Potomac Park. Instead, the AIM people kept on moving until they reached the BIA building. Somebody suggested that they seize the building as their embassy in Washington. There was a brief scuffle with the policemen guarding the basement door, but the lawmen were pushed back by the swarms of Indians, and the building was abandoned to the AIM. Within a few hours, the story of the Trail of Broken Treaties leaped from the back pages of newspapers to the top headlines, and radios across the nation reverberated with the sound of Indian drums and the high, quavering chants of the Sioux war dance.

I reached the building shortly after the news broke. The lower floors were crowded with hundreds of teenagers and a number of Indian veterans and activists in their twenties. Some of them were naïve, idealistic young people, some were out for a lark, and a few were hardcases looking for a chance to take a little bit of their resentment out on somebody. About fifty old people took the whole thing in stride, watching the youngsters with tolerant affection. There were children and babies, an old man on crutches, and several Vietnam veterans incapacitated by war wounds.

Upstairs, where the carpets were deep and no exposed steam pipes marred the smoothness of the ceilings, Harrison Loesch and John Crow were trying to face down the leaders of the take-over. Charges flew thick and fast on both sides. Clyde Bellecourt was shouting that the take-over was the government's fault because they had shunted the caravan into a rat-infested church. I rebutted that we had never said we would ask the government for facilities. Some young punk I'd never seen before shouted that Loesch wasn't leaving the room until the Indians got what they wanted. At this point, with a potential explosion building up on both sides, I suggested that we go downstairs to the auditorium where we could talk more comfortably and settle our Indian internal squabbles with a vote. I didn't think the Indian cause would be served if we all went to jail for kidnapping.

Loesch was rather scared, and with good reason, but he blustered his way through with a red face. Many of the Indians he was facing—probably for the first time in his life—were not AIM members, but tribal leaders and people with legitimate grievances. The Potawatomi tribe of Kansas had sent several tribal council members to protest the commissioner's orders to abolish their council in direct opposition to the so-called self-determination policy. Phillip Deer, an intelligent and responsible Creek Indian leader, protested the BIA's mistreatment of his tribe in Oklahoma. Many Indians from Washington State objected to the continued violation of their treaty-bound hunting and fishing rights. It couldn't have been very pleasant for Loesch, as a member of the Elks, a club that banned Indians and other nonwhites from membership, to be put on the spot by the people his other organization, the BIA, had been persecuting since 1834. Particularly not at election time. Loesch was finally released on the promise that he would try to secure accommodations for the caravan.

Part of the purpose of the Trail of Broken Treaties had been to exact commitments from both parties to improve the treatment of Indians. Letters had been sent to President Nixon and to Senator McGovern before the caravans even set out. Nixon wrote back stating rather curtly, through an aide, that he had done more for the American Indian than any president in this century and that he didn't intend to be available. As one Indian dryly observed, even if his claim were true it wasn't saying much. McGovern said he would try to be there, but when the demonstration turned into the BIA take-over he waffled and refused to meet with the AIM leaders, despite several irate phone calls from Means who threatened to expose him before the press as a phony liberal.

Candidates of every stripe were oddly silent about the take-over as election day drew near. Coming out for the Indians would have lost votes from the Western anti-Indians and from law-and-order types in general, while an attack on the caravan would have looked awfully bad to most liberals and nonwhite voters. As politicians will, they avoided the issue entirely.

By the morning of 2 November, the BIA was back to business as usual. AIM occupiers sent the women around to clean up the mess left in the wake of the scuffle. Loesch on his part agreed to let the Indians use the building until better quarters were found. He also arranged a discussion between the Indians and Bradley Patterson, executive assistant to Leonard Garment, a special assistant to Nixon, and Robert Robertson, executive director of the National Council on Indian Opportunity.

Everything seemed peaceful, but late in the afternoon, as Means ordered the Indians to secure the building against outsiders, some Washington police tried to barge in, prompted by the rumor that there was a policeman trapped inside. There was a brief scuffle, Indians were clubbed, and the police were roughly and forcibly evicted. An order immediately came from the White House's number-two man, John Ehrlichman, to pull back the riot police. AIM remained king of the hill.

At 8:15 P.M. the steering committee newly drawn up by AIM and Survival of American Indian members met with Loesch, Brad Patterson, and Robert Robertson. The Indians asked the three whites to leave while they began the meeting with an Indian prayer. At 11:00 P.M. the three whites left. They had decided not to commence a police action, but to start legal action to evict the Indians.

After 196 years of trickery, the Indians, and particularly the AIM leaders, had learned not to trust white promises. This lesson could be traced back to the *Mayflower* or Sand Creek, but there were more immediate memories to draw on. In 1971, the Minneapolis chapter and their supporters had suffered severe beatings during an attack by eighty U.S. marshals at the Twin Cities Naval Air Station, an abandoned base that AIM had wanted for a school. The AIM people took over the base and were told that a negotiating team from the office of Senator Walter Mondale would arrive at 10:00 A.M. Instead, riot police arrived at 5:00 A.M. and charged them, arresting sixteen men and brutalizing Indian women and children. The Survival of American Indian group had also been through duplicity. In 1970, Hank Adams was shot and severely injured by two white sportsmen. When he tried to press charges, the local police accused him of having attempted suicide.

Impelled by these examples, the Indians in the building did everything in their power to turn it into a fortress. Typewriters, file cabinets, food freezers, and boxes of stationery were stacked in front of the shattered glass doors and guarded by young men armed with makeshift clubs.

The idea of a static defense didn't appeal to me, and I attempted to interest the AIM leaders in another form of protest. We had just received a letter denying the Indians the right to hold traditional religious rites at the graves of Ira Hayes and John Rice. Hayes was famous for his role at Iwo Jima; Rice, a Winnebago, had fought in World War II and Korea but had been denied burial in an all-white cemetery in Nebraska. I thought that an appeal to federal courts on this insult to our religious freedom would accomplish more than the seizure of an office building. But the AIM leaders, who had taken over Commissioner Bruce's plush office and were lounging around like Napoleon and his marshals, were in no mood to go to court. Several of them made fun of the idea. I left in a mood of disgust and took up the case on my own.

At 11:00 A.M. on 3 November, U.S. district court Judge Howard Corcoran denied the temporary restraining order and forbade the religious ceremonies at Arlington. Terry Sulley, who coordinated legal services for the caravan, and Ralph Temple, another attorney, filed suit in appellate court that same afternoon on behalf of the Indian plaintiffs. The case of *Siaticum* v. *Laird* was on its way to becoming a legal landmark.

Meanwhile, back at the BIA building, the takeover was becoming a media event unto itself. Reporters from all over the nation and from as far away as Russia and Japan swarmed in, taking pictures and waiting for the AIM leaders to finish their seemingly endless closed meetings and to come down to the auditorium for press conferences. The scene was unforgettable—Indians in a mixture of regalia and army fatigues, reporters tripping over the convoluted wires of TV cameras, white hippies and other fringe elements meandering through the building where Indians slept in the halls; and, outside, mounted police drilling ominously on majestic black horses in the shadow of the Washington Monument. It was a sort of indoor Indian Woodstock, with just enough threat of violence to keep everyone's nerves tingling. The only people that didn't seem happy with the whole thing were the black policemen clustered rather guiltily outside the basement door.

Strange scenes were enacted. Means was in his glory, making speeches before the cameras of every network in the civilized world and pursued by blonde groupies with tape recorders and bogus press credentials. At one point, he was waylaid by a bearded hippie in a lavender sweater, a gold filigree necklace, and sandals who asked him to endorse a book about ecology.

"I gotta see a copy of this book before I endorse anything," Means growled. "We've been ripped off too many times before by things like this."

The hippie moaned that he didn't have a copy and gave Means a single, badly Xeroxed sheet of paper. The text on the page consisted of five or six paragraphs of misspelled clichés, laced with obscenities. Halfway through the second sentence Means seemed to realize that the man was mad.

"I ain't signin' nothing 'til I know where the money's going," Means barked, edging away from the freak, who began to trail him around the auditorium, moaning complaints about Means's rudeness. Means finally eluded the hippie and conferred with an Indian girl who had been watching the phones.

"We've gotten calls from several publishers, including an encyclopedia," the girl said. Means was jolted by the encyclopedia. He borrowed a dime from a reporter and went downstairs to the pay phone to investigate.

Meanwhile, a photographer from the Department of the Interior was roaming the building, armed with false press credentials, taking pictures of the worst damage he could find for subsequent use as antiactivist propaganda.

The influx of white hippies and street types finally got on everybody's nerves to such an extent that Vern Bellecourt clambered onto the podium and shouted orders to throw out any white person who didn't have a press pass. The Indians cheered good-naturedly, and a handful of security people with clubs and canes went around pointing to any non-Indian who didn't have credentials.

While the leaders parleyed in Bruce's office, the Indian teen-agers and old people sat around in utter boredom, too tired to stay awake and too tense or uncomfortable to sleep. The monotony was broken by a white medical technician with straggly brown hair and a feeble beard giving instructions about basic sanitation in such an arrogant tone that it was surprising that nobody punched him in the mouth. After a while Bellecourt came back from Bruce's office and made a speech.

"Many sold-out leaders on reservations are saying that we are not grass-roots Indians. Therefore, we are asking you, the grass-roots Indians, to vote on the 20 points we have drawn." The fear of the AIM leaders, who were mostly urban Indians, of not being grass-roots Indians amounted almost to paranoia. Some of the activists inside the building had little preprinted cards attached to their buttonholes that read I Am a Grass Roots Person.*

As the day wore on, riot police were assembled in the basements of federal buildings surrounding the BIA. The tension reached a high point as Means spoke

---

*The BIA claimed, of course, that most Indians opposed the take-over. But a BIA Indian employee told coauthor Koster that about 60 percent of the building's own staff supported AIM.

at the last of the day's interminable press conferences.

"We see no reason to leave, and so we're staying," he shouted. Wild cheers and drumbeats drowned out the rest of his statement. "Remember this," he told the reporters. "We Indians have never been afraid to die, because we know where we're going."

The biggest surprise of all came from Commissioner Louis Bruce, who decided to remain overnight in the building with the activists to show his sympathy with their goals and to try to prevent bloodshed. Bruce's decision was cheered by the activists. As riot police in outer-space helmets concentrated in the shelter of surrounding buildings, the AIM faction began to work on makeshift weapons. Spears were made of electrical insulation cable, chairs and table legs were broken up for clubs, and the seats were turned into shields. The federal forces cut all telephone lines except the line to the commissioner's office.

At about 8:30 P.M. the mayor's command post called me and advised that police were going in within twenty minutes unless the Indians left the building peacefully. I felt that the government meant exactly what they said, since they had never been reluctant to break Indian heads in the past, and I went to the BIA to try to talk the poorly armed activists out of a disastrous showdown with the police.

I entered the building with Alvin Josephy, an old friend and senior editor of *American Heritage* magazine. Alvin's books are popular with Indian people and his dedication to Indian people is long-standing. We passed the barricades of typewriters and furniture and saw that the roof was being torn apart so that chunks of tile could serve as missiles in case of attack. The building was a shambles.

Up in the office, the AIM leaders and other militants had assembled: Clyde and Vernon Bellecourt; Dennis Banks; Russ and Ted Means; Carter Camp, an AIM newcomer from Oklahoma; Sid Mills from Survival of Native Americans; Bobby Free; Herb Powless; and Mad Bear Anderson and Oren Lyons of the Iroquois. As I began to speak, they saw Alvin and asked what he was doing there.

"He's my friend, he's all right," I said. But several of them disagreed and he was taken outside and guarded by a huge militant armed with a club.

"What's your name?" the guard demanded.

"Josephy."

"Josephy? Alvin Josephy? You mean the guy that wrote *The Patriot Chiefs?*"

"That's right."

"Damn, I read your book. . . ." Alvin got along with his guard better than I did with the militant leaders. One after another, they disagreed with me violently. The two Bellecourts looked like they wanted to punch me. I concealed my anger and appealed to them to at least remove the women and babies. At first they refused, but at last they agreed to evacuate the women and children and the elderly people to the YMCA two blocks away.

I left the building feeling mighty low and praying that the Great Spirit would avert a massacre. When I returned the call to the mayor's command post, I was told that the Indians had refused to move and that Means had answered orders to leave the building by shouting "This is a good day to die."

The next day, 4 October, Commissioner Bruce was ordered to report to the Interior building across the street. His concern for the lives of demonstrators hadn't won him any sympathy from the Department of the Interior. Yet as the government's position slowly hardened, the American people began to show their sympathy. The YMCA set up a chow line and offered a suite of rooms. Marion Berry, chairman of the District of Columbia school board, issued an ultimatum to the government demanding protection for the Indians. Charles Cassell, D.C. delegate candidate did the same. Stokely Carmichael, former head of the Student Nonviolent Coordinating Committee (SNCC), appeared at the BIA and made a speech stating that the struggle of the Indian was central to civil rights in America. Dr. Benjamin Spock, the pediatrician and antiwar activist, showed up with a check. And, incongruously enough, the Reverend Carl McIntyre, the pro-Vietnam War minister showed up with a group of his followers and demonstrated in the Indian's behalf. Reinforced and buoyed up by this outburst of public support, the Trail of Broken Treaties leaders called for discussion of their twenty-point proposal and of their eight demands, which included the removal of Loesch, John Crow, and Robert Robertson.

Inside the building, Leonard Crow Dog, AIM's young medicine man, held a ceremony to paint the faces of the Indians who would face the riot police in what many expected would be a fight to the death. Russell and Ted Means were the only major AIM leaders who were seen with their faces painted. Most of the others who took this vow were young students and Vietnam veterans. None of them thought they could overcome the thirty-four thousand police available for use against them, but the face painting marked a commitment to go down swinging.

"If I go back to my reservation with my tail between my legs, without getting anything done here, the superintendent will slam the door in my face," Russ said. "Hell, he's done that already. So, those of us who have painted our faces have taken a vow to die for what we believe in."

But killing Indians had become unpopular in most places in America, especially just before a national election. Protests against what many people feared would be a massacre flooded into the White House by letter and phone, and nothing happened.

The one single hope that had sustained me through twenty-three years of activism was the federal court system. Historically, the courts had made efforts to keep the greedy Indian-haters in check after all else was lost, and the Supreme Court, which protected constitutional rights, was the one friend the Indian had left. My faith was renewed when the U.S. court of appeals in D.C. unanimously granted permission for the ceremonies at the Arlington graves of Ira Hayes and John Rice.

Inside the building, still in a state of semisiege, owing to crowding, bad nutrition, and the fact that most people couldn't sleep for the constant alarms and the ever-present threat of attack, there was an outbreak of strep throat. Many non-AIM people were becoming disenchanted with the AIM leadership, and in some cases the leaders were becoming disenchanted with each other. Word leaked out that some of the take-over leaders were sneaking out to spend the night in fashionable hotels.

On 5 November the Interior Department, urged on by the White House, offered the activists another deal: limited use of the BIA auditorium, use of the fine interdepartmental auditorium, installation of showers and trailer accommodations, and a meeting with the secretary of the interior, Rogers Morton. The Indians, still suspicious, refused the offer and tightened their security.

On the sixth, several chairmen from the National Tribal Chairman's Association sneaked into Washington to hold a press conference where they condemned the entire Trail of Broken Treaties. They then immediately changed their minds and pledged to support some of the twenty points proposed by the take-over leaders. That evening, the U.S. marshals served papers on twelve leaders of the Trail of Broken Treaties, ordering them to leave the building or face contempt proceedings. These court orders led to the breaking strain that caused the massive destruction to the BIA building. According to some of the activists, the rank-and-file Indians were watching an Indian-made film called *As Long as the Rivers Flow*. One scene showed Washington State police brutalizing Indian women and children during a fishing rights arrest. Something snapped in the audience, and people began to shout that if they were going to be beaten and possibly killed, they'd destroy the hated BIA building first. Men ran amok with clubs and hammers, smashing windows, shattering toilet bowls, and ripping files of records to shreds. In a matter of minutes, the BIA central office was littered with paper and chunks of broken furniture.

Some of the earlier damage had been done to fortify the building. But a great deal of it was in spontaneous outrage at the BIA and the government.

With the Indians once again preparing to fight to

the death, everything seemed lost. After conferring with the office staff, I made a last-ditch call to the White House. I reached Brad Patterson, and he listened intently and told me to stand by for an emergency call. Exactly at 4:30 P.M. the phone rang and I answered. Hans Walker, a Mandan from North Dakota said, "Get down to the Interior Department right away, it's an emergency!" Alvin Josephy and I charged out like the two battle-hardened marines we once were and rushed to the Interior Department. We met Hans at the C Street entrance and he escorted us to the solicitor's office.

The assistant solicitor came into the room and asked what could be done to stop the situation.

"The government had better not order the police to go into that building," I said. "The Indians in there are high on religion and are ready to die. They've got dynamite charges set in there and gas soaking into the rugs, and they'll blow up the whole building rather than surrender. Teen-agers will die by the hundreds. Old women and old men who came to get something done will be killed and there will be an international disgrace for the United States. We're here to plead for the White House to enter into negotiations to avert bloodshed."

Alvin could see that they thought I was bluffing, but he knew I was dead serious, and he agreed.

"I just can't believe that the night before election day, in the capital of this country, that you'd do such a stupid thing," he said. "You'd better stop everything and concentrate on defusing a very explosive situation. This can be done if the Indians meet with somebody meaningful. They have to meet with people from the White House who can speak for the president. Up until now all they've been speaking to is functionaries. They should meet with somebody who can talk directly for the president or for Mr. Ehrlichman."

He concurred in my statement that the assault could lead to a wholesale slaughter on both sides and urged them to cancel any attempt to evict the Indians from the building.

After the officials conferred, they told us that the

assault wouldn't take place. Shortly after this, we learned that the White House had agreed to negotiate and that the police had been ordered not to go anywhere near the building.

At 9:00 P.M. the selected negotiators for the Trail of Broken Treaties met with Leonard Garment, Brad Patterson, and Commissioner Bruce who agreed to discuss all points presented by the caravan except amnesty, which would be dealt with separately. Although tension remained strong on both sides, most of the Indians in the building heaved a collective sigh of relief. Hungry, weary, many of them sick, the building's defenders began to leave in small groups of four or five. Many would have fought to the death if attacked, but once negotiations began they felt that they'd done their part. Others had to be back home to keep their jobs. And some were disillusioned with the fragmented leadership of the various militant groups.

"We believed the AIM guys until we heard that all they wanted was publicity and money," remarked one young girl. "They sold the Indians out, so we're leaving."

On 7 November, with the election issue no longer a factor, the Trail of Broken Treaties agreed to leave the building by 9:00 P.M. on Wednesday, 8 November. The Federal Interagency Task Force had agreed to study a number of issues: eligibility of Indians for federal services; improvement of governmental service delivery speed; quality and effectiveness of federal programs; Indian self-government; and congressional implementation of necessary Indian legislation.

The negotiators submitted an estimate of $66,500 to the White House representatives as the cost of returning all caravan members to their homes. Arrangements were made to use the National Congress of American Indians as a conduit through which the White House could pass money to the caravan. Robert Howard, head of the OEO Indian Desk, and NCAI director Charles Trimble took the $66,500 into the BIA building in two suitcases and left hurriedly. The division of the money was a controversial issue both inside and outside the BIA. Conservative whites blasted the administration for "buying off" the activists, and the activists themselves fell to quarreling over the funds. Although the rank-and-file Indians of the caravan still in Washington received amounts ranging from $25 to $100, several activist leaders got sums of $5,000 and $10,000 for "traveling expenses." George Mitchell, cofounder of the AIM and a completely sincere and honest man, quit in disgust at the way some of the leaders divided up the money and at the way petty ego-tripping had marred the whole course of the Trail. Russell Means, who had done more than anyone else to hold the defense of the building together, was similarly disgusted, but he stayed on, grumbling to himself about the rip-off. As a final dirty job, he was delegated to try to explain the massive destruction.

Lurching out of the building, looking like he hadn't slept for a week, Means faced the reporters with glum defiance.

"I know you guys are going to have a field day with this," he said wearily, "but this destruction doesn't mean a damn thing, because papers . . . papers, and the words written on papers have never meant a damn thing to the lives of Indian people."

Banks and Means had one last card up their sleeves. As they left the building they announced that AIM had removed BIA files, which they said documented the corruption and apathy of federal officials in dealings with Indians. According to the story put out by other AIM leaders and later printed by Jack Anderson, Means had conned the Washington police into giving him a motorcycle escort—to prevent trouble—as he drove the papers out of town in a U-Haul truck. When the story got back to Means, he was rather acid about the whole thing.

"Some of my fellow leaders made sure I got full credit for that caper," he said. "That's why there's a secret indictment out on me right now."

On 10 November the White House ordered a full-scale investigation into the seizure and occupation of the BIA building. To publicize the matter, the NTCA was shown around the building to duly express horror at the destruction. The fact that it would not have happened had they done their jobs properly was never publicized.

The National Congress of American Indians, the nation's oldest and most respected Indian lobby, charged that the secretary of the interior, the Bureau of Land Management, and the National Council on Indian Opportunity had worked clandestinely to muster elected tribal leaders in support of the administration. The NCAI charges would surprise no one who knew that the national headquarters of the NTCA were in the executive offices of the president and that the puppet chairmen were receiving fifty thousand dollars in federal funding per meeting.

The same day, the NTCA, led by Rev. Webster Two Hawk, held its own press conference. Two Hawk urged the federal government not to speak to any Indian group except his own, to prosecute those who had occupied the BIA building, to prosecute those who stole the BIA files, and to continue business as usual. Two Hawk then moderated this statement by blaming the damage on the "irresponsible self-styled revolutionaries" who led the take-over. A great many right-wing groups seized on Two Hawk's statements and presented him to an unknowing public as a responsible Indian leader. Actually, he was no better than other AIM leaders, and many of his colleagues in the NTCA were almost as bad. It is doubtful that more than 10 percent of the NTCA leaders could survive a full-scale investigation into their tribal affairs; the amounts that many of them deprive their needy people of make $66,500 look like chicken feed.

The NCAI completed their Impact Survey Team report on the destruction of the building and laid the blame on the rage and frustration that all Indians felt toward the BIA. Navajo chairman Peter MacDonald, a Nixon Republican, criticized the Department of the Interior for constantly harping on the damage to the building as a cover for the ineptitude and corruption in the BIA and in Interior itself. He suggested that more attention be given to the Indians' legitimate grievances and less publicity aimed at the destructive tactics that some militants employed to rectify the situation.

The figures on the cost of the destruction were some of the least reliable in American history, or even in BIA history. On the second day of the seizure, when the Department of the Interior sent in their cameraman posing as a reporter, they had already charged Trail members with $250,000 worth of damage—this at a time when the destruction was limited to a few broken windows and a mess of papers on the floor. By the time the Trail ended, the figure had soared to $2.5 million, an amount compared to the San Francisco earthquake or the sack of Washington by the British in the War of 1812. During subsequent congressional hearings, the destruction was priced at $750,000. The actual cost is anybody's guess. But if a $4,000 plywood house can cost the BIA $14,000, anything is possible.

A few days after the last of the Indians pulled out, the BIA public relations staff, in a gem of an idea probably inspired by the mental linkup between "Indians" and "museums," set up a display of Indian artifacts of the take-over—bludgeons made from table legs, crude spears made from brooms and scissor blades, paper-cutter machetes, and so forth. If nothing else, the display proved that the rank-and-file people in the caravans didn't come to Washington expecting a fight, for better weapons could be found in a locker check of any urban high school. Later, at Wounded Knee, things would be different.

Repercussions shook the federal Indian agencies and the White House as the House of Representatives began a probe of the take-over. The White House invoked executive privilege against the appearance of five White House aides. In the Senate, James Abourezk, newly elected Democrat from South Dakota, requested that the BIA be made independent from the Department of the Interior.

Within the BIA, the once monolithic structure was shattered for good by factionalism and the publicity that the Trail had focused on the bureau. Crow and Bruce, long at odds, began to quarrel openly. Bruce announced that he was cutting the BIA staff, Crow countermanded this order. Finally, on 1 December, Secretary Rogers Morton suspended the authority of Crow, Bruce, and Loesch.

This news reached the last remnants of the Trail of Broken Treaties caravan while they were checking in at a Howard Johnson Motor Lodge in Tempe, Arizona. They were down to twenty-nine members, and when the word reached them they were too shocked to make a statement to the press. Times were getting tough for the caravan. Publicity about the BIA destruction and other irresponsible acts had cut into their funding, and for a while it looked as though they were finished. But they still had one act left to play.

On 8 December 1972 the secretary of the interior pledged to keep an open-door policy in receiving advice from all national Indian groups on policy decisions. The Trail of Broken Treaties goals of ridding the BIA of Loesch and Crow had been confirmed two days before, when the White House had cleared orders to fire Loesch, Crow, and Bruce.

As Jack Anderson's BIA columns began to appear, a new era seemed to be dawning in Washington. The documents signed by Leonard Garment and Brad Patterson and the Trail of Broken Treaties negotiators were testimony that Indians must be dealt with or fought. As the Indians of the past had died fighting to preserve their freedom, modern Indians had shown they were willing to die fighting to regain it.

# 10
# Wounded Knee

> This is a good day to die!
> —Crazy Horse, 1876

As Russell Means led the Oglala Sioux remnants of the Trail of Broken Treaties through the town of Pine Ridge, the seat of the tribal government at the Oglala reservation, he may have noticed a stir of activity around police headquarters.

Unknown to Means, tribal president Richard Wilson had secured a court order from the Oglala Sioux tribal court which prohibited Means or any other AIM member from speaking at or attending any public meeting.

Since the Oglala Sioux Landowners Association was meeting in Pine Ridge, Means, a member of this group, decided to attend and to report what had actually happened in Washington. Before he had a chance to speak his mind, he was arrested by BIA special officer Delmar Eastman for violating the court order.

This arrest was a blatant violation of the First Amendment, for it denied Means freedom of speech on the reservation where he was born and was an enrolled tribal member. I called the White House and demanded to know why Washington was allowing tribal officials to violate Means's constitutional rights. They claimed they had no knowledge of the facts but said they would bring the matter to the tribe's attention. The next day, Means was released.

Means next showed up in Scotts Bluff, where he was arrested again, this time by white Nebraska police. He charged that the police slid a loaded gun into his cell and dared him to make a break for it. "They wanted to off me during an attempted escape," he said. When he got out, he began to agitate about police and judicial conditions in western Nebraska and western South Dakota, the same issues I had raised in 1959. Under prodding by many Indian leaders, Sen. Edward Kennedy agreed to set up an FBI investigation of local law enforcement.

Means remained something of a man without a country. Back on his home reservation, President Wilson, with his special powers usurped from the tribal council, began to harass AIM members and their friends. One Sioux girl who supported AIM's activities had to leave her car, which bore an AIM bumper sticker, and walk for help when the car ran into a ditch. When she came back the car was riddled with bullet holes and inoperable. Wilson was so busy with his war on AIM that he didn't take time to do anything about the death of Wesley Bad Heart Bull.

Bad Heart Bull had had a fight with three white men in a bar in Buffalo Gap, South Dakota. On 21 January he was found lying in the street with a knife in his chest. The white authorities arrested Darold Schmitz, a thirty-year-old service station attendant, and charged him with second-degree manslaughter.

Wilson, as head of the tribe, did not respond in any manner. AIM, however, cared enough to declare 6 February 1973 as a day of mourning. AIM field director Dennis Banks sent out word for his forces to rally in Custer, the county seat for Buffalo Gap. The town of Custer had a bad name with Indian people, and the white townspeople were jittery as 6 February drew near. Lyn Gladstone, a reporter for the *Rapid City Journal,* filed a story that the AIM demonstration would not materialize. Although the people waiting in the cold were betting that nothing would happen, a camera crew began setting up for action.

Automobiles filled with Indians began arriving, and the Indians filed out to the courthouse. The county state's attorney, a balding, nervous man named Hobart Gates, met with Means, Banks, and Dave Hill, a stocky young Choctaw from Salt Lake City, as two hundred Indians, more than half of them women and children, waited outside in the falling snow.

"I'm going to prosecute to the fullest extent on this second-degree manslaughter," Gates said. "I assure you, I'll do everything in my power, I'll get every witness that'll help win this case when I prosecute him."

But the state authorities refused to heed an Indian who said he had witnessed the crime and would testify that it was murder. Means had had enough second-degree justice.

"I want to know why this white man who killed an Indian was charged with second-degree manslaughter instead of first-degree murder, and the only way you're going to get me out of here is to kill me!" he shouted.

All hell broke loose. Some say that a white policeman shoved Bad Heart Bull's mother, and some claim that the Indians tried to push their way into the courthouse and were roughly handled by police. A fight broke out with fists and clubs, and the Indians inside the courthouse tore nightsticks away from the police and started swinging. Banks leaped out a window and escaped in the snow. Means and Dave Hill took on the police inside the courthouse and knocked eleven of them down before being beaten themselves.

Outside, their followers tried to swarm up the courthouse steps and were repulsed by the police, who fired tear gas and used their riot sticks on women as well as men. The outraged Indians took over a gas station and made makeshift fire bombs. A mob of Indians tipped over two police cars and stole the shotguns inside. Others stoned the courthouse and set fire to the small chamber of commerce building.

When the unequal fight had ended, twenty-seven Indians were arrested and marched away through the snowy streets as smoke rolled up from burning buildings. Eleven police had been injured badly enough to see a doctor, and Means and Hill were hospitalized briefly and jailed.

The whites in Custer were terrified. Would-be vigilantes vowed to shoot any AIM member on sight, and the National Guard was mobilized and three blocking positions set up around Custer in case Means and company returned.

"It's kinda like fighting guerrilla warfare," said Mayor Gene Reese. "You never know what they're going to do or where they're going to strike."

After Ramon Roubideaux, a Sioux lawyer, had arranged bail for everyone in jail, AIM gathered in Rapid City to confront the city fathers and state agencies that were discriminating against the Lakota people, the Sioux. Because of personality clashes, the Indians of the area were split into several factions, and the AIM hoped to be able to unify them to get something done.

Mayor Don Barnett of Rapid City was wise enough to try to head off trouble. Although the AIM declared Rapid City a "demilitarized zone" (DMZ), fighting broke out after an Indian was hit over the head in a tavern, and four bars were sacked and vandalized. Forty Indians—including Bad Heart Bull's mother—were arrested during the Rapid City street brawling. Trouble threatened to get even worse as 150 Indians gathered outside the county jail, beating their drums and singing. They were incensed by the double standard of justice, exemplified by the fact that Wesley Bad Heart Bull's killer faced a maximum of ten years in jail, and Bad Heart Bull's mother faced a maximum forty-year sentence on riot charges. Police riot squads formed a line in front of the jail and spent most of their time trying to keep out of range of the TV cameras.

These events cast a pall of fear over South Dakota. Whites in many towns, perhaps plagued by guilty consciences and ludicrously ignorant about Indians anyway, wondered what sort of unspeakable vengeance AIM might exact for the past persecution of the Indians among them. The fear of a new Indian war led state law-enforcement officials to stop any and all Indians traveling toward Rapid City, without considering that hundreds of Indians from four Sioux reservations go there to shop. State patrolmen stopped Indians indiscriminately and in some cases ordered them to go back where they came from. Patrolmen stopped me twice on my way to visit my mother, who was forced to stay off-reservation near a heart specialist because there were no reservation facilities to treat her.

The entire Indian population was stirred by what had happened at Custer and Rapid City. Even the gentlest of Indians couldn't help but feel that Custer had it coming.

Things were also stirring back on the Pine Ridge reservation. On 21 February the tribal council was called into session to consider impeachment of Richard Wilson. Before the council meeting began, Wilson showed the film *Anarchy—USA,* a ninety-minute propaganda epic released by the John Birch Society that purports to link the U.S. civil rights movement with Communist take-overs in China, Algeria, and Cuba. The text is blatantly simplistic, and the film is salted with incredible still photographs of Arabs slaughtered by the FLN (the Arab terrorist group) in the 1950s—severed heads, a pretty girl with her throat cut, men castrated by blowtorches, a baby killed with a submachine gun. Among its other charges and implications, the film assumed that Dr. Martin Luther King was a Communist and that a fringe benefit of the civil rights movement was interracial sex. What all this had to do with AIM was never spelled out.

Five hundred Oglala Sioux had gathered for a fair impeachment hearing against Wilson and instead were treated to the film and to Wilson's marathon attacks on people he never named while he smeared them verbally.

Ever since Russell Means had returned home to the reservation from Cleveland and announced that he would run for chairman, there had been bad blood between him and Wilson. In November 1972, during the Trail of Broken Treaties, Wilson told a reporter from the *Minneapolis Tribune,* "They're a bunch of renegades—nothing but a bunch of spongers. Here in Pine Ridge, they bum off of my poor people. They're social misfits. Their lawlessness, their tactics of violence, give the rest of us a bad name."

AIM probably felt very sorry about giving Mr. Wilson a bad name, for he could obviously do well enough on his own. In the early 1960s he and his wife fled the reservation and spent several years in the Southwest after a conflict-of-interest case in which she was the director and he was a contract plumber for the Oglala Sioux Housing Authority. He came back and was forgiven. A few years later, Wilson and Robert Mousseaux, the tribal secretary, were brought up on charges of unlawfully converting tribal funds to the use of another individual. Charges against Wilson were later dismissed, but Mousseaux was convicted. By the time of the latest impeachment attempt, the traditional chiefs and tribal elders had reached the end of their rope with Wilson. His misuse of tribal funds, his management of the tribe without a budget, his violation of the tribal constitution by refusing to call meetings in accordance with the tribal law, and the goon squad he maintained to intimidate his opponents had antagonized even the most patient of the old Indian leaders.

A series of meetings were held in the Calico community near the Pine Ridge Agency. The old traditional chiefs and the Oglala Civil Rights Organization called down to AIM in Rapid City and asked them to come to Pine Ridge and try to straighten things out.

The first meeting between Means and Wilson ended when five of Wilson's supporters cornered the AIM leader in a parking lot at Pine Ridge and tried to beat him up. Means broke through their cordon and escaped.

On 27 February, the day after the parking lot incident, the village of Wounded Knee was invaded by armed forces of the Oglala Sioux and the American Indian Movement. The 200 activists seized control of the hamlet and began to dig in around Sacred Heart Church, the white wooden Catholic chapel that stood beside the graves of 146 men, women, and children killed by the army at the Wounded Knee Massacre.

Means went in fully expecting to die. "I hope by my death, and the deaths of all these Indian men and women, there will be an investigation into corruption on the reservations and there's no better place to start than Pine Ridge," he said.

The United States responded just as AIM had anticipated, sending in hundreds of FBI agents and U.S. marshals to confront the Indians holding Wounded Knee and eleven so-called hostages, many of them old friends of the Indians involved.

Wilson, the main target of this invasion, went absolutely wild. He began hiring his relatives and friends to act as police and vowed to raise a force of eight hundred guns to go in and wipe out the AIM "clowns." His threats were largely hot air. Before the siege of Wounded Knee even began, he had vowed to personally cut off Means's braids. Later, he said that when Means was captured he would have his head shaved, stuff him into a woman's dress, and dump him beyond the boundaries of the reservation, nevermore to return. Another time, he vowed to wipe out everyone at Wounded Knee if Washington would only give him clearance. When a reporter asked Means what he thought of the plumber's threats, Means retorted blandly, "I cannot comment on the ravings of a drunken paranoid."

Meanwhile, the U.S. marshals moved in to surround the besieged hamlet with armored personnel carriers that looked as if they could have crushed all of Wounded Knee in one sweep. The APCs with the .50-caliber machine guns were symbolic of the overreaction that brought Wounded Knee to stage center of the world. Other Indians and non-Indians alike began to sneak through the federal cordon bringing in food and more weapons to the defenders.

Inside Wounded Knee, the defenders set up a council to run the garrison. Banks was technically the highest-ranking AIM leader, but because of AIM's organization, Means was probably considered the principal leader at Wounded Knee. Means was an Oglala Sioux, duly enrolled at the Pine Ridge reservation, and Banks, a Chippewa from Minnesota, was an outsider. In theory, each AIM chapter is autonomous and supports all other chapters when the call goes out. In addition to Means and Banks, the leaders at Wounded Knee were Clyde Bellecourt, a Chippewa, and Carter Camp, a Ponca, both of AIM, and Pedro Bissonette, an Oglala and a leader of the local Oglala Civil Rights Organization. Leonard Crow Dog, a Brulé Sioux from the neighboring Rosebud reservation, was the medicine man for the besieged hamlet.

Carter Camp, acting as spokesman for the group, stated their initial position. The AIM leaders knew that the government could destroy them, but they were determined to fight to the death if necessary. AIM would not harm the hostages, but they would not release them until their demands were met. They demanded that Sen. Edward Kennedy lead an investigation of the BIA and the Department of the Interior in their handling of Indian reservations, that Senator William Fulbright investigate the 371 treaties that the government had failed to honor, and that the Oglala Sioux have the right to elect their own officials in free elections.

By way of comment, the FBI began to place sandbags and machine guns atop the BIA building at the Pine Ridge Agency, as if they expected a full-scale attack on the nearly deserted town.

Within a short time, the government had concentrated 250 FBI men, U.S. marshals, and BIA policemen from other reservations around Wounded Knee. Joseph Trimback, agent-in-charge of the Minneapolis FBI, met with AIM representatives under a cease-fire, but no agreements were reached. The government learned that the hostages included Clive Gildersleeve and his wife Agnes, proprietors of the hated Wounded Knee Trading Post, and Father Paul Manhart, the Jesuit priest in charge of the Sacred Heart Church.

U.S. attorney William Clayton disclosed that the government had arrested sixteen adults and a juvenile as they attempted to leave the village in connection with the burglary at the trading post.

The two Democratic senators from South Dakota, James Abourezk and George McGovern, arrived by helicopter in a rather theatrical attempt to obtain release of the hostages. McGovern seemed to be posing for the cameras as he disembarked from the chopper and walked into Wounded Knee. Unfortunately for his composure, his first contact with the AIM leaders was with Russell Means, who had never forgotten the way McGovern waffled on his promise at the BIA takeover or his years of bumbling on the Senate Indian Affairs Subcommittee.

"We asked to see Senator Abourezk," Means said. "We did not ask to see Senator McGovern. Senator McGovern typifies three individuals of the last century—General Crook, General Sheridan, and General Custer."

Nevertheless, McGovern stayed on through the all-night negotiations in the so-called DMZ around Wounded Knee, and the next day the hostages were released. Ten of the eleven hostages said they preferred to remain inside Wounded Knee.

On 2 March word reached the AIM leaders that the home of Aaron DeSersa, one of their supporters, had been fire-bombed and that DeSersa's wife had been burned and taken to the hospital. The AIM leaders put the blame on Wilson's goon squad. In addition to leading reporters into Wounded Knee through the back country, DeSersa was the editor of the *Shannon County News,* a small newspaper in which he had praised AIM and attacked Wilson. The paper's facilities, in DeSersa's home, were destroyed by the fire.

Later the same day, several reporters sneaked past the roadblocks set up by the U.S. marshals and learned that some of the former hostages were more frightened by the federal men ringing the hamlet than they were of the Indians involved in the take-over.

By 4 March newsmen were tripping over one another trying to answer the obvious questions about Wounded Knee. Were the AIM leaders simply playing games to get publicity, or were they serious? How many Indians on the reservation actually supported the stand taken by the traditional chiefs and the AIM spokesmen? Why did the U.S. send in marshals and FBI men to police an Indian matter? What was the truth about Wilson's goon squads?

All these questions should have been answered, durign or after the siege. Instead, the press people spent most of their time waiting for government press releases, rapping in the Pine Ridge parking lot, drinking coffee at a cafe owned by a non-Indian, and hunting for bootleg liquor.* Between marathon bull sessions and padding their expense accounts, they picked up enough government-supplied information and ravings from Dick Wilson to piece together a disjointed running commentary of the Wounded Knee incident.

AIM had always had a sort of love-hate relationship with the press, but at Wounded Knee the relationship deteriorated mostly into hate, on both sides. The reporters and the networks came in for heavy criticism by the Justice Department for the first heavy coverage of the incident, and some of the reporters seemed to try to play up a more critical view of AIM rather than jeopardize their source of government press releases. The TV crews, who provided visual coverage, thrived on photogenic scenes of Indians in war paint, with guns, and the grotesque APCs tearing through the tall grass. But pressure was exerted on them to try to play down coverage in an effort to ease tensions.

Some AIM leaders, long starved for publicity for their cause and also endowed with healthy egos, went out of their way to cooperate with newsmen. One constantly repeated tale centered around the capture of some whites who mysteriously showed up inside the AIM bastion. Two of them, middle-aged men carrying concealed handguns, claimed to be postal inspectors. Two others were white ranchers who said they were looking for lost stock. The Oglalas, remembering Norman Little Brave and a few other unsolved murders, feared that the whites might have entered Wounded

---

*Reporters' and Indians' cars left inside the FBI-BIA cordon while their owners went into Wounded Knee suffered from mysterious vandalism, including slashed or deflated tires and damage to distributors. One *Newsweek* story referred bluntly but briefly to this phenomenon, which quickly ceased, at least as far as newsmen's cars were concerned. Many Indians, none of whom dared to press formal charges, asserted that jewelry and other goods were removed from their cars or persons by federal forces.

In another interesting reaction to press coverage of the Wounded Knee incident, the government filed a number of felony charges against a *Boston Globe* reporter who was a passenger on one of the supply airdrops. The charges were dropped in July 1973, long after the Wounded Knee siege was over.

Knee with the idea of picking off a few Indians. After being held overnight, they were marched out of the hamlet at gunpoint and told not to return.

"Any spies who violate our borders will be subject to international law and will face a firing squad," Means warned as they left.

As the white prisoners were being marched away, one cameraman ran up, having missed their departure. Means obligingly had the prisoners marched back and forth until everyone had enough pictures.

Such incidents, and the instance where a TV cameraman helped the Indians slaughter rustled steers for food, created a furore. Right-wing commentators and government officials, not to mention the loudmouthed Mr. Wilson, began to scream that the newsmen were inciting the Indians to riot and prolonging the trouble. The final blow to cooperation between the AIM and the press came with an article in *Time* magazine stating that many newsmen felt they'd been hyped by overcooperative AIM leaders.

Newsmen love to think of themselves as hardheaded, cynical, and relentless in their pursuit of truth, even though many prefer to pursue it with maximum comfort and minimum risk. The insult to their objectivity and threats from the government, combined with the long stalemate in negotiations, caused them to take a new tack. By the second month of the Wounded Knee siege, the news overview had been revised considerably. Means and Banks were no longer portrayed as doomed heroes battling oppression but as a couple of urban toughs trying to seize power. The coverage veered from one unreal extreme to the other, never bothering to assess the facts.

Some of the worst hatchet jobs came from young feminist-oriented writers working for slick magazines. After discovering to their shock that Indians no longer lived in tepees, they arrived inside Wounded Knee and found Means sitting around in a trailer house reading comic books when he wasn't doing his trick on guard duty. Their disillusionment was complete when they heard him talk and realized that his flip, sarcastic jargon bore little or no relation to the oratory quoted in *Touch the Earth*. Moreover, young female reporters tend to think of themselves as the advance guard of the feminine liberation movement, and Means's unabashed male chauvinism is blatantly obvious to anyone who has spent ten minutes in his company. Banks's good-luck beret with its Playboy-bunny patch spelled things out even more clearly.

Many reporters were also put off by Leonard Crow Dog, AIM's medicine man. They seemed to think that Crow Dog was some sort of publicity stunt. Crow Dog, whatever his faults, is a totally sincere medicine man, an illiterate full blood who speaks English with a Sioux accent. Many people, white and Indian, can attest to his spiritual powers.

AIM was caught in a bind. They needed the newsmen and their attention focused on Wounded Knee to prevent a massive crackdown, but as the siege wore on AIM leaders began to have the feeling that they were going to get screwed every time they talked to a reporter. "They're treating this thing like a goddam comic opera," Means fumed.

The White House first sent Ralph Erickson, a special assistant to the U.S. attorney general, to negotiate with the Indians. On 4 March Means said, "We don't want to deal with the lower echelon flunkies of the federal government any longer. They are not dependable. They don't show up for meetings. American Indian Movement negotiations will have to be with the secretary of the interior and the White House, with congressmen and senators in attendance."

Means was referring to the fact that Erickson had sent the North and South Dakota U.S. attorneys to deal with AIM and had himself stayed on in Pine Ridge.

At the beginning of his tenure as negotiator, Erickson took a moderate tack: "The Justice Department feels that it is important to avoid overreaction. We are not interested in charging persons who unknowingly or unwillingly were involved. There is no spirit of vengeance. But even if we wished, we could not close our eyes to the criminal acts of planning, leading, and executing the raid."

In an apparent effort to undermine the morale of the defenders, the Justice Department announced that Indians inside Wounded Knee could depart without their weapons and with no threat of immediate arrest. A grand jury would determine charges at a later date. The weapons were supposed to be stacked and tagged with the owners' names so that they could be returned at a future date. The AIM leaders interpreted this as a ruse, which in effect would amount to signing a confession with each name tag.

"We decided that Indian people were more important to us than jail terms," Carter Camp said. The AIM leaders publicly burned the government offer in the Sacred Heart Church as their followers cheered.

The standoff lasted until the seventh of March. The Indians dug in around the church with two concentric circles of trenches and bunkers protected by sandbags. Molotov cocktails were made of soda bottles—not the best material, for the bottles are too thick to break easily when they strike. Meals were served inside the Sacred Heart Church, which was also the dormitory for most of the defenders.

Between dawn and sunrise on 7 March a light Cessna single-engine plane landed inside the Oglala perimeter, suffering some damage to the nose and tail. The occupants, a Dr. Cummings and Paul Davids, the pilot, unloaded three hundred pounds of pinto beans, brown beans, flour, sugar, condensed milk, cooking oil, canned fruit, and toilet paper. Most of the food was paid for by Michigan Indians who sympathized with the Wounded Knee defenders. Dr. Cummings, a surgeon, had packed some buffalo meat from his home freezer.

The plane took off and made its escape before full light exposed it to the FBI and the marshals on the surrounding heights. The next day Cummings and Davids were both arrested at their homes and charged with obstructing and impeding federal officers under the Civil Disobedience Act of 1968. The rumor that they had transported guns into Wounded Knee was totally false, as the FBI later admitted, but the government was taking no chances.

On 7 March the federal government issued an ultimatum ordering AIM and the Oglalas to move out of Wounded Knee before nightfall on 8 March. The government moved six APCs with .50-caliber guns into position and sent word to ready a dozen more in Martin, a few miles away. It looked like the showdown.

The AIM leaders held a rally inside the church to prepare for whatever came.

"We came here and bet our lives that there would be historic change for our nation," Means said. "The government can massacre us, or it can meet our basic human demands. Either way, there will be historic change."

"We are the keepers of the whole Western Hemisphere—we must know this," Crow Dog said. "We are nature people, happy people. It is the white man who wants to change all that, and that is why we must stay here. For myself, I am not afraid to die. If I die here at Wounded Knee, I will go where Crazy Horse and Sitting Bull and our grandfathers are." The activists cheered wildly.

Tension mounted as the deadline neared.

"We never attempted to say we can overthrow the U.S. government militarily," Means said. "The treatment by the government has not changed from Wounded Knee to My Lai and back to Wounded Knee again. We may just be here for the rest of our lives."

Working feverishly, the militants reinforced their barricades. Some sang war songs. Others walked around with prayers on their lips. Many, if not all, expected it to be their last night on earth. Some of the men were Vietnam veterans, and they must have felt a curious bitterness about digging in to face the fire of the same country they had risked death for in Asia.

Across the country, thousands of Indians and non-Indians were stirred to action. In at least ninety places around America, Indian activists prepared to rise against the government if Wounded Knee fell. In Los Angeles, the Indians and other minorities planned to storm and hold the Justice Department building. In

North Carolina, a band of Tuscaroras rode through the streets of a small town smashing windows in protest over the treatment of the Oglalas.*

As newspapers and TV screens brought home the shocking picture of armored personnel carriers moving toward a band of badly armed Indians, the public reacted with a vast outburst of sympathy for the defenders of the besieged hamlet. Veteran Western Union operators reported that the flood of telegrams to the White House urging restraint and voicing support for the activists was the greatest outpouring of public emotion in their memory.

Just before the deadline on Thursday, 8 March the government backed down in its announced plans to assault the hamlet. Unfortunately, they hadn't realized the precariousness of their own position. The Indians had been watching every federal post with cocked rifles and dynamite charges with six-second fuses ready to be heaved into the APCs and bunkers. The AIM leaders were able to contact their patrols and call off the sniper attacks in time, but, thanks to the government and Wilson factionists who destroyed their telephone lines, they were unable to reach the Indian blocking forces waiting miles outside Wounded Knee to assault government troops from the rear if the federal attack began. Promptly at the deadline, the blocking force came rolling past the outlying federal barricades in cars and trucks, and both sides opened fire. The government's .50-caliber machine guns and M-16s raked over Wounded Knee, tearing through buildings and kicking up spurts of dust. Frantic radio messages were sent by government forces trying to reach Means. Banks replied that he was out on the firing line trying to get the Indians to cease fire.

Two Indians were wounded in the impromptu fire fight. One of them, Webster Poor Bear, was a Vietnam veteran. His father Enos Poor Bear, a former tribal chairman, came out to Wounded Knee and spoke to the activists and newsmen.

---

*In apparent retaliation, white night riders burned a school long used by the Tuscaroras.

"My son went through Vietnam without getting a scratch, and now he gets shot by the same government that sent him there. I think he should get a medal for what he did at Wounded Knee."

Negotiations began again. While the government and the activists talked, the traditional chiefs and their followers circulated a petition calling for a referendum to rescind the tribe's 1934 IRA constitution. They hoped to bring the confrontation to an end before any Indians or federal men were killed.

While the talks went on, the government shot up flares all through the night to illuminate the hillsides. These flares set a number of prairie fires, destroying the grass around the hamlet and burning one log house to the ground. Fire fights broke out every night, with thousands of rounds expended on both sides.

The news media habitually reported that each side blamed the other for these gunfights and left it at that. This perplexed many Indian people in and out of Wounded Knee. One Onondaga girl from New York State who spent a month inside the village said that she thought the FBI and the marshals fired first on every occasion except one.

> I was sitting in a bunker talking to this reporter and all of sudden firing broke out. You could see the tracers from the government's .50-caliber machine guns coming down at us from the hill, so we crawled back to the church where they had a radio set up for the newsmen. The reporter got on the radio and told them there was a fire fight going on, and they asked him, "Who started it?" and he said, "I don't know who started it." How could he say that when he was sitting right there with me and we both heard the feds fire first?

On 10 March the Justice Department announced that they were lifting the siege of Wounded Knee because many of the government's objectives had been accomplished. Dennis Banks was jubilant.

"We have won a moral victory," he said. "The government has agreed to pull its troops away, to pull out its armored personnel carriers, and to pull away its military vehicles. We will have free access to come and go as we please."

The young militants in Wounded Knee staged a war dance and held a barbecue to celebrate their triumph and to give thanks for the fact that they were still alive.

The government had promised to investigate the charges against the BIA's tribal government at Pine Ridge and to investigate several other AIM grievances. The Indian people rejoiced because the government admitted being wrong and had apparently decided that people's lives on both sides were more important than saving face.

I was in Saint John's Hospital in Rapid City recovering from surgery when the Wounded Knee clash began. On 11 March I joined hundreds of other people in driving to Wounded Knee to meet those who took part and see the village for myself.

I was appalled at the change that had taken place since my last trip there. The trading post, the church, and the log houses had all been riddled with federal bullets, and it was a miracle that only two of the defenders had been hit. The quality of the entrenchments was not very good. Some of the barricades and obstacles were made of cinder block. I winced to think what would have happened to anyone crouched behind these cinder blocks if they were struck by large-caliber slugs. Their shattered chunks would have been almost as lethal as bullets. Inside the perimeter was the AIM "tank," a U-Haul van the activists had plastered with mud as camouflage and used for patrol work. Anyone sitting over the front-mounted engine of the "tank" would have been roasted alive if a single tracer hit it.

When word got out of my presence at Wounded Knee, Dennis Banks came over and asked me to say a few words. Rather emotionally, I told those gathered there that I was going to Washington to tell the White House that it was one hell of a day when Indians had to arm themselves to see justice done to their own tribal councils.

Unknown to anyone, I had been advising presidential aide Bradley Patterson of the situation as I gathered information from those I knew to be trustworthy. Almost everything that went on in Rapid City, Rosebud, and Nebraska was known to me. My own son had been inside Wounded Knee until he was seriously hurt. I asked him why he joined such a dangerous activity.

"Dad, look at you," he said with conviction and anger in his voice. "For twenty years you've done more than anyone else I know, but nothing has really changed like you want it to. So I decided to take a gun and see what I could do to change things this way!"

At that moment, I could have easily joined the ranks of armed Sioux, but I knew that there was a great necessity to keep some channel of negotiation open. Nevertheless, I vowed that things would change no matter what it took.

Wilson's dictatorial regime made it extremely dangerous for someone like myself to be seen driving around the Pine Ridge reservation, but I wanted to get the story that the newsmen had neglected, of how the Indian people really felt. I spent a full day traveling through Holy Rosary, Calico, and Manderson which is just over the hill from Wounded Knee. I also visited Kyle and Wanblee. Everywhere I went, at every home I visited, the people said that they opposed the Wilson administration and would support the activists at Wounded Knee.

On the evening of 11 March the truce broke down and the federal forces returned to the hills around Wounded Knee. Their pretext was the wounding of an FBI agent, Curtis Fitzgerald. According to the news story, Fitzgerald had spotted the AIM "tank" and thought he recognized it as a truck either overdue at the rental agency or stolen. He took off after it, and the FBI car and the tank exchanged fire. Fitzgerald's car seemed to show five bullets going out through the windshield and one coming in from outside.

The feds made what Ed Sullivan would call "a really big show" out of Fitzgerald's misfortune. He was flown by helicopter to Ellsworth Air Force Base at Rapid City with an enormous bandage swathed around his head and face. Oddly enough, he had been shot in the wrist. Again, each side claimed the other had fired first.

The pursuit of the U-Haul van struck most of the Indians as a pretext for renewing hostilities and punishing AIM and the Oglala militants. I had to share this view, because the day the shoot-out took place, I had seen the U.S. marshals taking pictures of every car that entered Wounded Knee. My friend Abe Bordeaux and I had deliberately parked near the marshals and eaten lunch while we observed them. One of the marshals was a woman who tried to keep us from seeing her face. She bore a strange resemblance to a woman who had been inside Wounded Knee with press credentials. With all this surveillance going on, I doubted that the government had adopted an attitude of wanting to forgive and forget.

As the feds closed in for the second round, four hundred supporters rallied at Wounded Knee. Six of the eight district chairmen withdrew their support from the tribal council and threw in with the occupiers, which meant that the Oglala militants had three times more support from the tribe's own elected officials than Wilson did. A majority of those who represented the local districts had repudiated the Dick Wilson regime and declared themselves a free and sovereign nation. Means announced that three Oglala Sioux—Chief Frank Fools Crow, Matt King, and Frank Kills Enemy—had left for New York City to seek support for their cause from the United Nations.

Wayne Colburn, chief U.S. marshal, announced that his three hundred men had lost patience with the stubborn Oglala garrison at Wounded Knee.

"I'm sure as hell planning on changing their life-style," Colburn said. "If this means starving, if it means being cold, not reading the evening papers, not being able to watch television, not making telephone calls, not being able to get soap to wash their clothes with, that's what's going to be done." Nobody had the heart to tell Colburn that doing without food and electricity was already part of the Pine Ridge life-style and didn't represent any change for most of the defenders. Recent figures indicate that only about 10 percent of the families on Pine Ridge reservation have electricity and 5 percent have running water. Since the average family income is about two thousand dollars a year and most of the houses are substandard, being hungry and cold is not a novel experience.

Within Wounded Knee, spirits were high. Reporters from Japan and other countries were sending out photographs and news stories that supported the Oglala and condemned their treatment by the United States government. All over Africa the story hit the front pages. Dubious rumors even flew that the Arab nations had threatened to cut off the U.S. oil supply if the government didn't deal honorably with the Indian people.

Chief Frank Fools Crow, a renowned medicine man, was a center of strength for those Indians who wanted to set aside the demeaning Indian Reorganization Act and live according to the Sioux Treaty of 1868. A tall, handsome man of seventy-eight, Fools Crow, long braids flowing beneath his big brown cowboy hat, was a living symbol of the dignity of traditional Indian government and religion. Led by Fools Crow and backed by the AIM and the Oglala militants, the traditional chiefs demanded that the government deal with the Indians on the basis of the solemn treaties, which, according to Supreme Court rulings, are part of the law of the land.

The next in a long line of government spokesmen, Harlington Wood, said that talks would continue. "There will be no move to take Wounded Knee while negotiations are in progress."

The Reverend John Adams, a United Methodist minister from Washington, D.C., arranged new meetings between AIM and the government.

Wilson, however, continued to agitate for violence. In Pine Ridge, Wilson's rump council, shorn of six of its eight district chairmen, enacted several resolutions. They first asked the BIA police to remove all nontribesmen from the reservation. This meant that the churchmen trying to resolve the situation peacefully would have to go. Wilson characterized the National Council of Churches as "dope pushers." "Or if they're not pushing it, they're sure as hell using it," he said.

The second resolution held AIM responsible for all acts of violence. It was a purely political ploy, attempting to show that whatever segment of the Indian community Wilson represented was anti-AIM.

On 15 March a terrible blizzard swept most of western South Dakota, cutting Wounded Knee off from the rest of the world, even though the barricades had been lifted again. U.S. attorney William Clayton announced that a grand jury had returned thirteen indictments against thirty-one persons involved in the take-over. Charges specified in the indictments included burglary, larceny, conspiracy, and civil disorder. Kidnapping was not among the charges mentioned, although several of the former hostages testified at hearings on Wounded Knee.

After a TV broadcast disclosed that the Indians at Wounded Knee were low on food and fuel and facing a critical shortage of insulin for several diabetic women, Jack Hushen, director of public relations for the Justice Department, announced that the National Council of Churches would be allowed to bring food, fuel, and medical supplies into the village.* No progress was reported in the negotiations.

On the Rosebud reservation, ninety miles away, there was a flurry of activity. Crow Dog's Paradise was the center of supplies for Wounded Knee, with trucks, pickups, and carloads of people moving in and out at all hours of the day and night. Armed guards watched the fence lines near the highways. It was common to meet young men there who said they had served in Wounded Knee but had rotated with their buddies to come out for a shower and a change of clothes. The government's supposedly watertight barricade around the hamlet was more or less of a joke to the Indian people who knew every inch of the ground.

---

*Means told coauthor Koster that the Red Cross caravan that got through brought in a huge load of Spam—the same monotonous fare Indians receive as U.S. Department of Agriculture surplus commodities.

Seated in the well-known Abourezk Store in Mission, a hundred miles from Wounded Knee, it was impossible not to notice that Indians with cars from Washington, Oregon, Oklahoma, North Carolina, Illinois, California, New York, and many other states were moving through, buying supplies and heading out in the direction of the federal siege. Mission was the last real Indian town before hitting the border of the Pine Ridge police state set up by Wilson and the government.

One group, in thirty-seven vehicles, requested housing at Saint Francis Mission, a Catholic Indian school located seven miles from Rosebud, where Wilson's buddy Rev. Webster Two Hawk sat shakily in his plush office, powerless to stop the use of his reservation as a staging area. Another group of forty-one carloads from Oklahoma stopped in Mission seeking information on how to reach Wounded Knee without running afoul of the feds. The local AIM chapter, on duty for just such a purpose, was able to give them perfect directions.

Back on Pine Ridge, Wilson issued orders for his special squads to sweep the reservation and pick up or chase out all undesirables, with special attention given to the representatives of the National Council of Churches who were acting as a liaison between the government and the militants.

On 17 March Harlington Wood returned from a sudden flight to Washington. Rumor had it that the White House had intervened. Washington denied this and said that the Justice Department was calling the shots. Wood drove hurriedly from the plane to the AIM checkpoint where AIM attorney Ramon Roubideaux and Dennis Banks were waiting for him.

"This is the best I could do for you," Wood said cryptically. "If you want to see me again, I'll come back at any time. It will be at your pleasure." He drove back to the agency at Pine Ridge as Banks and Roubideaux took the offer back to Sacred Heart Church.

The Indians branded the U.S. offer a call for total surrender and capitulation. "In essence, what they offered us was to fly us to jail," Means said. The offer was rejected.

Fire fights between the Indians and the government became almost a nightly occurrence. In one of these gun duels, Rocky Madrid, a twenty-six-year-old Chicano acting as an AIM medic was hit inside the perimeter.

"He was running forward, unarmed, to see if any of our people had been hit and he was hit by a spent round from an M-16," Means said. "He was lucky, man, that that round was spent. When an M-16 round hits flesh it tumbles and tears the hell out of you, but in this case it just plowed along between his skin and his abdominal wall and didn't break through to his stomach. Crow Dog took the bullet out."

On 19 March residents of the Pine Ridge reservation handed BIA superintendent Stanley Lyman a petition requesting a referendum to determine whether to dissolve the present tribal system of government that stemmed from the Indian Reorganization Act and to establish a new form of government for the Oglala. The fourteen hundred signatures on the petition fulfilled all legal requirements for a referendum.*

Meanwhile, the people of Rosebud reservation were ready to defy the government blockade. They announced that an armed party would march on Wounded Knee bearing food and medicine.

At Pine Ridge, AIM attorney Ramon Roubideaux declared that a double-barreled attack would be launched. Rosebud's people would move on Wounded Knee five hundred strong, while lawyers, including William Kunstler and Mark Lane, would begin a legal assault on the Justice Department's handling of the incident.

The marshals and FBI agents were making an impression, mostly unfavorable, on the surrounding communities. In Hot Springs, complaints began to flow in that these federal men had spent their leisure time

---

*To justify refusal to take action on this legally binding petition, the BIA field officials falsified voter eligibility figures, according to subsequent investigation by Senator Abourezk.

defaming Indians, insulting Indian women, and drinking heavily in public. In Rushville, Nebraska, twenty-six miles from Pine Ridge, similar reports began to flow in. Since I was in touch with the White House, I advised Brad Patterson of this and he told me to contact Kent Frizzell, who was in command of the federal forces on the reservation.

On 26 March a fifty-year-old U.S. marshal, Lloyd Grimm, was shot in the chest and seriously wounded at a roadblock near Wounded Knee during the heaviest fire fight of the siege. He was rushed from the scene.

Means and Banks were rumored to have slipped out of Wounded Knee on the night of the twenty-sixth, and a group in Rapid City made a bid to settle the situation. Some said that the two AIM leaders had escaped to Cuba; others said they had attended a meeting on the Rosebud reservation. The government spread rumors that Means and Banks had returned with white supporters and taken back command of the Wounded Knee garrison from Pedro Bissonette at gunpoint. All the rumors later proved ridiculous. When a few reporters sneaked into Wounded Knee they found Means, Banks, and Bissonette still in charge.

Once started, the rumors of dissension grew. Senator Abourezk charged that AIM guards were holding a hundred Oglala people who wanted to leave Wounded Knee. Roubideaux denied this. Meanwhile, Marlon Brando had focused publicity by sending a supposedly Apache actress to refuse his Academy Award for *The Godfather* because of the way films had stereotyped the American Indian and because of events at Wounded Knee.* Brando said he might go to Wounded Knee personally but later decided against it, explaining that if Wilson's Indians captured him and threw him off the reservation the general public might be led to believe that his help had been irrationally rejected by AIM and the Oglalas.

The drama of Wounded Knee was now so heavy

---

*The actress later turned out to be the daughter of a Filipino father and a white mother, and she had been crowned Miss American Vampire in Palisades Park, New Jersey, in 1971.

and the plot so thickened that everyone seemed to forget the original reason for the take-over. Radio stations ran "Wounded Knee" commercials—"Look out. An Indian's going to run the barricade in that pickup truck."—and the *New York Daily News* shortened the name of the hamlet to "The Knee" in their headlines. The Wounded Knee take-over had almost become a cliché, and no one reflected on the causes: the leasing arrangements that cheated Indians out of the income on their own lands; the crooked trading posts; the dictatorial tribal councils; and the nepotism that kept the full bloods out of the only jobs available while the chairmen hired their friends and relatives.

Although the White House had little to say publicly about Wounded Knee, the government was acutely embarrassed. During the second month of the siege, an Indian dance troupe headed for a goodwill tour of Western Europe had their plans changed by the State Department. The dancers were neither militants nor members of the AIM or the Oglala Sioux tribe, but they were Indians, and their presence in Europe would have called attention to the situation in South Dakota.

After an infinity of fire fights that seemed to tear the South Dakota night apart with tracers and riddled every house in the hamlet, the government and the occupiers reached a peace pact that was signed on 6 April by Frizzell for the government and by Means, Camp, Bissonette, Crow Dog, and others for the Oglalas. Banks did not sign. As described by the government, the pact called for the following:

- Russell Means would submit to arrest and go to Washington, D.C., for meetings with White House representatives. A disarmament program would start as soon as Means called to report that talks were going on. There would be a thirty- to sixty-day delay in the arrests of those who would be indicted by the federal grand jury.
- A federal investigation of Indian affairs on Pine Ridge and an audit of the tribal books would take place.
- The Justice Department would consider and, where appropriate, protect the legal rights of individual Oglala Sioux Indians by bringing civil suits against

unlawful acts by the tribal council and federal government.

• A presidential treaty commission would reexamine the Treaty of 1868.

• A meeting would be held in Washington in May between Indian leaders and White House representatives to discuss Indian affairs.

"I pray to my Father in Heaven, as you do to your Great Spirit, that the agreement we are about to sign is not full of empty words, and that the promises will be fulfilled," Frizzell said as he smoked a sacred pipe with AIM leaders.

Within a few days, hopes for peace collapsed. Means's version of the treaty was that he was to call Wounded Knee and authorize the surrender of weapons only after negotiations were successfully under way. But the White House staff claimed that the surrender of weapons was a preliminary necessity before the talks began. Means refused to ask the defenders to give up, and the White House refused to talk until they did.

"Tell them that the Indians' last treaty with the government lasted all of 72 hours," Means said as he left the White House grounds. "The government broke it before the ink was dry."

Means's next stop was a House Indian Affairs Subcommittee hearing on Wounded Knee and the Trail of Broken Treaties. The chairman, Representative James Haley of Florida, seemed more interested in insulting Means than in determining where the blame lay for the whole episode. "Mr. Means . . ." Haley said, "you and your bunch of hoodlums belong in a federal penitentiary."

Means traveled around the counrty trying to gather funds and rally support for the Wounded Knee takeover. The conditions of his twenty-five-thousand-dollar bail forbade him to reenter the besieged village.

"I've heard that there's a contract out on my life right now," he said in New York. "That's the best thing that could possibly happen to me. It would make me a martyr."

While Means moved around the country, Indians continued to move in and out of Wounded Knee.

On 18 April three single-engine planes flew out of the dawn from three different directions and converged over the hamlet to drop supplies. Parachutes bearing food packages fell within the perimeter, and firing began from the federal lines as the Indians inside Wounded Knee rushed to pick them up. A government helicopter took off, supposedly in pursuit of the planes, and passed over the Sacred Heart Church, which was filled with women and children, firing machine guns through the roof.

Inside the church, a man named Frank Clearwater was sleeping after an arduous journey into the village. A bullet struck him in the head and seriously wounded him. A cease-fire was called and Clearwater was rushed to a Rapid City hospital. He died of his wounds a week later. Six others were injured in the foray.

"The position of the U.S. marshals is that they will not subject themselves to the kind of planned assault on all positions without returning fire more quickly," said Stanley Pottinger, the chief federal negotiator now in charge.

In Cleveland, Ohio, Means called for volunteers to march on Wounded Knee over the Easter weekend.

Senator McGovern, touring his home state, called on federal authorities to clear the occupiers out of Wounded Knee before angry citizens did the job first. As Easter neared, the federal government moved their roadblocks in around Wounded Knee to control any problems that might arise.

Wilson began to have his own problems with the federal officials as eight of his men were arrested for manning an illegal roadblock outside Wounded Knee. When he learned of this, on the morning of 23 April, he said, "I'm fed up with the Justice Department." Later he said that Pine Ridge police would reestablish their own roadblocks. Wilson continued to interfere with the Community Relations Service personnel of the Justice Department who were serving as mediators between the two armed camps.

When the news of Clearwater's death came out, the Indian negotiators called for a four-day suspension and truce on 25 April to bury him. The Oglala Sioux council, Wilson's puppet government, immediately refused Clearwater burial on the Pine Ridge reservation because he was not a Sioux.

On another front Vernon Bellecourt and a group of marchers, Indians and non-Indians, forty-nine miles east of Pine Ridge were blocked by Delmar Eastman, a BIA police officer, and told that the Oglala Sioux Tribal Council had a court order enjoining any marchers from entering the reservation. The marchers turned back to Rosebud.

To appease Wilson and to bring the occupation to an end, the federal government allowed the Wilson forces to man the perimeter around Wounded Knee. Few Indians cared to take part in the suppression of Wounded Knee, so most of Wilson's vigilantes were white ranchers who had a vested interest in keeping the status quo at Pine Ridge. Any hint of reform threatened their cheap leases to graze cattle on Indian land.

In California, disgusted with trying to raise funds from a public that seemed to be hardened to the Indians' privations, Means made a fiery speech at the Janus Steps of UCLA. After making bitter fun of the college students who turned out to take photos of "your friendly local militant" with expensive cameras, he announced that he was going back to Wounded Knee to bury Frank Clearwater's body and that if the government tried to stop him they could expect a fight. Shortly after the speech his bail was revoked. He was pulled over on the Los Angeles Freeway and arrested by the FBI.

With Wilson's people on the perimeter of Wounded Knee, the activists prepared for the worst.

Buddy LaMonte was a thirty-one-year-old army veteran, the only boy among Mrs. Agnes LaMonte's eight children. Although he was not a member of AIM, he and his mother had offered Means a place to live when Means came back from the BIA take-over, and he had taken his phone calls at their home.*

"He [Buddy] wanted to go to Wounded Knee to be

*In this capacity, he became friendly with coauthor Koster.

with his people," Mrs. LaMonte said. "Before he left, he said, 'Mom, I'm going to buy you a trailer house, so you'll have a home to go to.' I have enlargement of the heart and sugar [diabetes], so it didn't seem right for him to be thinking about someplace for me to go when I could die any time and he was still a young man. So I said, 'What about you, where are you going to live?' and he said, 'I'm just going to travel around, don't worry about me.' But he told his nephew and nieces, 'If anything happened to me, I want to be buried at Wounded Knee.' "

"He had asthma, he was always coughing and coughing," Mrs. LaMonte said. "I kept sending him mentholated cough drops the whole time he was there."

On 27 April, with CS gas being lobbed into Wounded Knee, Buddy LaMonte emerged from an underground bunker coughing and choking.

Indians monitoring a police-band radio heard a voice they say was a U.S. marshal's. "There's one flushed out of that bunker. Get him. He's a good target."

A heavy burst of machine-gun fire slammed Buddy LaMonte into the ground. By the time anyone reached him, he was dead.

Clearwater's funeral procession was diverted to Rosebud where the Crow Dog family offered land for his grave. But Buddy LaMonte got his last wish. He was buried at Wounded Knee, near the graves of the 1890 massacre victims, with a flag over his coffin and three volleys fired over his grave by the Oglala militants. Mrs. LaMonte, tears running down her face, begged the AIM and Oglala militants to end the fighting before anyone else was killed.

On 7 May the AIM and Oglala people began laying down their weapons and ended the seventy-day confrontation. The day before the surrender, Crow Dog and Carter Camp had given themselves up to Wayne Colburn and were taken into Rapid City for arrest and arraignment. Kent Frizzell had called me to request that I come to Wounded Knee with two FBI agents in an attempt to find eight graves that were rumored to be around the perimeter. The activists who spoke of these graves believed they contained the bodies of Indians murdered by white vigilantes or Wilson's men. Federal and Wilson forces thought they contained would-be defectors. They were never shown to exist.

As we proceeded into Wounded Knee on Monday, 7 May, no one was manning the AIM roadblock and the main village seemed deserted. The Community Relations Service man climbed out and ordered the rest of us to stay in the car.

Suddenly a voice said, "You're all right, Bob, get out and step ten paces away east."

I didn't know the voice, but I did as he ordered. The FBI men were frisked and then we began our mission.

Someone said that Crow Dog wanted to see me, so I went over to the log house where I found Leonard lying very sick. After talking a while, he told me he wanted to speak to me away from the federal men. We went into the log house. Crow Dog said he wanted to turn himself in, but he wanted to stay with his people until they all gave up on the following day. I advised him to go immediately and get it over with. Ramon Roubideaux appeared to make the trip with Carter Camp, so Crow Dog joined them. For all practical purposes, Wounded Knee II was over.

Although many of the Indian people inside were still carrying weapons, Dennis Banks was nowhere to be seen. I asked one fellow where he was.

"He's gone," the man said simply.

Later I learned that Banks and sixty other militants had escaped during the night, trying to slip through the heavy ring of federal and vigilante forces. Fourteen of the activists were captured with a variety of weapons. The others disappeared without a trace.

The federal officers were faked out when they went in to collect the weapons neatly stacked inside the village. They found a little toy bow-and-arrow set, several Matty Mattel plastic M-16s, carved wooden replicas of rifles, and eight decrepit .22s. The machine guns, assault rifles, and high-powered hunting weapons with telescopic sights were nowhere to be found.

Four CBS newsmen were among the twenty-eight

people packed into a school bus and dragged off to Rapid City for arraignment before a U.S. magistrate. The only major leaders missing were Means, already in the Minnehaha County Jail, and Banks, who had disappeared like the gray ghost.

The ruins of the burned-out trading post reminded me of the burned-out tepees after the 1890 massacre, and the bags of uncollected trash could have passed for the blanket-shrouded bodies that the Seventh Cavalry left in the snow that bitter winter. I seemed to be walking into the past as my eyes took in the bare terrain around Wounded Knee.

The eight graves were promptly forgotten by everyone but me. I swore I wouldn't give up the search until I had cleared up the mystery, and I remembered the tears of an Oglala mother who told me that her eighteen-year-old son was gone and that he had never run away before. The search for the graves was postponed deliberately until a new tribal administration could be seated in April 1974.

After the take-over ended, the chiefs led by Fools Crow began to prepare for the meetings that would be held on 17–18 May with a presidentially appointed delegate. Because I had personally saved the Sioux Nation's claim before the United States Court of Claims in 1955 by firing an incompetent lawyer and remanding the claim back to the docket for retrial, I had a special interest in the negotiations on the Treaty of 1868, which was our claim's foundation. I decided to follow the negotiations closely.

The government forces tried to recoup their moral defeat at Wounded Knee by harping on the destruction of the village and of the Oglala people's homes. They offered reporters a guided tour of the hamlet, just as they had at the BIA building, carefully pointing out the damage to the church, excrement in people's homes, senseless vandalism to furniture and sentimental objects, and wholesale theft. With Means in isolation, Camp, Bissonette, and Crow Dog in jail, and Banks presumed to be hiding in Canada, there was no one around to refute these charges. But strangely enough, when I had toured the village as the AIM faction was leaving, before the government came in, I hadn't noticed most of the damage. The church and some of the buildings had been riddled from the outside by government .50-caliber machine guns, and one log house had been set afire and burned by a government flare. Other than that, the only damage I saw was the ruined trading post and the bags of litter and stripped carcasses of steers, which obviously couldn't be removed under gunfire.

During the days that we were waiting for the White House meeting, harassment of the Oglala people by Wilson's police continued. Each time I met with the traditional Sioux leaders at Fools Crow's camp, some new offense was reported, often committed by men who had sworn oaths as law officers to protect their people.

On 17 May there was a large crowd assembled at 9 A.M. waiting for the arrival of the presidential delegates, headed by Bradley Patterson. When the party arrived, all but Patterson were requested to remain on the helicopter. The chiefs wanted to ask him some questions about the authority he had come with, and they made no secret of their resentment of the presence of BIA and Interior Department people with him. Patterson answered the chiefs by saying that the president had appointed all the negotiators to report back to him about the meeting.

The traditional leaders began the meeting with a Sioux prayer. Then the Indians began to speak, explaining what the Wilson type of government had done to the reservation and the traditional people. Ms. Bobby Greenberg, a lady lawyer, remained silent as she listened to the Indians' complaints. The main thrust was that the chiefs and other Oglalas were disgusted with the BIA's puppet tribal council and were prepared to do whatever was necessary to return to a tribal government of Indian origin.

All the Indians present, from Fools Crow to Mrs. LaMonte, emphasized this wish and said that the Indian Reorganization Act of 1934 was a violation of the Sioux Treaty of 1868. The Treaty of 1868 is silent on the form of government, which means that the right to self-government is reserved for the Sioux Nation. Time after time the leaders called attention to the petition, with fourteen hundred signatures, requesting the secretary of the interior to call for a referendum to rescind the tribe's constitution. I also challenged the government to follow through and call for a referendum on tribal government.

During the meeting several resolutions were enacted. The government was asked to fulfill treaty obligations, to suspend Wilson's government until an investigation had been completed, and to cause a full-scale investigation of Indian affairs. Another resolution asked the president to establish a presidential treaty commission to investigate the settlement of treaty obligations.

Specifically, this resolution emphasized that the Indian Claims Commission was wasting millions of dollars by making the Indians prove that these treaties existed and by paying tribes to hire expert witnesses to testify against the government. There is no court system in the world more asinine than the Indian Claims Commission, which, by using government money to defeat the government, borders on comedy. The fact that the commission was staffed by men like Arthur Watkins, Utah's famous Indian-hating ex-senator, adds another touch of the ridiculous. If the whole farce were replaced by a treaty commission, America would win a reputation for honesty, and the taxpayers would save money.

The presidential negotiating party left to assess what they had heard, and they promised to meet with us again on 30 May.

Instead, they sent a letter, delivered by a U.S. marshal to Matt King, chairman of the treaty council. The letter, on White House stationery, was an insult to the intelligence of the Sioux people. It questioned the need for a treaty commission and in fact said that the government saw no need for one.

The chiefs' treaty council appointed seven men to answer this letter. The reply fully explained, in legal terms, the actual necessity of a presidential treaty commission and in general set the record straight for the president's information.

There were 428 people facing charges over Wounded Knee as the summer began. Most of them were released on reasonable bail, but the bond set for the real or imagined leaders of the take-over was astronomical —$125,000 for Russell Means; $150,000 for Pedro Bissonette, already facing charges for a fistfight with an off-duty federal official; and $35,000 for Crow Dog. AIM's legal team, headed by Ramon Roubideaux, worked for a month to get the AIM and Oglala leaders out of jail and onto the streets where they could tell their own story.

Seven or eight of the protest leaders were in jail for close to a month, and Means, the first major leader to be arrested, set the record with thirty-nine days. The terms of his bail forbade him to go back to the reservation or to leave South Dakota.

Shortly after he got out, Means issued a blast at the marshals for vandalizing the village and trying to blame the damage on the activists. But no one in the press seemed too interested in him unless he had a gun in his hand, and his statement received less publicity than his smallest gesture during the Wounded Knee siege.

Wilson's goons operated boldly on Pine Ridge, under the noses of the federal officials still there. They chased one carload of Indian women down the Big Foot Trail at a hundred miles an hour until the women reached Pine Ridge and pulled up in front of the police station.

"Wilson's goons are after us," one woman yelled to a passing U.S. marshal.

"Don't call them goons," the marshal reproved.

"They pointed a gun at us. Aren't you going to do something about it?" the Indian woman asked.

"Well, I've got to hear their side of the story first," the marshal said.

In July, Sacred Heart Church, which had survived the machine guns and flares of the two-month siege, burned to the ground. The reservation people who supported AIM said that Wilson's people had done it. The .50-caliber federal bullet holes that honeycombed the church were a silent indictment of the government. Some believed that the fire was caused by arson, to destroy the incriminating battle damage. Fifty-caliber machine guns are not supposed to be used in quelling domestic disturbances.

Father Paul Manhart, the Jesuit priest at the church, said that he was staying in Wounded Knee and would gather funds to rebuild the church. Mrs. LaMonte, herself almost destitute, said she would help.

"I go to Wounded Knee to pray a lot," she said. "I pray by Frank Clearwater's grave too. Mrs. Clearwater told me she wanted to come live here to be near where it all happened, and I told her to come and live with me so we could keep one another company. You know, Indian people don't have much, but if we have anything at all, we like to share it."

# 11
# Business as Usual

> The American Indian commands respect for his rights only so long as he inspires terror for his rifle.
>
> —Col. George Crook, circa 1873

The White House never met with the traditional leaders to renegotiate the Sioux Treaty of 1868. Leonard Garment, the White House attorney usually sent out to deal with recalcitrant Indians, discovered the act of Congress that had abolished treaty making with Indian nations in 1871. He notified the Sioux traditionals and militants that treaties were no longer to be negotiated and advised them to talk to the various congressional committees. The Sioux traditionals replied that they were not asking for the negotiations of new treaties, they were merely asking that the treaties now in force be fulfilled. But by this time, the guns had been silent so long that Washington began to get hard of hearing again where Indians were concerned.

The fact that Garment or his bosses dared to make such a cavalier turnabout and to violate the conditions of the Wounded Knee armistice were not all rooted in a 102-year-old act of Congress. AIM's one negotiating point had always been that the government could not afford an Indian massacre in 1973, after the public in America and the world had shown itself to be strongly sympathetic to the Indians. But with the AIM leaders in jail, in hiding outside the United States, or scattered to the four winds, there was no one to bring the world's attention down on Wounded Knee or the Pine Ridge reservation. TV newsmen and wire-service reporters, the critical element in whipping up mass indignation, had started to pull out long before the siege ended. By the time the second treaty council was scheduled after the first talks in May, press coverage had trickled down to drips and drops of mostly inaccurate statements made by people who didn't understand the complex legal situation or have any real knowledge of the people involved.

Moreover, the government could hardly have failed to notice the slump in AIM's popularity that followed hard on the heels of the capitulation.

Part of this slump was undoubtedly a psychological letdown. Many Indian people, inured to a lifetime of police brutality and raised on a history of genocide, literally expected the activists at Wounded Knee to be wiped out to the last man by the FBI and marshals. During the siege itself, especially during the first tense weeks, support for the Wounded Knee defenders was almost unanimous among Indians. The only exceptions seemed to be some BIA employees and the immediate relatives of the more corrupt tribal officials. In many cases, whole tribes, like the Onondaga Nation of New York State, announced their support for AIM and urged the government to knuckle under. But as the siege wore on, press coverage became less hysterical and more cynical. Many Indians not on the scene became less enthusiastic.

The lack of any immediate results were probably another major factor. Independent of Garment's canceled treaty council, Senator James Abourezk held hearings in Rapid City on 16 June. Abourezk, a South Dakota Democrat whose family ran a trading post, was known to be sympathetic to the Indians and critical of the BIA.

One of the witnesses testifying at Abourezk's hearing was Russell Means, recently freed on bond after thirty-nine days in jail.

"The Justice Department is not doing anything," Means said. "The situation is as bad as before the takeover and it only serves to give the suffering Indian people more reason to put their life on the line. We just keep dealing with rhetoric, not action."

Another witness was Charles Red Cloud, a traditional elder in his seventies.

"A lot of money is coming to the reservation in the name of our people. Nobody knows where the money goes. Our people are poorer than ever. People here wonder where their next meal is coming from. They have no future."

In addition to discerning that the Indians were dissatisfied with the aftermath of Wounded Knee, Abourezk got some interesting insights into how the BIA operates. The approaches to the hearing were flanked by menacing uniformed BIA police in four cars who took pictures of the Indian people coming to testify.

"This is one of the most reprehensible things I've seen," Abourezk said. "People are afraid to testify here. They're being intimidated by the BIA police." The senator shooed away the Indian police and confiscated their film.

He also plowed up some peculiarities in voter enrollment at Pine Ridge. In 1969, there were 3,104 Pine Ridge residents eligible to vote. When AIM supporteres petitioned to revoke the tribal constitution during Wounded Knee II, thinking they had the necessary number of votes, the BIA declared that, as of 1973, there were 9,518 eligible voters. Since there are only about 11,000 people residing on the reservation and the voting age is still twenty-one this figure struck Abourezk as rather unusual. He drew the obvious conclusion.

"It looks to me like the BIA is making the voter-eligibility figures higher and lower when it wants. In this case the BIA is a law unto itself." Had anyone in the government noticed this disparity during the siege, a peaceful settlement might have saved the lives of Frank Clearwater and Buddy LaMonte.

Carl Stoiber, an attorney for the Justice Department, told the hearing that there had been fifty-five complaints of civil rights violations since the end of the Wounded Knee take-over. Most were charges of harassment or police brutality by Dick Wilson's BIA police or goons.

Three cases had been forwarded to Washington for possible action, twenty-one were still pending, and the others had been dropped.

Chairman Dick, reading a prepared statement, piously declared that he knew nothing about any police brutality or harassment. The whole thing, he said cryptically, had been caused by the white man's greed for land and gold.

The traditional chiefs told Leonard Garment the same story that their people had told Stoiber. Garment told them they should have more faith in fact-finding teams and the Justice Department. The mass media slept through the whole thing. And AIM's support slowly dwindled. A UPI reporter told a writer from *Race Relations Reporter* that the word was out: AIM wasn't worth covering.

At the outset, the people of Pine Ridge and Rosebud had been overwhelmingly in favor of AIM's goals, if dubious about their methods. But many were horrified by the destruction found inside the hamlet of Wounded Knee, so amply and enthusiastically publicized by government officials on the scene. No newsmen seemed to put two and two together well enough to realize that much of the damage was a result of the fighting and that garbage trucks and fire engines weren't available to people under direct fire from .50-caliber machine guns and M-16s. For those who were too obtuse to grasp what the federal marshals were trying to point out on their guided tours of trash-strewn houses, Dick Wilson was on hand to explain it all: "They're clowns! Bums! This is the way they live!"

No newsman seemed to be objective enough—or brave enough—to publicize the AIM leaders' charges that the feds or Wilson's men had deliberately trashed the village, destroyed property, and expanded on actual battle damage to discredit AIM and the Oglala activists.

"Of course the feds did it, man," Means told one reporter. "We're not stupid. We wouldn't be dumb enough to do something like that to our own people that supported us."

Media backlash hurt AIM, and all Indian activists, at this crucial point. One "think piece," nailed together by two UPI reporters on a weekend trip to the reservation, seemed to be a deliberate effort to put an end forever to government charges that newsmen were overly sympathetic to the militants. This gem of nonobjective journalism quoted at length three sources: a white rancher who feeds his cattle Indian grass at bargain-basement lease prices, a Catholic priest in a mission largely supported by mail-order donations solicited by sucker list, and none other than Dick Wilson himself. There was not a single quote from any AIM leader anywhere in the article. The only statement from anyone who didn't have vested interests in seeing AIM put down as badly as possible was from Ramon Roubideaux: "Dick Wilson should be stood up against a wall and shot!"

When an independent reporter asked Roubideaux, a usually genial man, about the UPI quote, Roubideaux replied, "It's out of context, of course, it's only a small part of what I said. But I do feel that way. Dick Wilson is a dictator."

But the incident that reduced sympathy for AIM to low ebb was the shooting of Clyde Bellecourt. Carter Camp, the activist arrested for the shooting, had been elected chairman of AIM at the Oklahoma convention only a few days before he allegedly fired a .38 into Bellecourt's stomach.

The shooting took place on the Rosebud reservation, where Camp, Bellecourt, Means, and other activists had been staying with friends. The AIM leaders had been agitated for several months because they believed that someone fairly high in AIM's power structure was an informer. One government spy, a Chicano posing as an Indian, had already been exposed when Hank Adams and a newsman named Les Whitten were fingered to the FBI and arrested as they tried to return some of the stolen BIA files to the government's custody on 21 January. Jack Anderson, Whitten's mentor, raised hell about suppression of the media, and both men were released in a matter of hours. Subsequent events seemed to show that other informers were still at large, and, for several reasons, suspicion fell on Camp.

Camp was a relatively unknown figure to the other AIM leaders, most of whom had been acquaintances—though not always friends—for three or four years. George Mitchell, cofounder of AIM, was leery of Camp and considered him an excessively violent interloper.

"Nobody every heard of him before the Trail of Broken Treaties," Mitchell remembered after the shooting took place. "I think he said he was a tank driver in the Army, and that he grew up in California." Mitchell, among others, particularly disliked Camp's almost Pavlovian reflex of reaching for a gun at the slightest provocation. He had previously threatened several people, including one of the female legal assistants to the Trail, for no apparent reason. The other leaders' failure to kick him out, or control him, pointed up one of AIM's great weaknesses, their lack of any semblance of internal discipline.

On 25 August, while staying at Rosebud, Camp did his gun-pulling act for a customer in a service station in Mission, South Dakota, and was arrested by a BIA policeman. The speed with which he was returned to the street, a matter of hours, led some of the other AIM leaders to increase their suspicions. On the twenty-sixth, Camp got into an argument with Clyde Bellecourt, and the powerfully built Chippewa took Camp's gun away from him and threw him out of the AIM billet.

The next morning, Camp and two friends returned to the house where Bellecourt and Means were sleeping. Camp asked Bellecourt to come outside. A moment later, Means and others in the house heard a single shot, and Bellecourt lurched back into the house holding his stomach, blood gushing through his fingers. Means and the others rushed him to the Baptist Hospital in Winner, a largely white town on the reservation. Doctors removed a .38 dumdum bullet from his body in a four-hour operation. The bullet had missed his vital organs except for the pancreas.

Meanwhile, Camp was picked up, unarmed, by the police. He was charged with assault with a deadly weapon.

Bellecourt was treated by Dr. Constance Pinkerman, a Cherokee-Choctaw anesthesiologist, and by Crow Dog, AIM's medicine man, after two white doctors had removed the bullet. The white surgeon who extracted the slug reported that he had received irate phone calls from whites who criticized him for saving Bellecourt's life. The hospital administration later considered evicting the seriously wounded AIM leader, but they were deterred by protests from their medical staff.

The other AIM leaders, including Russell Means and Vernon Bellecourt, held a vigil on the hospital lawn to forestall what they feared might be a second assassination attempt. Means had declared that the shooting was part of a federal plot to kill or discredit AIM leaders. "We knew it was coming, but we didn't expect it would be from this close," he said. AIM dropouts, disgusted with the whole thing, put it down as another quarrel over money or power.

During the second day of the hospital vigil, Means and Bellecourt were arrested for their part in the Custer County Courthouse brawl that preceded Wounded Knee. Means was hauled off to appear in Custer County Circuit Court, where he demanded that his $15,000 bail be reduced. He was rearrested in court and had $95,000 more tacked onto his bond. Eventually, he got it reduced to $10,000 and was freed on bail. He now faced a possible maximum of 180 years in jail for the Wounded Knee and Custer incidents, on charges including burglary, larceny, assault, impeding federal officers, arson, unauthorized firearms, motor-vehicle theft, and conspiracy.

While all this was going on, Means, the two Bellecourts, and Camp, the cutting edge of armed protest, were all out of circulation. Garment decided to cancel the scheduled September meeting with traditionals and AIM leaders.

Clyde Bellecourt recovered after a lengthy hospital

stay, and he refused to testify against Camp, saying that he had spent 14½ years in reform school and prison and couldn't do that to anyone else. But the National Council of Churches revoked Camp's bond from Wounded Knee charges and he went back to jail anyway.*

The shooting and the resultant arrests not only made it easier for the government to ignore its promise to meet with Indian leaders, but a large number of Indians and non-Indians previously sympathetic to AIM were alienated. In New York City, several groups that had made verbal commitments to help finance AIM withdrew their offers as soon as the news of the shooting broke. In South Dakota, George McGovern cocked an eye toward the 1974 senatorial elections and blasted AIM as "rip-off artists who are exploiting the Indian problem for their own selfish needs" and as "violent lawbreakers." He also accused AIM of claiming to act in the spirit of Dr. Martin Luther King and being a disgrace to Dr. King's memory. Although this may have been an oblique reference to Rev. Ralph Abernathy's trip to Wounded Knee, it was a puzzling statement because no AIM leader had ever been known to invoke the spirit of Dr. King. AIM's stated heroes were always Indians—Tecumseh, Crazy Horse, Sitting Bull, Chief Joseph, and the hundreds of others who died fighting for Indian freedom in the past. The reference to Dr. King was a curve ball, a shabby attempt to win back conservative white voters by catering to their fear of AIM and their prejudice against both Indians and blacks.

Another factor that catered to local prejudices was not McGovern's doing, but AIM's. The heavy influx of New Left leftovers who hurried west to jump on the Wounded Knee bandwagon, both during and after the siege, did more than a little to alienate other Indians and to convince right-wing westerners (and easterners) that the AIM activists actually had Communist ties.

---

*Camp was set free on reduced bond late in December and cooperated with other AIM leaders as if nothing had happened.

This was, of course, ridiculous. No Communist group would ever tolerate the constant squabbles, jockeying for the limelight, and financial double-dealing that went on among some elements of the AIM leadership. At worst, as at best, AIM was a uniquely Indian organization. But the arrival of the New Left was resented by many of the more conservative Indians and even by some sincere white liberals with long records of support for Indians. You didn't have to be a master psychologist to realize the effect on a South Dakota jury of having William Kunstler or Mark Lane as an attorney. Some members of AIM's legal advisory staff, who had worked with the activists since before the Trail of Broken Treaties, tried to warn the headstrong militants that association with people like Kunstler and Lane would ultimately do more harm than good. But the short view—that big-name attorneys would bring in more publicity and money—won out, at least initially.* While Means was doing his thirty-nine days in jail, Kunstler was commuting between the U.S. Virgin Islands, where he helped defend some blacks charged with shooting white tourists, and New York, where he took part in a poetry reading to raise funds for a broad spectrum of left-liberal causes.

"My distinguished counsel was telling people that I wanted to stay in jail," Means snorted. "Hell, anybody that knows me has to realize that's bull——!" But he refused to give Kunstler the sack.

While other lawyers and the AIM leaders vied for the limelight, the weight of the actual legal complications arising from charges against Wounded Knee activists fell on the Wounded Knee Legal Defense/Offense

---

*During the siege, Dick Wilson issued a press release which read in part: "There is no doubt that Wounded Knee is a major Communist thrust. . . . News reporters and TV cameramen . . . can destroy a Nation by the propaganda of lies and hate they broadcast for every crackpot, screwball, and Communist-front organization who wants to take a swat at our American way of Life!" The May 1973 issue of *American Opinion*, the John Birch Society's house organ, was dedicated to Mr. Wilson and those who agreed with him.

Team, headed by Ramon Roubideaux. Roubideaux, who had served as a negotiator during the Wounded Knee siege, and had briefly been arrested for possession of a .38 pistol, was, in a less flamboyant way, as interesting a character as some of the militants he was defending. A smallish, sad-eyed man of Sioux and French ancestry, he had been picked as an observer for ungainly P-61 night-fighter planes on the World War II Italian front because of his superb eyesight. While on leave as a second lieutenant, he was evicted from a white dance hall in South Dakota because he was an Indian. It was this, he said, that decided him on a career as a lawyer, and after his discharge he studied law in Washington, D.C. Despite membership in a number of the usual white businessmen's clubs and organizations, he became more and more drawn to Indian activism and to Indian religion.

To Roubideaux, who was well versed in how things were done in conservative South Dakota, fell the thankless task of trying to be a buffer between anti-Indian South Dakota whites and the often antiwhite leaders of AIM.

"I've dealt with some big ego problems in my day, but this AIM bunch is the limit," Roubideaux said. He admitted that he actively disliked some of his wards. Banks, he said, was the best and most tractable of the lot.

"He's a very level-headed man. I see great things for him. Means is an honest man, but he's just too militant. I set up a dinner for him to speak to these Rapid City businessmen, and he told them that if we didn't get the Black Hills back by 1976, he'll take them back at gunpoint. Man, you just don't *say* things like that in South Dakota, because these guys have guns too! I thought somebody might shoot us right on the spot!"

Roubideaux relaxed from his troubles of trying to tone Means down and render him fit for white consumption by taking Banks on a fund-raising tour of Alaska, where Indians and Eskimos had recently received large payments in return for ceded rights to all but forty million acres of the state.* A few days after they returned from Alaska, the unpredictable Banks put in a second disappearance.

Back on the reservations, harassment of AIM people continued. In July, Clarence and Vernal Cross and William Spotted Eagle were asleep in a parked car. They were rousted by BIA police, and in the process of arresting them the Indian police shot Vernal Cross twice and then sprayed him with chemical Mace. His brother Clarence was fatally wounded and died several weeks after the shooting. The matter received almost no national publicity.

The kind of law and order that people at Pine Ridge had to tolerate could be summed up in the sufferings of Mrs. Agnes LaMonte, whose son Buddy had been killed at Wounded Knee.

In mid-September, Russell Means definitely announced that he would run against Dick Wilson for tribal chairman. Shortly after the announcement, white police from Custer County barged onto the reservation, unopposed by BIA police, and began to arrest anyone suspected of having taken part in the burning at Custer the previous February. One of Mrs. LaMonte's daughters was arrested right out of her living room. The white police, on the reservation illegally to begin with, didn't even let her put on her shoes before they dragged her off to jail. Mrs. LaMonte was less worried about the charges than about the fact that her daughter might be beaten or raped by the white police—a fear not uncommon on Pine Ridge. Her daughter was later freed on bond.

On 21 October Mrs. LaMonte and her sister, Mrs. Jenny Leading Fighter, were sitting in their car at a stop sign in the town of Pine Ridge. A car with three

---

*Senator Henry "Scoop" Jackson (Democrat, Washington), friend of oppressed Soviet Jews and other groups with extensive voter and financial support in the U.S., had sponsored a bill that would have pared the Native People's share of the land down to ten million acres, instead of the sixty million acres that the Native People had demanded. Police and game wardens in his state also have trouble recognizing Indians' treaty rights to fish the rivers.

alleged Wilson goons rammed their car broadside, injuring both women. Mrs. Leading Fighter was hospitalized for two days. Mrs. LaMonte refused to be taken to the hospital and asked to be taken home.

BIA police removed three rifles from the attackers' car and found five more high-powered weapons, equipped with telescopic sights, in the trunk. The three men were released without being charged.

"I think it was deliberate," Mrs. LaMonte said of the collision. "They were all goons. They were running wild drunk all afternoon."

"If we pick up a gun, we'd be put in jail," one of her daughters said sullenly. "But them, they go around free like that."

Many other incidents or harassments were less subtle. A few weeks before Mrs. LaMonte's collision, nine-year-old Mary Ann Little Bear was hit in the face by a shotgun blast as she and her father were riding in their car past the scene of a council meeting. Her father drove to Pine Ridge and summoned the BIA police, pointing out the house the shot had come from. Inside were three Wilson supporters. There were no arrests. Mary Ann Little Bear lost one of her eyes.

In May, with the siege just over, Frank Fools Crow, the seventy-eight-year-old medicine man friendly to AIM, was trailed as he drove away from his home. A car with three Wilson supporters smashed into the rear of Fools Crow's car as he pulled into a gas station.

Severt Young Bear, a prominent AIM supporter, had his house shot up on so many different nights that he had to ask friends to stand guard with loaded rifles every night. No one was ever apprehended by the BIA police.

The man was not arrested or charged. There were literally dozens of other beatings or property damages and threats too numerous to count. But the breaking point seems to have come with the killing of Pedro Bissonette.

Bissonette, a thirty-three-year-old ex-Golden Gloves boxer, was a leader of the Oglala Civil Rights Association that had invited AIM onto the Pine Ridge reservation, precipitating the Wounded Knee siege. Most people were impressed by his politeness, but perhaps because of his activism, he had had more than his share of run-ins with tribal police. On 17 October he was shot to death by BIA police at a roadblock.

According to the BIA police, he was killed while resisting arrest when the BIA police tried to serve him with two fugitive warrants, one dating from Wounded Knee and the other related to firing a gun in the air in a barroom brawl.

The activist version circulating among people on the reservation was that Bissonette had been pursued by BIA police who fired at him. He fired a shot in return and then escaped. Later, the Indians said, he was caught coming through a roadblock. The activists charged that the police had held him down and fired seven pistol shots into his chest. Radical attorney Mark Lane, working with the AIM faction, said that he had seen the wounds in Bissonette's chest and that they were caused by separate pistol shots. But Dr. W. B. Brown, a pathologist who performed the autopsy in Scotts Bluff, Nebraska, said that death had been caused by a single shotgun blast.

"I found seven pellets," Dr. Brown said. "They were buckshot, not rifle or pistol bullets. Seven pellets is the normal load for that type of cartridge."

Some four hundred mourners filed past Bissonette's closed casket as it lay in a tepee in front of his mother's home, three miles from Pine Ridge. The government had sought a court order to bar AIM leaders from the funeral, but a federal judge had denied the request. At the Roman Catholic funeral mass, Pedro's mother Suzie sat beside Russell Means and his brothers, Ted, Dale, and Bill. Dennis Banks, now back in the United States, had been barred from the reservation by Delmar Eastman, special officer in charge of the BIA police, who said that Banks, a Chippewa, would be arrested on sight if he attempted to enter the Pine Ridge Sioux reservation. The Indian funeral procession detoured to the edge of the reservation, so that Banks could view Pedro's body. He sat beside the opened casket, gazing at Bissonette's face for a short time before the procession went on its way.

Three days after Bissonette's death, two BIA policemen stopped a car filled with young Sioux men. As they were questioning the car's occupants, a second car sped by and the men inside opened fire. Both BIA policemen were wounded. The car with the gunmen escaped. In the next few days, several BIA policemen reported that their houses had been hit by rifle fire.

Another bizarre incident occurred just after Bissonette's funeral. As the guests were preparing to leave the Bissonette place, AIM security guards captured a drunken Sioux teen-ager in an old jalopy trying to drive onto the Bissonette family's land. The boy said, under AIM interrogation, that Dick Wilson had given him whiskey and paid him fifty dollars to disrupt the AIM leaders' visit to the reservation, in hopes of bringing about either a mass arrest or a showdown between the Means brothers and the BIA police. Armed with the kid's testimony, Wounded Knee Legal Defense attorneys demanded that the federal authorities arrest Dick Wilson for conspiracy and for bootlegging, since dispensing whiskey on the reservation is illegal. Their bid at a legal counterattack had all the political naïveté of the Children's Crusade and was equally unsuccessful. Wilson was not arrested.

Contrary to most people's impressions, episodes of violence and near-violence escalated after Wounded Knee, rather than melting away, and not only in Sioux country. During the first days of the siege, two young New Mexico Navajos, Larry Casuse and Bob Nakatine had kidnapped Emmett Garcia, the mayor of Gallup. The pair and their hostage took shelter in a liquor store and in the gunfight that followed Casuse was killed—police said he committed suicide—and Garcia was wounded and hospitalized. The young Navajos said they were trying to force Garcia to do something about the liquor trade in Gallup, which was debauching so many of their people.

Violence was narrowly averted in two other incidents. In the summer of 1973, two separate groups of activists took over two different government buildings—

a hospital in New Mexico and a state office in Des Moines, Iowa. In both cases the activists barged in carrying guns but left peacefully after their grievances were discussed. About the same time, armed Chippewas faced down white sportsmen trespassing on their Minnesota reservation and chased them out.

By the winter of 1973, the government seemed to be treading very cautiously where Indian activists with guns were concerned. In December, forty armed U.S. forest rangers from the Southwest were sent to California in response to unsubstantiated stories from lumberjacks that heavily armed Indians were prowling through the gloomy green woods setting forest fires. The forty rangers arrested all they could find of the mysterious war party—two married couples and a twenty-one-year-old man from the Pit River tribe of California—and then stayed on to protect the leery loggers from the hundred or more armed Indians believed to be loitering in the vicinity of Lassen National Park. The whole episode had a quality reminiscent of Chief Seattle's speech, in which he told the whites that the ghosts of his people would never leave the white man alone in the country they had so loved in life. And the forest rangers had no power over ghosts.*

Whether as a result of Wounded Knee, or as a variation on the theme of the rebirth of Indian pride, constructive changes were also taking place all over America. One of the most important changes, both in national and local terms, was the downfall of Webster Two Hawk.

Two Hawk, the first president of Nixon's NTCA, was the definitive Uncle Tomahawk of the 1970s. A few weeks after he flew into Washington, D.C., at the taxpayer's expense, to denounce the Trail of Broken Treaties, he returned to ride in Nixon's second inaugural parade, straddling a pathetic horse that must

---

*In 1971, Russell Means gleefully accepted part of the blame for the National Parks Service's creation of a forty-man special task force to protect America's natural wonderlands from "hippies, vandals, Indians, and nudists." Means didn't enumerate which other groups he represented. Task Force Lassen Forest may be the same group.

have come from a Washington hackney cab and wearing an Indian suit that could only have come from a costume shop. A warbonnet fluttered over Rev. Two Hawk's close-cropped crew cut. The effect was one of monstrous parody, a middle-class clergyman posing for "The End of the Trail."

This could have been prophetic, because Two Hawk was indeed near the end of his own political trail. I filed against him for the office of tribal chairman of the Rosebud reservation. When some of the people heard I was running, they told Two Hawk to his face that they didn't even want to sign his nominating petition. The August primary, which winnowed seven preliminary candidates down to two finalists, showed Two Hawk lagging behind me as we both qualified for the final election. On 23 October I beat Two Hawk by close to three hundred votes. The incumbent might have delighted conservative commentators by his attacks on me, on AIM, and on any Indian who dared to question the status quo, but he couldn't win an election on his own reservation, despite his access to almost unlimited federal funds. There wasn't enough money in the mint to bribe the people of Rosebud into accepting another term of Two Hawk, or to second his endorsements of the status quo with their votes.

Things were moving all over Indian country. In mid-August, the Justice Department announced the formation of the Office of Indian Rights, a special branch of the Justice Department, to protect and foster the civil rights of Indians.

Justice Department officials, apparently anxious to shore up the crumbling cliché that violence never solved anything, alleged that an Office of Indian Rights had been in the works long before Wounded Knee. Actually, the genesis may well have begun when Father Theodore Hesburgh resigned as chairman of the U.S. Civil Rights commission and several other officials issued statements criticizing civil rights policies in relation to Indians.

"Sooner or later, there's going to have to be a confrontation between the Civil Rights Commission and the Civil Service Commission, and sooner or later there's going to have to be a confrontation between the Civil Rights Commission and the Bureau of Indian Affairs," said civil rights official Maurice Mitchell.

Well there might be. A U.S. Civil Rights Commission report in mid-May of 1973 pointed out that many private employers hired non-Indians for jobs on the reservations even when plenty of willing Indians were available. A Phelps-Dodge Corporation copper mine near the Navajo reservation was found to have employed 96 Indians out of a work force of 1,258 people. The cities of Tucson and Phoenix were also cited for employment discrimination. In New Mexico, Indians were found to account for 7 percent of the state's population, but only 2 percent of the state's jobs. Even the New Mexico post office, the traditional employer of minorities, employed only 34 Indians out of 2,573 postal workers. The only jobs Indians seemed to qualify for in New Mexico were those that involved dancing in regalia for tourists. In the neighboring state of Arizona, the post office employed only 34 Indians out of a work force of 5,000.

The figures for the Southwest, bad as they were, didn't detract from South Dakota's standing as the Mississippi of the North, and of Rapid City as the capital of anti-Indian racism. George McGovern's hypocritical admiration of Dr. Martin Luther King didn't extend to outrage over the blatant segregation of the Sioux Addition. This Indian shantytown sprang up four miles outside of Rapid City because the city's great white fathers purchased the land there and made it available to Indians in order to keep them out of white neighborhoods. Rapid City has three hospitals—two for whites and the Sioux Sanitorium for Indians. The unemployment rate of the Rapid City Indians, who migrated to the outskirts looking for any work at all, is 22.3 percent, compared to 5.3 percent for Rapid City whites.

Most activists didn't put too much stock in the new Office of Indian Rights. Its director, Carl Stoiber, a former Rhodes scholar, had done a number of investigations of complaints against Wilson's goons just after Wounded Knee, but the abuses complained of didn't abate. Ramon Roubideaux said flatly that the Office of Indian Rights looked like window dressing, an attempt to quash a legitimate investigation by a nongovernment source.

But other changes were coming. On 16 October 1973 the U.S. House of Representatives voted 404 to 3 to repeal the disastrous termination of the Menominee tribe of Wisconsin, a measure that nonviolent Indians had pleaded for—in vain—since the dark days of the Eisenhower administration.

"The idea was to make Indians as much like white people as we could and then cut them off from the Federal relationship," said Rep. Lloyd Meeds, a Washington State Democrat. He added that the actual results had been to leave the Menominees "tottering on the brink of collapse."

Congressional sources said that measures to repeal termination of other tribes might be more difficult because the other tribes terminated had had their tribal land broken up into allotments; the Menominees had been organized as a corporation and their tribal lands kept more or less intact.

On 22 December the Menominee repeal became official when President Nixon signed it. Nixon said in a written statement that the signing represented a clear reversal of the policy of forcibly terminating Indian tribal status. He admitted that the Menominees had not entered into the termination willingly, and he saluted the tribe and its leaders for their "persuasiveness and perseverance in using the tools of the political process." He didn't mention that the Menominees and others had worked for repeal of termination for almost twenty years before Wounded Knee II.

In Congressman Meeds's own state, federal attorneys began an effort to have the U.S. Supreme Court curtail sport fishing in the Puyallup River so that the local Indians might be assured an adequate supply of fish for food. The Washington State Game Department had persisted in its ban of Indian net fishing for steelhead trout, prompting bitter Indians to ask if the steelhead had come over on the *Mayflower*. State courts had maintained that sports fishery had left no more fish than were necessary for the survival of the species. The Puyallup people's attorneys tried to reverse the odd logic that put rich white he-men's rights to have fun killing fish before the Indian's treaty rights to eat.

On the huge Navajo reservation, the tribal leaders finally won control over the school boards to the extent that they were able to scrap an outmoded dress code forbidding girls to wear slacks, even when they had to ride for hours on unheated school buses. And in Oklahoma, where conservative white school board members kept Indian boys out of school for refusing to cut their hair, the families of the boys involved began to demand probes of the Johnson-O'Malley Act funds that Congress appropriated to compenstate public schools for educating Indians. The Indian families charged that Johnson-O'Malley funds were being misused and should be withheld from districts that restricted Indians' rights to free expression of their culture.

In New England, a quiet change took place, almost unnoticed except by the Indians and the descendants of the Pilgrims. Since 1970, when Russell Means launched his own career and started a new Indian tradition by storming the *Mayflower II* and kicking sand on Plymouth Rock, Thanksgiving Day had been the National Day of Mourning to Indians, a field day on which they rallied at Plymouth Plantation and told *Mayflower* families and reporters that they didn't feel very thankful for the coming of the white man. In 1971, Indians had marched quietly in a drizzle but had been upstaged by Vietnam Veterans against the War. In 1972, a few weeks after the Trail of Broken Treaties, New England Indians stormed the *Mayflower II* as Means had in 1970, ripping flags and spitting on Plymouth Rock.

But in 1973, the unexpected happened, *Mayflower* families, who had spent the past three Thanksgivings desperately trying to appear oblivious to shouting, spitting, flag-ripping, ship-storming Indians, changed their tack. They invited the Indians to a church service at the First Parish Church, where a Passamaquoddy Indian, Wayne Newell, delivered a sermon.

"I think that the blessings that God has given all of us

have been corrupted by us, so that these once-blessings are now things that perhaps will destroy this Nation if we don't reexamine their value," Newell said, as the first tremors of the energy crisis were being felt across the country. Whatever they may have thought, the descendants of the Pilgrims listened politely.

By December 1973, as the year of Wounded Knee drew to a close, things were really moving. On 5 December the U.S. Senate passed legislation establishing an American Indian Policy Review Commission, aimed at studying the legal and historical background of the unique relationship between the Indian people and the federal government, in order to bring about a fundamental reform.

The legislation, which was forwarded to the House of Representatives, had been introduced by Senator Abourezk. It called for a commission of Senate and House members from both parties and of five members of the Indian community.

Ironically, while Abourezk was introducing such potentially important legislation, McGovern, back in South Dakota, was telling white audiences at state colleges that Indian treaties were scraps of paper.

"I think the treaties were abrogated by an act of Congress over 100 years ago and that it's ridiculous to talk about the Treaty of 1868 being carried out," McGovern said early in December, showing the same colossal ignorance that had made a joke of his tenure on the Indian Affairs Subcommittee. Congress had not abrogated the treaties in 1871. Congress had terminated future treaty making with the Indian tribes as sovereign nations from that year forward. McGovern's statement also ignored the existence of the Indian Claims Commission, which had been around since 1946.* Lack

---

*In December 1973 the Indian Claims Commission paid the Sac and Fox tribe almost two million dollars in compensation for 3.65 million acres of land that the tribe ceded to the U.S. 169 years before. That's over fifty cents per acre. On 19 February 1974 the Commission awarded the Sioux Nation $17.1 million for its land claim based upon the 7.5 million acres lost under the 1868 Treaty. In addition, the Commission awarded the Sioux Nation five percent interest because of the violation of the Fifth Amend-

of national news coverage prevented the American public from seeing a rare spectacle—George McGovern coming on with the same pitch as the less-cultured members of the John Birch Society.

Back in Washington, Sen. Edward Kennedy dropped another clue as to why massive expenditure of federal funds didn't alleviate Indian poverty.

"Indian educators and tribal leaders, as well as parents and teachers, have been unable to discover what portion of the funds appropriated for the Indian education programs really reaches and benefits Indian children," Kennedy said, opening a hearing of the Senate Judiciary Subcommittee on Indian Education Accountability on 13 December. The subcommittee, he said, had encountered a maze studded with obstacles and riddled with dead ends, and they had concluded that nobody in the Office of Education or the BIA really knew the answers to the questions they were asked.

Some of the mysterious discoveries made by the subcommittee included the following:

- In Alaska, $2.8 million in federal funds distributed by the BIA were neither spent nor accounted for by the state. The BIA accepted a report of this strange situation without requiring any action by the state.
- An audit of twenty-three Oklahoma school districts showed that 14 percent of the federal money earmarked for Indian education under the Johnson-O'Malley Act went to ineligible students—in other words, non-Indian students were getting the money appropriated for Indians. Senator Kennedy added that 106 other Oklahoma school districts were apparently doing the same thing, and the BIA had done nothing about it.
- In two New Mexico school districts, $166,000 in surplus funds were received over a two-year period, and the money just disappeared.

---

ment to the Constitution. (Just compensation was not paid when the land was taken.) To add to this award, the Commission allowed $450,000 for the mineral rights lost in 1868 plus five percent interest on that amount, making a total award of $102 million.

The BIA, Kennedy pointed out, has more than seven thousand employees paid for dealing with education and related matters, yet BIA officials claimed that they lacked the manpower to provide accurate reports. The basic products of Indian education, Kennedy concluded, were "a handful of unmet needs and dashed expectations."

The BIA had been the target of attacks by everyone from Means and Banks to Senators Kennedy and Barry Goldwater all through 1973,* but responses to the attacks were rarely quoted in rebuttal. This was because the BIA had been a hydra without a centralized head since December 1972, when Secretary of the Interior Rogers Morton had pressured Commissioner Louis Bruce and Deputy Commissioner John O. Crow into resigning. For most of the interim year, Marvin Franklin, an Oklahoma oilman with some Indian connections and many Republican connections had served as acting chairman. Franklin had stated publicly and frequently that he wouldn't accept an appointment as full-time commissioner of Indian affairs—possibly because such an appointment might have touched off another insurrection on the scale of the Trail of Broken Treaties.

Around 20 October Franklin made one of his rare public stands, opposing a plan to reform the BIA by trimming off some of its extraneous fat. The reform plan, drawn up by John Seidl, a Department of the Interior official, would have cut the BIA staff in half and passed the payroll savings on to the Indian people. Further, it would have replaced the eleven area offices created in the 1940s with six new area offices, thus reducing the area office staff from 2,000 to 560. Franklin seemed horrified by Seidl's plan to pass poverty funds directly to poor people and said the plan was "diametrically opposed to all the things I believe to be beneficial to the American Indian."

Oddly enough, Seidl's plan bore a strange resem-

---

*In September 1973 Sen. Barry Goldwater, addressing Indians from four states at Scottsdale, Arizona, said that the federal bureaucracy was laggard and insensitive. "It is difficult," he said, "to deal with a bureaucracy which possesses greater centralized power than even organized labor or the political parties."

blance to a plan that Commissioner Bruce had been working on when he was sacked in 1972. It even sounded vaguely like the much-touted Nixon doctrine of eliminating excessive bureaucracy. But anyone who remembered the BIA's fantastic abilities to save itself at the Indian people's expense during the 1940s and 1950s wouldn't have been too surprised to see Seidl's plan die on the drawing board. Like the science-fiction computers that seize control from the technicians who supposedly run them, the BIA had long since become a self-contained, self-serving entity whose goal was not to serve the Indian people but to survive and grow ever larger.

In December 1973, almost a year to the day after Bruce and Crow were fired, a thirty-four-year-old Athabascan Indian from Alaska was sworn in to the $36,000-a-year job of commissioner of Indian affairs. Morris Thompson, a former area director from the BIA's Juneau office, was the fourth Indian and the youngest man ever to hold the job. Indians across the nation paused to watch and evaluate his performance.

His first press conference didn't seem auspicious. Thompson said he would meet with any Indian who had "reasonable objectives," but he said he would prefer to rely on the advice of such established groups as the National Tribal Chairman's Association. The new commissioner declined to say whether he thought AIM was a help or a hindrance in working for constructive change. In other bids for popularity with the White House, Thompson said that Nixon's administration had reversed the trend of erosion of the Indian land base—a dubious claim, for termination had in effect ended under John Kennedy, and millions of acres were still being leased to white ranchers in 1973. Thompson also called for action on Nixon's 8 July 1970 message—the standard cop-out so dear to the hearts of all Republican bureaucrats. Thompson even suggested that if he were promoted to a position as assistant secretary of the interior for Indian affairs, he would have more clout in solving Indian problems. About the only constructive suggestion he made was that Indian students should be educated as close to home as possible, and that off-reservation boarding schools should be phased out gradually, but not immediately. In brief, it looked like business as usual at Boone's Apple Farm.

Back on the Pine Ridge reservation Russell Means's campaign for tribal chairman continued. Candidates announced and then dropped out with bewildering swiftness. When voting regulations were finally set up on 27 November 1973, the candidates were given until 21 December to collect three hundred signatures to qualify them for placement on the ballot. There were five candidates left, although as many as thirteen had been running in the early fall.

While Means ran for office, his attorneys ran around trying to keep him out of jail. At a pretrial hearing in Sioux Falls, Wounded Knee Legal Defense attorneys subpoenaed former U.S. attorney general Richard Kleindienst. Kleindienst had served as the nation's top lawman through most of Wounded Knee, but he resigned on 30 April during the first explosion of the Watergate furore. Investigating Watergate, Kleindienst had concluded that there was no evidence of federal crimes beyond the original six defendants—Hunt, Liddy, and company. His appraisal of the Wounded Knee situation seemed similarly myopic. Under oath, Kleindienst testified that he didn't recall being told about the blockade Dick Wilson's goons had thrown around the besieged hamlet to cut off food and medical supplies to the AIM and Oglala defenders. This indicates that Kleindienst must have been too busy with Watergate to read the papers, for the goon barricades had been extensively photographed and described by AP reporters and other newsmen.*

After failing to recall a few other controversial items, Kleindienst refreshed his memory enough to flatly deny making a statement that "Grand Jury indictments are being used to bargain with the Indians at Wounded

---

*AP also produced a picture of what looked like a Sheridan tank at the same time that the government was telling reporters there were no tanks in the area.

Knee" as quoted by an AP reporter. He stated that it had been his policy to avoid a confrontation regardless of the apparent aggravations. Yet he admitted that federal forces had fired 500,000 rounds of ammunition into the tiny hamlet of Wounded Knee—several thousand times the number of bullets fired at the 1890 massacre and quite possibly the heaviest concentration of small-arms fire in any North American land battle. Half a million bullets fired into an area filled with women and children seemed like a monstrous overreaction to a bunch of protesters who hadn't inflicted a single fatality on the federal forces. Kleindienst, however, said that although he had discussed the Wounded Knee affair almost daily with Justice Department officials, he had considered himself responsible for the overall situation rather than for specific details.

The Wounded Knee defense attorneys had called on Kleindienst to testify, seeking to establish evidence of what they termed "bad faith prosecution." This meant that the lawyers alleged that the government was using the expensive trials and massive potential sentences—up to 180 years for Means and Banks—to silence the AIM leadership. The defense attorneys charged that the government was using selective enforcement by employing criminal statutes against AIM leaders and Oglala militants, but not against Wilson's goons, and that the government condoned harassment of activists by Wilson's followers and by white authorities off-reservation. In light of the Justice Department's miserable record of failure in prosecuting the perpetrators of all the beatings and sniper attacks on the Pine Ridge reservation, it looked like the Wounded Knee Legal Defense Committee had a pretty good case. But the attempt to legally prove "bad faith prosecution" was unsuccessful. The AIM attorneys pointed out that they had only been allowed to subpoena five witnesses instead of the twenty they had sought, and this weakened their case.

Another subpoenaed witness proved less cooperative than Kleindienst. The Reverend Paul Boe, a fifty-eight-year-old Lutheran minister from Minneapolis, was ordered to testify before a different federal grand jury about the occupation of Wounded Knee, but he refused.

"I contend all the federal government wants is my testimony for evidence against AIM members," Boe said. "The grand jury has already indicted more than 100 persons. The government just wants the evidence now to convict them."

Reverend Boe said that his testimony would jeopardize the five years of trust between his church and AIM; he was sentenced to fourteen months in jail on 19 December 1973. The sentence was stayed until 2 January so he could put his affairs in order or file an appeal. The American Lutheran Church decided to support Boe, but mail from parishioners ran three to one against him. Some of the negative mail consisted of copies of the same form letter with different signatures—a favorite trick of "grass-roots" archconservatives, whose poll-stuffing techniques found their best-known exposure when the Committee to Re-Elect the President got caught rigging a radio poll to show support for the mining of Haiphong harbor.

Despite the government's clumsy efforts and the continued epidemic of foot-in-mouth disease among federal officials, AIM didn't exactly prosper. The Indian activists' cause wasn't furthered by their own lack of cohesion. It seemed that nobody really knew who had the action, or where AIM was going.

George Mitchell, the theorist-in-exile, explained in retrospect that he had drafted AIM's constitution and bylaws so that each AIM chapter was autonomous. He did this to prevent exactly the kind of fractional infighting and ego-tripping that eventually drove him out of AIM. The other AIM leaders, for reasons best known to themselves, disregarded Mitchell's careful planning and set up a whole slate of national offices, which led to some inflated egos and a great deal of confusion. After Clyde Bellecourt was shot, Carter Camp was removed from his titular office as chairman and replaced by John Trudell, a young Santee Sioux navy veteran. Trudell had been one of the coalition of Indian leaders who ran things at Alcatraz after Richard

Oakes left. Reporters who had been on Alcatraz remembered him as a sincere, likable young man who sometimes let other, more venal leaders bully him rather than provoke trouble. On the basis of his individual personality he was one of the best of the AIM people, but very little was heard from him as far as publicity went. The press continued to quote Means, Banks, and Vernon Bellecourt as if each of them were the lone leader of AIM.

Thus while Means was running for office on Pine Ridge, Vernon Bellecourt was in Minneapolis vowing to turn AIM into an "educational organization" to teach white people about the beauty of Indian culture. A few weeks after Vern's speech of pacific intent, Banks showed up in Tucson, Arizona, vowing to bring massed firepower against the Alaska pipeline.

"The Indian response to the Alaska pipeline running across Indian land will make Wounded Knee look like a Boy Scout picnic," Banks said. "The current situation has been provoked by the oil industry so it can establish price controls and increase its holdings."

About the same time as Banks declared war on the pipeline, Means turned up in Washington, D.C., at the National Press Club threatening the nation's bicentennial celebration.

"If by 1976 the treaty issue is not justly dealt with, the planned birthday celebration by white Americans will be an unhappy celebration," Means said.

This was not a new theme. Means had said the same thing during the BIA take-over, and Vern Bellecourt had elaborated a few weeks after the Trail of Broken Treaties by threatening to "blow out the candles on America's birthday cake." But Wounded Knee and the incidents that followed had lent new credence to these threats, particularly since the week of 4 July 1976 would be the hundredth anniversary of the Indians' proudest holiday—Custer's Last Stand.

When reporters asked Means about the results of Wounded Knee, he cited increased housing construction and funds to the bilingual school program. Earlier, Dick Wilson had charged that Wounded Knee had been a setback to Indian progress, but it is a matter of record that by the autumn of 1973, the government was constructing fifty-six new two-, three-, and four-bedroom houses on the Pine Ridge reservation.

A few days after Means spoke, Banks, also in Washington, issued a proclamation urging Indians to stay away from bars during the Christmas holidays.

"With the coming of the white man's holidays, there will be mounting pressure on Indians throughout the United States to continue self-genocide with white man's whiskey," he said. "Alcohol is the dominant causative factor in the decimation and destruction of Indian people. Boycott white men's bars and other sources of this destructive poison!"

Where AIM was going by year's end was a mystery. The popularity of the organization had fluctuated wildly in the Indian world, reaching its apogee during the first days of the Wounded Knee siege and its nadir with the shooting of Clyde Bellecourt.* By the fall of 1973, some of the more conventional leaders had worked their way around to accepting AIM for what it was—not a spiritual crusade or a national lobby, but a free-lance army, with both the virtues and vices of a military organization.

"Before now, we could exhaust every appeal to the government and then sit back and wait without any hope of anything happening," said one member of the National Congress of American Indians. "Now, we can always threaten to call in AIM as a last resort."

More Indians died before the often-postponed Pine Ridge tribal primary could take place. On 10 November 1973 Phillip Little Crow, an AIM supporter, was beaten to death and an alleged Wilson supporter was charged with voluntary manslaughter. On 15 November Pat Hart, a friend of Pedro Bissonette, was shot in the stomach by an unseen sniper and his wounds required ten hours of surgery. On 20 November Allison Little Fast Horse, a fifteen-year-old AIM supporter,

---

*On 28 December AIM sponsored an all-day "happening" in Atlanta, Georgia, featuring several movie stars and a number of lesser rock groups. The AIM leadership hoped to draw 117,000 people. The festival bombed and they barely made expenses.

was found dead in a wayside ditch with a bullet through his heart.

On 22 January 1974 the tribal primary finally took place and winnowed the twelve candidates for the tribal chairman's $15,000-a-year job down to two—Russell Means and Dick Wilson. The official tally read: Means 667 votes, Wilson 511, and Gerald One Feather 367. Means was jubilant—"I'm the champ!"—but claimed that Wilson's hand-picked election workers had juggled the figures. AIM sources charged that the actual score was Means 930, One Feather 624, and Wilson 540. Means was dubious about the future. "Without the intervention of outside observers," he said, "the people of Pine Ridge will face two more years of Wilson's police state." Yet Brad Patterson of the White House refused to send a special task force to ensure an honest election, lest the administration be charged with "meddling."

Meanwhile, on 5 February results of a study by a private accounting firm, hired by the Department of the Interior to audit the Pine Ridge tribal books, disclosed that the tribal records were such a mess that it was impossible to either prove or disprove AIM's charges of corruption against Dick Wilson.

On 7 February the run-off election pitted Wilson against Means. From the outset, AIM supporters and other Oglalas charged corruption. They said that Wilson supporters had enrolled non-Indians to vote and had barred AIM voters and officials from the polling places. When a Wilson backer barred a registered Indian woman from a polling place in Pine Ridge, she punched him in the nose.

Drunks showed their friends crisp twenty-dollar bills they had been given to vote for Wilson. BIA policemen arrived from outlying districts and stuffed wads of paper ballots into the wooden boxes without signing register books. One district, Potato Creek, showed forty registered voters but cast 83 votes.

In the off-reservation town of Whiteclay, Nebraska, a shot fired at an AIM member named Milo Goings missed him and struck a nine-year-old boy named Harold Weasel Bear in the face.

Throughout the day, Means carried the outlying districts. However, the final count was 1,709 votes for Wilson and 1,530 votes for Means. Wilson, the first incumbent to win reelection since 1935, toted it up as a victory for law and order, and left the reservation to celebrate in Rapid City. Within days of his triumph, AIM followers and their families were being threatened and beaten up, and old people who had backed Means or other Wilson opponents were being threatened at gunpoint and told to leave the reservation.

Reporters found Means at his home district of Porcupine. An eagle feather fluttered from his braids as light snow fell. "I have no faith in a recount," Means said. "The government pulled out all the stops to make sure I didn't win this election. But I believe the American Indian Movement won an overwhelming victory even with the existing results of this election. The press has continually, continually claimed that we were a band of two hundred outsiders at Wounded Knee in 1973. The 1500 votes, according to this illegal election, have verified and vindicated and exonerated the American Indian Movement on the Pine Ridge reservation."

# 12
# The Rebirth of the Indian

Come, my brothers, let us see what kind of world we make for our children.

—Sitting Bull

All the treaties, all the laws, all the federal regulations, and all the federal policies in existence cannot justify the criminal acts of tribal and federal government officials who knowingly deceive those who have placed their trust in them.

There are few tribal governments in this nation that are free of corruption, malfeasance, maladministration, and oppression of the tribe's members. These facts are known at least in part by federal officials at one of the four levels of Indian affairs, yet nothing is done. The average bureaucrat is now fully aware that the field of Indian affairs is a runaway disaster area which grows worse with every passing hour. The bureaucrats, like many knowledgeable Indians, are also aware that the new self-determination policy is in direct conflict with laws now in force covering Indian affairs.

Many people, including those in the White House and the Department of the Interior, misunderstand the Indians who oppose the government's operations and policies. Many people try to create an impression that all Indian activists are dangerous leftists, star-struck publicity hounds, or maladjusted troublemakers. Whatever the failings of some of the individuals involved, the activist demonstrations of recent years have been motivated by Indian nationalism; that is, the love of the Indian for his own people and tradition. One has only to exercise some hindsight to analyze the reasons for the recent outbursts. The contents of this book, and the documents in the appendixes should serve to answer most of the quesions that fly through the intelligent citizen's mind when some Indian element swings into action.

And this is important. If the government and the public do not heed the cry of the Indian before much more time passes, the activists will be driven underground for an all-out battle that could turn any area with a sizable Indian population into a "little Northern Ireland." The gears of our society are so meshed and so complex that even a small band of dedicated fanatics could throw the whole social order out of line. It might be wise for the government and white America to reflect that those who are without hope are also without fear.

The United States must stop its constant attempts to cover up serious crimes committed by Indian leaders in responsible positions, by BIA employees who are only interested in using their jobs for gain, and by corporate interests who exploit Indian land, water, and minerals. Indians throughout the country know that there has been a complete breakdown in law and order on the reservations because the Justice Department has not been carrying through its responsibility to the Indians under the guardianship of the United States.

Indians are seeking control of their destiny, of their property, and of tribal government with a distinct desire to have the president and Congress hold their land in trust until they are ready to determine their own future, provided that Congress enacts legislation guaranteeing that no termination will take place without the consent of the tribe affected.

Sometimes through violent actions, more often through legal complaints, Indians are demanding changes in the outmoded laws that restrict Indians while the federal and tribal governments circumvent these laws at will.

To correct the situation, the president should recommend to Congress that an entire new Indian act be adopted and that the outmoded laws be rescinded. The title of this new legislation is unimportant, but the contents should signal that the citizens of the United States, expressing their will through Congress, desire to do the following:

1. Abolish the BIA and replace it with a secretary of Indian affairs, an autonomous organization outside of the Department of the Interior. This would eliminate the tremendous conflict of interest between Interior's stewardship over the Indians and their responsiblility for timber, minerals, water, grazing, parks, and other resources.
2. The Department of Indian Affairs should be staffed by ten Indians, elected by the Indians who reside in the present geographic areas now known as area offices. These ten Indians would act to protect the best interests of their people and would be answerable to the reservation and urban communities.
3. New laws should be enacted making elected tribal officials accountable to their respective tribes and to the federal government for all tribal property and finances.
4. Congress should enact a national Indian election law protecting those who seek political office and Indian voters from election fraud or threats. This law should make it a crime to buy votes or to bribe election officials.
5. Legislation should give the individual Indian new freedom to manage his property under the trusteeship of the government.
6. Congress should guarantee that federal appropriations will remain at their present level, with contractual agreements between the tribe and the government.
7. Congress should enact new tribal enabling acts giving each tribe the right to adopt its own form of government, providing that such governments adhere to the principles of the Constitution of the United States.
8. Congress should enact a "New Indian Finance Act" and appropriate $500 million for the purpose of lifting the Indians to an economic level equal to that of their non-Indian counterparts.

9. Last but not least, Congress should enact a jurisdictional act giving the U.S. district courts jurisdiction over all matters arising from Indian affairs concerning tribal government.

These laws, once enacted, would cure 98 percent of the serious situations that could potentially create violence or personal political grievances. Indians would lose their fear of termination, a new era would lead to cultural pride and economic development, and the Indian would be able to fit in with society and still retain his unique heritage.

Americans must realize that Indians are human beings who desire to maintain their culture and at the same time possess a full understanding of the white man's goal of excellence. The Great Spirit has protected his red children from extermination for a reason; Indians have the ability to live in both the spiritual and the natural worlds without exploiting either. This is a lesson we must teach our brothers.

We seek help so that we too can enjoy the fruits of our land. We must not abuse our land and its resources, and we must not destroy our air and water, nor should we undertake the blind and unreasoning pursuit of profit, which can lead to disaster for all living creatures. We must restore trust, self-discipline, and faith to all mankind so that we can live in harmony with our Maker.

Indians have been trying to reach the people of this nation for more than a century, but the white man's ears have been stopped up by greed, prejudice, or apathy. Indians have been crying for help until they have been forced into violence to win the attention they need to survive. Yet the Indian has always realized that lust, love, and hate create enough violence in this world without making violence a necessary condition for social change. For this reason we ask that all good and decent people join the Indian cause by talking to their neighbors and enlisting their help in solving the problems that the government has created for the Indian.

Your church, club, or civic organizaiton may mean

the difference between life and death for some Indians. Get in touch with those whose positions of public trust can benefit the Indian. Letters or phone calls to the president, your senators, representatives, state legislators, and town councilmen can help more than you realize. The time to act is now. Help us forestall any more Wounded Knees.

# APPENDIXES

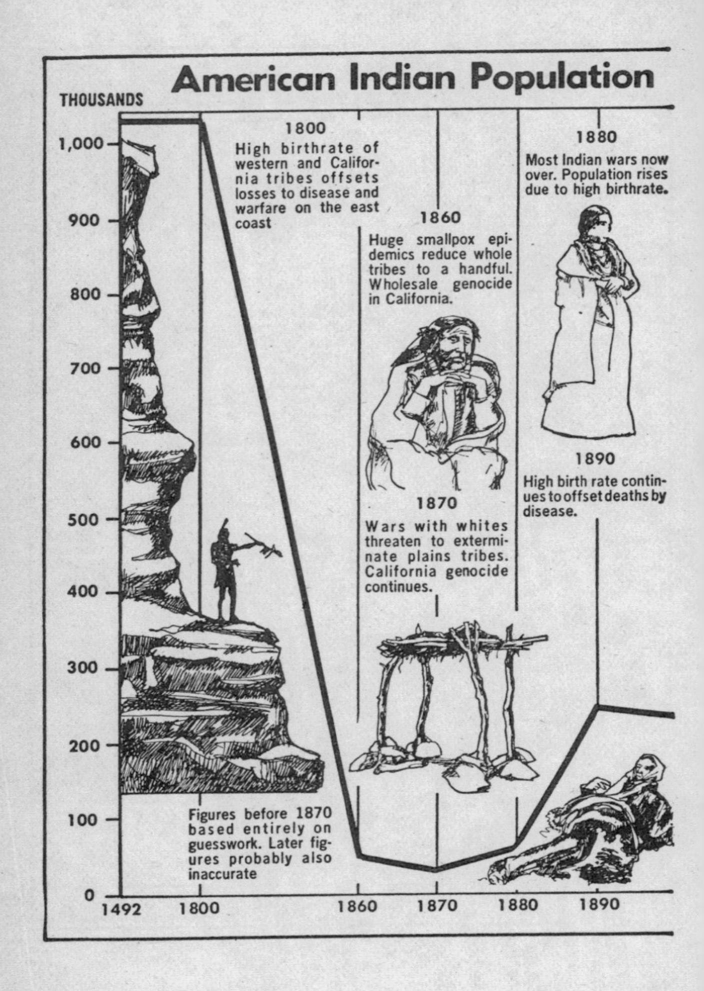
American Indian Population
THOUSANDS
1,000
900
800
700
600
500
400
300
200
100
0
1492
1800
1860
1870
1880
1890
1800
High birthrate of western and California tribes offsets losses to disease and warfare on the east coast
1860
Huge smallpox epidemics reduce whole tribes to a handful. Wholesale genocide in California.
1870
Wars with whites threaten to exterminate plains tribes. California genocide continues.
1880
Most Indian wars now over. Population rises due to high birthrate.
1890
High birth rate continues to offset deaths by disease.
Figures before 1870 based entirely on guesswork. Later figures probably also inaccurate

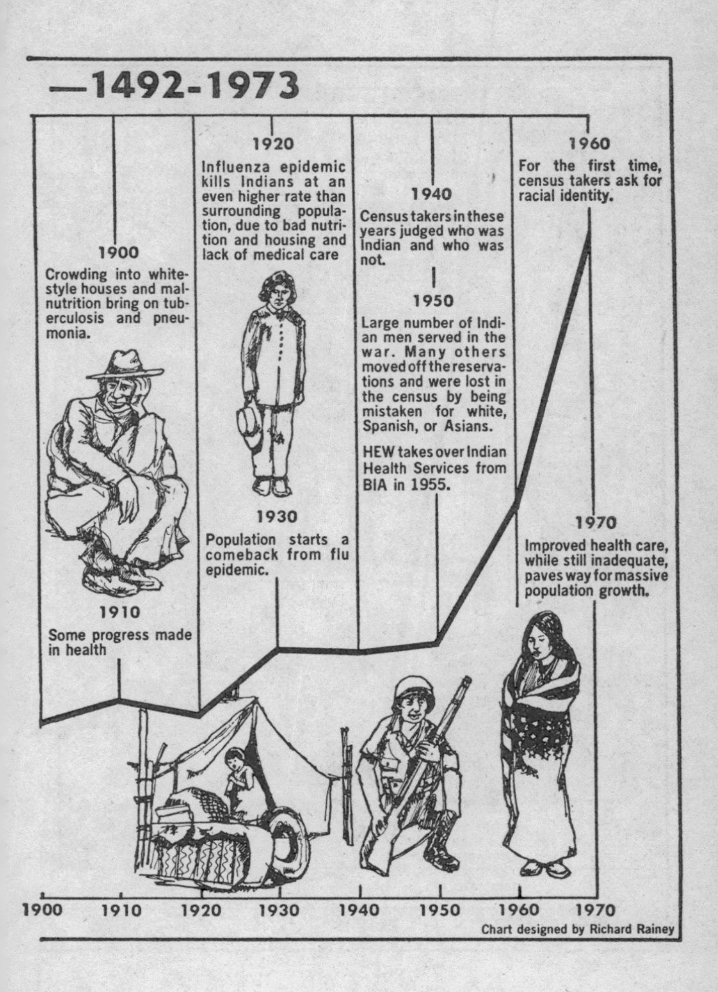
—1492-1973
1900
Crowding into white-style houses and malnutrition bring on tuberculosis and pneumonia.
1910
Some progress made in health
1920
Influenza epidemic kills Indians at an even higher rate than surrounding population, due to bad nutrition and housing and lack of medical care
1930
Population starts a comeback from flu epidemic.
1940
Census takers in these years judged who was Indian and who was not.
1950
Large number of Indian men served in the war. Many others moved off the reservations and were lost in the census by being mistaken for white, Spanish, or Asians.
HEW takes over Indian Health Services from BIA in 1955.
1960
For the first time, census takers ask for racial identity.
1970
Improved health care, while still inadequate, paves way for massive population growth.
1900
1910
1920
1930
1940
1950
1960
1970
Chart designed by Richard Rainey

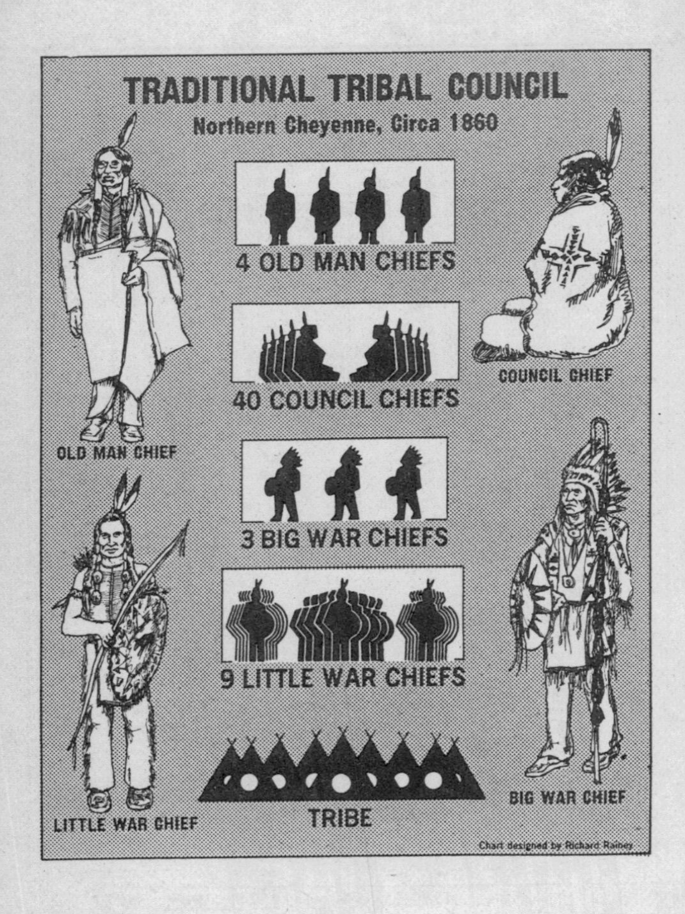
TRADITIONAL TRIBAL COUNCIL
Northern Cheyenne, Circa 1860
4 OLD MAN CHIEFS
40 COUNCIL CHIEFS
3 BIG WAR CHIEFS
9 LITTLE WAR CHIEFS
TRIBE
OLD MAN CHIEF
COUNCIL CHIEF
LITTLE WAR CHIEF
BIG WAR CHIEF
Chart designed by Richard Rainey

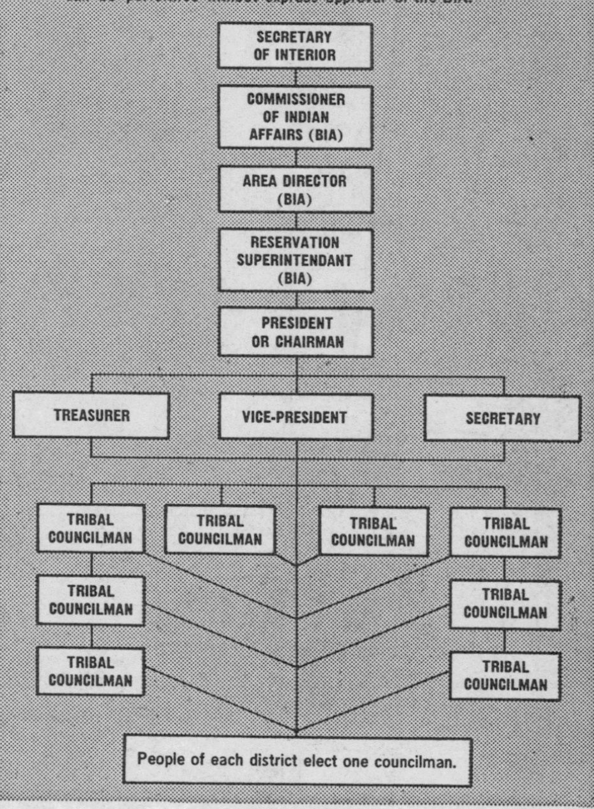
TRIBAL GOVERNMENT TODAY
(Under Indian Reorganization Act Of 1934)
'No act of tribal government except taxation of tribal members can be performed without express approval of the BIA.'
SECRETARY OF INTERIOR
COMMISSIONER OF INDIAN AFFAIRS (BIA)
AREA DIRECTOR (BIA)
RESERVATION SUPERINTENDANT (BIA)
PRESIDENT OR CHAIRMAN
TREASURER
VICE-PRESIDENT
SECRETARY
TRIBAL COUNCILMAN
TRIBAL COUNCILMAN
TRIBAL COUNCILMAN
TRIBAL COUNCILMAN
TRIBAL COUNCILMAN
TRIBAL COUNCILMAN
TRIBAL COUNCILMAN
TRIBAL COUNCILMAN
People of each district elect one councilman.

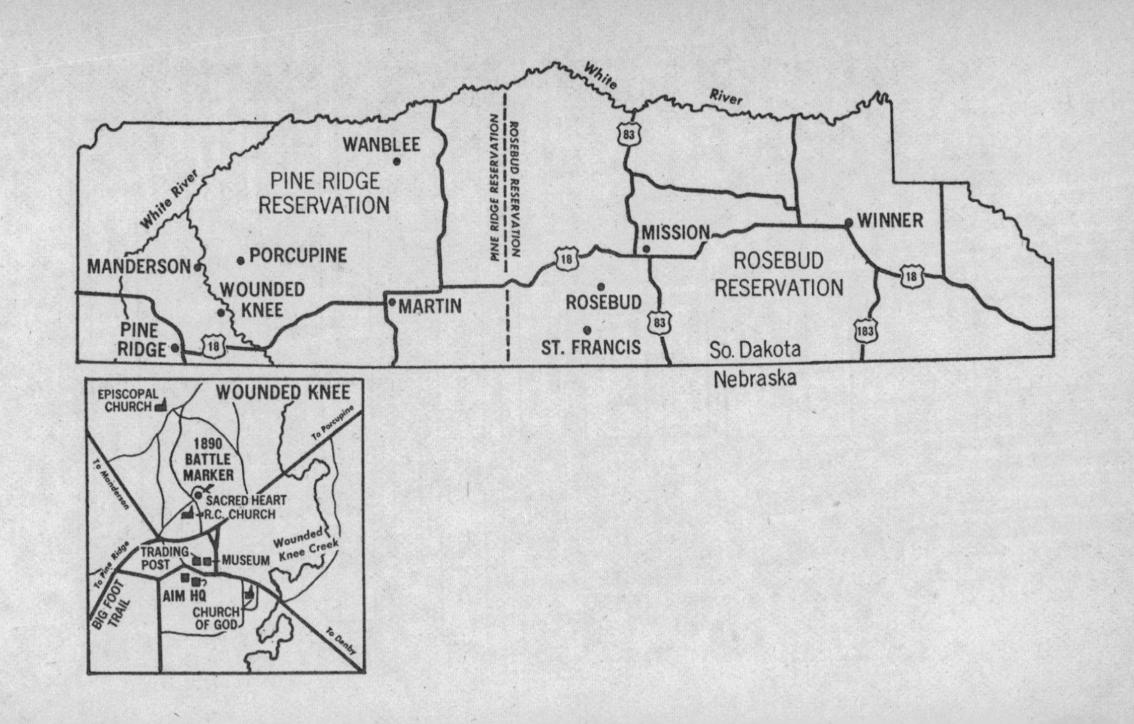
White River
White
River
WANBLEE
PINE RIDGE RESERVATION
PINE RIDGE RESERVATION
ROSEBUD RESERVATION
83
MISSION
WINNER
MANDERSON
PORCUPINE
WOUNDED KNEE
18
ROSEBUD RESERVATION
MARTIN
ROSEBUD
PINE RIDGE
18
83
ST. FRANCIS
183
So. Dakota
Nebraska
WOUNDED KNEE
EPISCOPAL CHURCH
1890 BATTLE MARKER
To Porcupine
To Manderson
SACRED HEART R.C. CHURCH
Wounded Knee Creek
To Pine Ridge
TRADING POST
MUSEUM
AIM HQ
BIG FOOT TRAIL
CHURCH OF GOD
To Denby

# The Sioux Treaty of 1868

Almost everyone has heard of Indian treaties, but relatively few Americans have ever had the chance to actually examine one. The Sioux Treaty of 1868, the most famous of all Indian treaties, is central to Sioux land claims and to the whole Wounded Knee incident.

The Treaty of 1868 marked the conclusion of Red Cloud's War, in which the Sioux, Cheyenne, and Arapaho fought the U.S. Army to a stalemate. Note that the army withdrew from their forts in Indian territory and closed down the Bozeman Trail (Article 16). Note also that the approval of three-quarters of all adult male Indians is required before the treaty can be set aside. Activists and traditionals contend—and the claim seems irrefutable—that because the three-quarters majority was never obtained in any document after the Sioux Treaty of 1868, none of the subsequent agreements are valid. Thus they claim that the Agreement of 1877 (by which the Sioux lost the Black Hills); the Dawes Allotment Act of 1887-89, which broke up the Great Sioux Reservation established by the Treaty of 1868; and the Indian Reorganization Act of 1934, which altered the form of government, are all technically illegal as far as the Sioux Nation is concerned.

The articles providing children with schools on the reservation (Article 7) and adults with cows and oxen for farming (Article 10) were never honored while the treaty was recognized by the whites. Article 16, which kept the army out, was violated by an expedition in which General Custer went prospecting for gold in the sacred Black Hills. And the whole treaty was scrapped (illegally, by the treaty's own terms) in 1877, the year after Custer's Last Stand.

---

## TREATY WITH THE SIOUX—BRULE, OGLALA, MINICONJOU, YANKTONAI, HUNKPAPA, BLACKFEET, CUTHEAD, TWO KETTLE, SANS ARCS, AND SANTEE—AND ARAPAHO, 1868.

April 29, 1868. 15 Stats., 635. Ratified, February 16, 1869. Proclaimed, February 24, 1869.

Articles of a treaty made and concluded by and between Lieutenant-General William T. Sherman, General S. Harney, General Alfred H. Terry, General C. C. Augur, J. B. Henderson, Nathaniel G. Taylor, John B. Sanborn, and Samuel F. Tappan, duly appointed commissioners on the part of the United States, and the different bands of the Sioux Nation of Indians, by their chiefs and head-men, whose names are hereto subscribed, they being duly authorized to act in the premises.

ARTICLE 1. From this day forward all war between the parties to this agreement shall forever cease. The Government of the United States desires peace, and its honor is hereby pledged to keep it. The Indians desire peace, and they now pledge their honor to maintain it.

If bad men among the whites, or among other people subject to the authority of the United States, shall commit any wrong upon the person or property of the Indians, the United States will, upon proof made to the agent and forwarded to the Commissioner of Indian Affairs at Washington City, proceed at once to cause the offender to be arrested and punished according to the laws of the United States, and also re-imburse the injured person for the loss sustained.

If bad men among the Indians shall commit a wrong or depredation upon the person or property of any one, white, black, or Indian, subject to the authority of the United States, and at peace therewith, the Indians herein named solemnly agree that they will, upon proof made to their agent and notice by him, deliver up the wrong-doer to the United States, to be tried and punished according to its laws; and in case they wilfully refuse so to do, the person injured shall be re-imbursed for his loss from the annuities or other moneys due or to become due to them under this or other treaties made with the United States. And the President, on advising with the Commissioner of

Indian Affairs, shall prescribe such rules and regulations for ascertaining damages under the provisions of this article as in his judgment may be proper. But no one sustaining loss while violating the provisions of this treaty or the laws of the United States shall be re-imbursed therefor.

ARTICLE 2. The United States agrees that the following district of country, to wit, viz: commencing on the east bank of the Missouri River where the forty-sixth parallel of north latitude crosses the same, thence along low-water mark down said east bank to a point opposite where the northern line of the State of Nebraska strikes the river, thence west across said river, and along the northern line of Nebraska to the one hundred and fourth degree of longitude west from Greenwich, thence north on said meridian to a point where the forty-sixth parallel of north latitude intercepts the same, thence due east along said parallel to the place of beginning: and in addition thereto, all existing reservations on the east bank of said river shall be, and the same is, set apart for the absolute and undisturbed use and occupation of the Indians herein named, and for such other friendly tribes or individual Indians as from time to time they may be willing, with the consent of the United States, to admit amongst them; and the United States now solemnly agrees that no persons except those herein designated and authorized so to do, and except such officers, agents, and employes of the Government as may be authorized to enter upon Indian reservations in discharge of duties enjoined by law, shall ever be permitted to pass over, settle upon, or reside in the territory described in this article, or in such territory as may be added to this reservation for the use of said Indians, and henceforth they will and do hereby relinquish all claims or right in and to any portion of the United States or Territories, except such as is embraced within the limits aforesaid, and except as hereinafter provided.

ARTICLE 3. If it should appear from actual survey or other satisfactory examination of said tract of land that it contains less than one hundred and sixty acres of tillable land for each person who, at the time, may be authorized to reside on it under the provision of this treaty, and a very considerable number of such persons shall be disposed to commence cultivating the soil as farmers, the United States agrees to set apart, for the use of said Indians, as herein provided, such additional quantity of arable land, adjoining to said reservation, or as near to the same as it can be obtained, as may be required to provide the necessary amount.

ARTICLE 4. The United States agrees, at its own proper expense, to construct at some place on the Missouri River, near the center of said reservation, where timber and water may be convenient, the following buildings, to wit: a warehouse, a storeroom for the use of the agent in storing goods belonging to the Indians, to cost not less than twenty-five hundred dollars; an agency-building for the residence of the agent, to cost not exceeding three thousand dollars; a residence for the physician, to cost not more than three thousand dollars: and five other buildings, for a carpenter, farmer, blacksmith, miller, and engineer, each to cost not exceeding two thousand dollars; also a schoolhouse or mission-building, so soon as a sufficient number of children can be induced by the agent to attend school, which shall not cost exceeding five thousand dollars.

The United States agrees further to cause to be erected on said reservation, near the other buildings herein authorized, a good steam circular-saw mill, with a grist-mill and shingle-machine attached to the same, to cost not exceeding eight thousand dollars.

ARTICLE 5. The United States agrees that the agent for said Indians shall in the future make his home at the agency-building; that he shall reside among them, and keep an office open at all times for the purpose of prompt and diligent inquiry into such matters of complaint by and against the Indians as may be presented for investigation under the provisions of their treaty stipulations, as also for the faithful discharge of other duties enjoined on him by law. In all cases of depredation on persons or property he shall cause the evidence to be taken in writing and forwarded, together with his findings, to the Commissioner of Indian Affairs, whose decision, subject to the revision of the Secretary of the Interior, shall be binding on the parties to this treaty.

ARTICLE 6. If any individual belonging to said tribes of Indians, or legally incorporated with them, being the head of a family shall desire to commence farming, he shall have the privilege to select, in the presence and with the assistance of the agent then in charge, a tract of land within said reservation, not exceeding three hundred and twenty acres in extent, which tract, when so selected, certified, and recorded in the "land book," as herein directed, shall cease to be held in common, but the same may be occupied and held in the exclusive possession of the person selecting it, and of his family, so long as he or they may continue to cultivate it.

Any person over eighteen years of age, not being the head of a family may in like manner select and cause to be certified to him or her, for purposes of cultivation, a quantity of land not exceeding eighty acres in extent, and thereupon be entitled to the exclusive possession of the same as above directed.

For each tract of land so selected a certificate, containing a description thereof and the name of the person selecting it, with a certificate endorsed thereon that the same has been recorded, shall be delivered to the party entitled to it, by the agent, after the same shall have been recorded by him in a book to be kept in his office, subject to inspection, which said book shall be known as the "Sioux Land-Book."

The President may, at any time, order a survey of the reservation, and when so surveyed, Congress shall provide for protecting the rights of said settlers in their improvements, and may fix the character of the title held by each. The United States may pass such laws on the subject of alienation and descent of property between the Indians and their descendants as may be thought proper. And it is further stipulated that any male Indians, over eighteen years of age, of any band or tribe that is or shall hereafter become a party to this treaty, who now is or who shall hereafter become a resident or occupant of any reservation or Territory not included in the tract of country designated and described in this treaty for the permanent home of the Indians, which is not mineral land, nor reserved by the United States for special purposes other than Indian occupation, and who shall have made improvements thereon of the value of two hundred dollars or more, and continuously occupied the same as a homestead for the term of three years, shall be entitled to receive from the United States a patent for one hundred and sixty acres of land including his said improvements, the same to be in the form of the legal subdivisions of the surveys of the public lands. Upon application in writing, sustained by the proof of two disinterested witnesses made for the register of the local land-office when the land sought to be entered is within a land district, and when the tract sought to be entered is not in any land district, then upon said application and proof being made to the Commissioner of the General Land-Office, and the right of such Indian or Indians to enter such tract or tracts of land shall accrue and be perfect from the date of his first improvements thereon, and shall continue as long as he continues his residence and improvements, and no longer. And any Indian or Indians receiving a patent for land under the foregoing provisions, shall thereby and from thenceforth become and be a citizen of the United States, and be entitled to all the privileges and immunities of such citizens, and shall, at the same time, retain all his rights to benefits accruing to Indians under this treaty.

ARTICLE 7. In order to insure the civilization of the Indians entering into this treaty, the necessity of education is admitted, especially of such of them as are or may be settled on said agricultural reservations, and they therefore pledge themselves to compel their children, male and female, between the ages of six and sixteen years, to attend school; and it is hereby made the duty of the agent for said Indians to see that this stipulation is strictly complied with; and the United States agrees that for every thirty children between said ages who can be induced or compelled to attend school, a house shall be provided and a teacher competent to teach the elementary branches of an English education shall be furnished, who will reside among said Indians, and faithfully discharge his or her duties as a teacher. The provisions of this article to continue for not less than twenty years.

ARTICLE 8. When the head of a family or lodge shall have selected lands and received his certificate as above directed, and the agent shall be satisfied that he intends in good faith to commence cultivating the soil for a living, he shall be entitled to receive seeds and agricultural implements for the first year, not exceeding in value one hundred dollars, and for each succeeding year he shall continue to farm, for a period of three years more, he shall be entitled to receive seeds and implements as aforesaid, not exceeding in value twenty-five dollars.

And it is further stipulated that such persons as commence farming shall receive instruction from the farmer herein provided for, and whenever more than one hundred persons shall enter upon the cultivation of the soil, a second blacksmith shall be provided, with such iron, steel, and other material as may be needed.

ARTICLE 9. At any time after ten years from the making of this treaty, the United States shall have the privilege of withdrawing the physician, farmer, blacksmith, carpenter, engineer, and miller herein provided for, but in case of such withdrawal, an additional sum thereafter of ten thousand dollars per annum shall be devoted to the education of said Indians, and the Commissioner of Indian Affairs shall, upon careful inquiry into their condition, make such rules and regulations for the expenditure of said sum as will best promote the educational and moral improvement of said tribes.

ARTICLE 10. In lieu of all sums of money or other annuities provided to be paid to the Indians herein named, under any treaty or treaties heretofore made, the United States agrees to deliver at the agency-house on the reservation herein named, on or before the first day of August of each year, for thirty years the following articles, to wit:

For each male person over fourteen years of age, a suit of good substantial woolen clothing, consisting of coat, pantaloons, flannel shirt, hat, and a pair of home-made socks.

For each female over twelve years of age, a flannel skirt, or the goods necessary to make it, a pair of woolen hose, twelve yards of calico, and twelve yards of cotton domestics.

For the boys and girls under the ages named, such flannel and cotton goods as may be needed to make each a suit as aforesaid, together with a pair of woolen hose for each.

And in order that the Commissioner of Indian Affairs may be able to estimate properly for the articles herein named, it shall be the duty of the agent each year to forward to him a full and exact census of the Indians, on which the estimate from year to year can be based.

And in addition to the clothing herein named, the sum of ten dollars for each person entitled to the beneficial effects of this treaty shall be annually appropriated for a period of thirty years, while such persons roam and hunt, and twenty dollars for each person who engages in farming, to be used by the Secretary of the Interior in the purchase of such articles as from time to time the condition and necessities of the Indians may indicate to be proper. And if within the thirty years, at any time, it shall appear that the amount of money needed for clothing under this article can be appropriated to better uses for the Indians named herein, Congress may, by law, change the appropriation to other purposes; but in no event shall the amount of this appropriation be withdrawn or discontinued for the period named. And the President shall annually detail an officer of the Army to be present and attest the delivery of all the goods herein named to the Indians, and he shall inspect and report on the quantity and quality of the goods and the manner of their delivery. And it is hereby expressly stipulated that each Indian over the age of four years, who shall have removed to and settled permanently upon said reservation and complied with the stipulations of this treaty, shall be entitled to receive from the United States, for the period of four years after he shall have settled upon said reservation one pound of meat and one pound of flour per day, provided the Indians cannot furnish their own subsistence at an earlier date. And it is further stipulated that the United States will furnish and deliver to each lodge of Indians or family of persons legally incorporated with them, who shall remove to the reservation herein described and commence farming, one good American cow, and one good well-broken pair of American oxen within sixty days after such lodge or family shall have so settled upon said reservation.

ARTICLE 11. In consideration of the advantages and benefits conferred by this treaty, and the many pledges of friendship by the United States, the tribes who are parties to this agreement hereby stipulate that they will relinquish all right to occupy permanently the territory outside their reservation as herein defined, but yet reserve the right to hunt on any lands north of North Platte, and on the Republican Fork of the Smoky Hill River, so long as the buffalo may range thereon in such numbers as to justify the chase. And they, the said Indians, further, expressly agree:

1st. That they will withdraw all opposition to the construction of the railroads now being built on the plains.

2nd. That they will permit the peaceful construction of any railroad not passing over their reservation as herein defined.

3rd. That they will not attack any persons at home, or travelling, nor molest or disturb any wagon-trains, coaches, mules, or cattle belonging to the people of the United States, or to persons friendly therewith.

4th. They will never capture, or carry off from the settlements, white women and children.

5th. They will never kill or scalp white men, nor attempt to do them harm.

6th. They withdraw all pretense of opposition to the construction of the railroad now being built along the Platte River and westward to the Pacific Ocean, and they will not in future object to the construction of railroads, wagon-roads, mail-stations, or other works of utility or necessity, which may be ordered or permitted by the laws of the United States. But should such roads or other works be constructed on the lands of their reservation, the Government will pay the tribe whatever amount of damage may be assessed by three disinterested commissioners to be appointed by the President for that purpose, one of said commissioners to be a chief or head-man of the tribe.

7th. They agreed to withdraw all opposition to the military posts or roads now established south of the North Platte River, or that may be established, not in violation of treaties heretofore made or hereafter to be made with any of the Indian tribes.

ARTICLE 12. No treaty for the cession of any portion or part of the reservation herein described which may be held in common shall be of any validity or force as against the said Indians, unless executed and signed by at least three-fourths of all the adult male Indians, occupying or interested in the same; and no cession by the tribe shall be understood or construed in such manner as to deprive, without his consent, any individual member of the tribe of his rights to any tract of land selected by him, as provided in Article 6 of this treaty.

ARTICLE 13. The United States hereby agrees to furnish annually to the Indians the physician, teachers, carpenter, miller, engineer, farmer, and blacksmiths as herein contemplated, and that such appropriations shall be made from time to time, on the estimates of the Secretary of the Interior, as will be sufficient to employ such persons.

ARTICLE 14. It is agreed that the sum of five hundred dollars annually, for three years from date, shall be expanded in presents to the ten persons of said tribe who in the judgment of the agent may grow the most valuable crops for the respective year.

ARTICLE 15. The Indians herein named agree that when the agency-house or other buildings shall be constructed on the reservation named, they will regard said reservation their permanent home, and they will make no permanent settlement elsewhere; but they shall have the right, subject to the conditions and modifications of this treaty, to hunt, as stipulated in Article 11 hereof.

ARTICLE 16. The United States hereby agrees and stipulates that the country north of the North Platte River and east of the summits of the Big Horn Mountains shall be held and considered to be unceded Indian territory, and also stipulated and agrees that no white person or persons shall be permitted to settle upon or occupy any portion of the same; or without the consent of the Indians first had and obtained, to pass through the same; and it is further agreed by the United States that within ninety days after the conclusion of peace with all the bands of the Sioux Nation, the military posts now established in the territory in this article named shall be abandoned, and that the road leading to them and by them to the settlement in the Territory of Montana shall be closed.

ARTICLE 17. It is hereby expressly understood and agreed by and between the respective parties to this treaty that the execution of this treaty and its ratification by the United States Senate shall have the effect, and shall be construed as abrogating and annulling all treaties and agreements heretofore entered into between the respective parties hereto, so far as such treaties and agreements obligate the United States to furnish and provide money, clothing, or other articles of property to such Indians and bands of Indians as become parties to this treaty, but no further.

In testimony of all which, we, the said commissioners, and we, the chiefs and headmen of the Brule band of the Sioux nation, have hereunto set our hands and seals at Fort Laramie, Dakota Territory, this twenty-ninth day of April, in the year one thousand eight hundred and sixty-eight.

The Treaty bears the signatures of the following Indian leaders:

Brule Band of Sioux by the chiefs and headmen, at Fort Laramie, April 29, 1968.

Ogallalah Band of Sioux by the chiefs and headmen, at Fort Laramie, May 25, 1868.

Minneconjon Band of Sioux by the chiefs and headmen, at Fort Laramie, May 26, 1868.

Yanctonais Band of Sioux by the chiefs and headmen, Nov. 6, 1868.

On November 6, 1868, other Ogalallahs signed at Fort Laramie, November 6, 1868.

Uncpapa Band of Sioux by the chiefs and headmen; (no date given).

Blackfeet Band of Sioux by the chiefs and headmen; (no date given).

Cutheads Band of Sioux by the chiefs and headmen; (no date given).

Two Kettle Band of Sioux by the chiefs and headmen; (no date given).

Sans Arch Band of Sioux by the chiefs and headmen; (no date given).

Santee Band of Sioux by the chiefs and headmen; (no date given).

Ratified, February 16, 1869
Proclaimed, February 24, 1869

# Termination Resolution, 1953

The policy of termination is the major bugbear of tribal Indians today. The policy stems from the legislation below, which was enacted into law under President Eisenhower.

Termination was doubly damaging. Those tribes actually terminated suffered economic disasters. Tribes not terminated but facing the ax backslid and stalled on any measures that could bring them closer to self-sufficiency and hence closer to termination and the end of federal trust relationships that protected their land and funded hospitals, schools, government, and roads.

The termination policy was ballyhooed as a long-overdue attempt to bring the Indian into the American mainstream—the same justification for every other land grab since the Dawes Allotment Act of 1887–89. But Indians rallied almost unanimously against it. The Menominis, the first tribe to be terminated, had their termination repealed on 22 December 1973 by President Nixon, after the House of Representatives had voted 404 to 3 in favor of repealing it. The future of the other terminated tribes is still conjectural.

Note that the resolution explicitly mentions treaties and seems to indicate that they are still in force, in marked contrast to other instances in which treaties are ignored.

---

HOUSE CONCURRENT RESOLUTION 108, 83rd Congress, First Session, passed August 1, 1953.

Whereas it is the policy of Congress, as rapidly as possible, to make the Indians within the territorial limits of the United States subject to the same laws and entitled to the same privileges and responsibilities as are applicable to other citizens of the United States, to end their status as wards of the United States, and to grant them all the rights and prerogatives pertaining to American citizenship; and

Whereas the Indians within the territorial limits of the United States should assume their full responsibilities as American citizens; Now, therefore, be it

RESOLVED BY THE HOUSE OF REPRESENTATIVES (THE SENATE CONCURRING), That it is declared to be the sense of Congress that, at the earliest possible time, all of the Indian tribes and the individual members thereof located within the States of California, Florida, New York, and Texas, and all of the following named Indian tribes and individuals thereof, should be freed from Federal supervision and control and from all disabilities and limitations specially applicable to Indians: The Flathead Tribe of Montana, the Klamath Tribe of Oregon, the Menominee Tribe of Wisconsin, the Potowatamie Tribe of Kansas and Nebraska, and those members of the Chippewa Tribe who are on the Turtle Mountain Reservation, North Dakota. It is further declared to be the sense of Congress that, upon the release of such tribes and individual members thereof from such disabilities and limitations, all offices of the Bureau of Indian Affairs in the States of California, Florida, New York, and Texas, and all other offices of the Bureau of Indian Affairs whose primary purpose was to serve any Indian tribe or individual Indian freed from Federal supervision should be abolished. It is further declared to be the sense of Congress that the Secretary of the Interior should examine all existing legislation dealing with such Indians, and treaties between the Government of the United States and each such tribe, and report to Congress at the earliest practicable date, but not later than January 1, 1954, his recommendation for such legislation as, in his judgment, may be necessary to accomplish the purposes of this resolution.

Attest: LYLE O. SNADER,
Clerk of the House of Representatives.
Attest: J. MARK TRICE,
Secretary of the Senate.

# Glossary of Names and Abbreviations

AIM. American Indian Movement. The largest and best-known militant-activist group, founded by Dennis Banks and George Mitchell in Minneapolis, July 1968. AIM claims seventy-two chapters as of late 1973, and some say the organization has as many as 100,000 members, but these figures are not dependable.

AK-47. A Soviet-bloc automatic rifle used by the militants at Wounded Knee. Weight, 10.4 pounds; range, 500-plus yards; cyclic rate of fire, 600 rounds per minute; caliber, 7.62.

Allotment. A parcel of land assigned to an individual Indian, as opposed to tribal land which is communally owned.

APC. Armored personnel carrier. A vehicle used by the government at Wounded Knee. The model in use, the M-113, mounts a .50-caliber M-2 machine gun, has a speed of forty miles per hour, carries thirteen men, and is amphibious and bulletproof against small-arms fire.

Apple. An Indian who copies whites or emulates middle-class white values and life-style: "red on the outside, white on the inside."

BIA. Bureau of Indian Affairs. The subsidiary of the Department of the Interior that has charge of almost all dealings with reservation Indians.

BLM. Bureau of Land Management. A subsidiary of the Department of the Interior, which is the parent department of the BIA.

Buy Indian Act. A law authorizing the secretary of the interior to purchase goods and services directly from Indians. Misinterpretation of the act, which never mentions contracts, has led to heavy and dangerous indebtedness on the part of tribes and Indians.

Chairman. The elected head of the IRA-mandated tribal council—not to be confused with *chief*.

Chief. A traditional Indian leader, either chosen by other traditional leaders and the tribe at large, or, more rarely, gaining the position through heredity.

*Hanblecheyapi*. The Sioux vision quest.

Heirship Act. A proposed bill that would have allowed individual reservation Indians to sell their individual allotments to non-Indians. Crushed by President John Kennedy at the urging of responsible Indian leaders, including coauthor Burnette, then head of the NCAI.

IAM. *Indian Affairs Manual;* BIA's handbook for dealing with Indians.

Indian Agent. The white official who formerly ran the Indian reservation. The title of agent has been superseded by the title *superintendent* since the 1930s.

Indian police. Law enforcement officers recruited from the reservations and paid by the BIA.

Indian Removal Act. Legislation enacted in 1830 which evicted the tribes east of the Mississippi from their homes.

*Inipi*. The sacred sweat lodge of the Sioux, used for religious purification.

IRA. Indian Reorganization Act. The New Deal legislation that created the present system of tribal government.

*Ishna Ta Awi Cha Lowan*. Sioux ceremony initiating a girl to womanhood.

Lakota. The Sioux name for the Teton Sioux people and language. The Teton (grassland) Sioux are those of western South Dakota, including the peoples of Pine Ridge, Rosebud, Standing Rock, Crow Creek, Lower Brulé, and Cheyenne River reservations.

M-1. The standard U.S. infantry rifle in World War II and Korea, revived for Wounded Knee because such modern rifles as the M-16 lacked the range for sniping in open country. Weight, eleven pounds; rate of fire, semiautomatic; range, over a thousand yards; caliber, .30.

M-2. The .50-caliber Browning machine gun used at Wounded Knee by the government forces. Designed for use as an antiaircraft gun, the M-2 is only supposed to be used in case of declared war, because the bullets have so much penetrating power that their effect cannot be localized. One bullet may go through the target individual and hit someone on the other side of him several hundred yards away. The M-2 weighs eighty-two pounds, has a cyclic rate of fire of 450 rounds per minute, and has a range of over two miles against ground targets.

M-16. A U.S. automatic weapon used by both sides at Wounded Knee. Weight, about seven pounds; range, 500 yards; rate of fire, 760 rounds per minute; caliber, .223 (5.5 mm).

M-60. Standard U.S. machine gun, used at Wounded Knee. Weight, twenty-three pounds; range, over a thousand yards; rate of fire, 600 rounds per minute; caliber, 7.62 mm. Developed from the German MG-42.

NCAI. National Congress of American Indians. An independent Indian-run group that lobbies for Indian rights and keeps an eye on Congress. Organized in 1944, it is largely supported by tribal people and governments.

NIYC. National Indian Youth Council. An Indian-run student group dedicated to lobbying for Indian rights and improving the Indian's image. Founded in 1961 by ten Indian college students in Albuquerque, New Mexico, it has several thousand members today.

NTCA. National Tribal Chairman's Association. An organization formed in 1969 at the behest of the Nixon administration to voice tribal leaders' opinions. Activists have often charged NTCA leaders with being "Uncle Tomahawks."

One-to-One Program. A federal program under which Indians supply labor and the government supplies materials and funds to build houses on the reservations.

PHS. Public Health Service of the Department of Health, Education, and Welfare. PHS has been responsible for Indian health on the reservation since 1955.

Purchase Order. A credit slip for income from leased land, it allowed an Indian to purchase certain restricted types of food.

Range Unit. A section of grazing land.

Relocation. Federal programs under which Indians are offered monetary inducements to leave their reservations to move to urban areas. The two main results: Indian slums and skid rows, and the modern urban militants.

Reservation. A tract of land set aside for Indian use.

Revolving Credit Fund. The BIA's loan bank for reservation Indians.

Schmoehawk. A non-Indian who poses as an Indian for commercial gain. A fake. No slur on any actual tribe is intended by the expression.

Sun Dance. Yearly religious festival of the Sioux and other plains tribes.

Superintendent. The (usually white) BIA official who represents the Bureau of Indian Affairs on the individual reservation. Because of the way the Indian Reorganization Act charters and constitutions are written, the superintendent on most reservations has the final say on any transaction involving money and can thus keep the tribe in an economic headlock.

Surplus Commodities. Agricultural products bought up by the government and redistributed to poor people, including Indians.

Uncle Tomahawk. An Indian yes-man. One who parrots whatever sentiment he thinks whites in power positions want to hear.

*Tapa Wanka Yap*. Sioux name for a sacred ball game.

Termination. Policy of ending the federal relationship with reservation Indians. The results of termination have usually been tragic for the Indian tribes involved and expensive for the states in which the terminated reservations are located.

Trail of Tears. Death march in which the Five Civilized Tribes were evicted from the Southeast and marched to Oklahoma in the 1830s. One Cherokee in four died on the trail.

Treaty. An agreement arrived at by negotiation between two sovereign nations.

UNA. United Native Americans, a San Francisco-based activist group organized by Lee Brightman, involved in social and academic programs.

*Yuwipi.* The spirit ceremony of the Sioux. The name means, literally, "tied up," because the medicine man is bound hand and foot while the ceremony takes place.

# Chronology

1778. The Continental Congress signs the first Indian treaty with the Delaware Nation. Like most of the 370 treaties that follow, it is broken within a few years.

1830. The case of *Worcester* v. *Georgia* causes the U.S. Supreme Court to recognize Indian tribes as sovereign nations with the right to govern their own internal affairs.

1834. The Bureau of Indian Affairs is organized within the War Department.

1849. The Bureau of Indian Affairs is transferred from the War Department to the newly formed Department of the Interior.

1851. The Laramie Treaty Council defines the hunting grounds of the various plains tribes.

1868. The U.S. signs the Sioux Treaty of 1868, giving the Teton Sioux the Black Hills and recognizing that a three-fourths majority vote of tribesmen is necessary to change the treaty.

1871. Congress ends treaty making with Indians as sovereign nations. Henceforward, all covenants will be called *agreements*.

1877. The U.S. scraps the Sioux Treaty of 1868 after the army and settlers have already violated it flagrantly, leading to Custer's Last Stand. The U.S. fails to obtain the necessary number of signatures to end the treaty, despite orders to Indians to "sign or starve."

1879. A lower court rules in the case of *Standing Bear* v. *Crook* that an individual Indian has the same constitutional rights as a non-Indian.

1880. The Decision of Ex Parte Crow Dog establishes federal jurisdiction on Indian reservations in cases of seven major crimes—murder, rape, burglary, and the like. Indian police forces formed by BIA.

1887. The Dawes Allotment Act breaks up Great Sioux Reservation and many others, giving "surplus" land to whites. Again, required number of tribal signatures are not obtained.

1924. All Indians become citizens, whether they want to or not. Land seizures follow as individual allotments become taxable.

1926. The Merriam Report delineates Indian poverty, unemployment, lack of health care and education.

1934. The Indian Reorganization Act, pushed through as part of the New Deal, creates the present form of tribal government. The act is approved only because many traditionals protest it by boycotting the referendum.

1942. The U.S. seizes five hundred square miles of the Pine Ridge reservation for a practice bombing range.

1944. The National Congress of American Indians is formed as an Indian lobbying group.

1950s. The relocation policy of moving Indians to cities begins. Indian slums and skid rows spring up all over the West Coast and Midwest.

1953. The law forbidding Indians to purchase liquor off-reservation is repealed. White whiskey towns spring up around dry reservations.

1953–54. The termination policy of ending federal services to reservations begins. Reservations terminated usually become economic disaster areas.

1955. The responsibility for Indian health is transferred from the BIA to the U.S. Public Health Service.

1960–63. President John Kennedy extends federal housing assistance to reservations, increases amounts of surplus commodities, and helps kill heirship bill.

1961. The National Indian Youth Council, first all-Indian youth protest group is formed in New Mexico.

1968. A congressional investigation of Indian education finds "a national disgrace."

1968, July. The American Indian Movement is organized by Dennis Banks and George Mitchell in Minneapolis.

1969, November. Indians of All Tribes, a San Francisco activist group, seizes Alcatraz Island to dramatize Indian problems and to set up a cultural center.

1970, 8 July. President Nixon makes a landmark speech disowning termination and relocation policies. But corruption on the reservations flourishes.

1970, November. Russell Means, AIM leader, begins a new Indian tradition by capturing the *Mayflower II* and annoying *Mayflower* families on Thanksgiving at Plymouth, Massachusetts.

1971, May. Russell and Ted Means, Clyde Bellecourt, Mitchell Zephier, and Sylvester Smells are arrested for holding prayer vigil atop Mount Rushmore in the Black Hills.

1971, May. The last holdouts are evicted from Alcatraz by federal forces. They take over an abandoned missile site and are again evicted.

1971, May. Police battle displaced Indians in Chicago and evict them from a park they had been living in.

1971, 22 September. Russell and Ted Means lead sixty AIM and NIYC Indians in brief, harshly suppressed attempt to storm the office of John Crow, deputy commissioner of Indian affairs, in Washington, D.C.

1971, fall and winter. Onondaga Indians and friends stop expansion of Route 81 across their reservation just outside Syracuse, New York.

1972, February. Thirteen hundred Indians led by Russell Means and Dennis Banks take over Gordon, Nebraska, to protest humiliation and murder of Raymond Yellow Thunder.

1972, April. The AIM leadership becomes fragmented in a dispute over the use of guns at a Cass Lake, Minnesota, protest.

1972, 1–8 November. AIM leaders and other activists turn the peaceful Trail of Broken Treaties into a violent seizure of the BIA building in Washington. They hold the building for a week and depart with the files, and $66,500 in cash given them by White House.

1973, 6 February. Means and Banks show up at Custer, South Dakota, to protest the killing of Wesley Bad Heart Bull. Fighting breaks out and Indians burn three buildings and damage two police cars.

1973, 27 February. AIM leaders and two hundred armed followers capture the hamlet of Wounded Knee at gunpoint to dramatize poverty, corruption, and oppression at Pine Ridge reservation.

# Bibliography

To attempt a bibliography for a book like this is to court futility. In the first place, both authors—Robert Burnette in particular—were a part of the events described. Moreover, much of the information was gathered in day-to-day living or in conversations, lectures, and harangues that could never be footnoted. The following list is intended to convey some idea of the broad range of books, periodicals, and contacts that contribute to the total picture rather than as an exhaustive list of research resources for the edification of future scholars.

Listing all the periodicals that contributed information or perspective would be impossible, and providing dates and issue numbers would impose a breaking strain on the bibliographers' already surfeited tolerance for precision. No endorsement is implied by mentioning any particular book or magazine, for some of the articles were biased, inaccurate, and silly, just as others were fair and honest. Among those that fell within our ken were *Time, Life, Newsweek, National Geographic, Harper's, American West, American Heritage, American Opinion, TV Guide, U.S. News and World Report, Mankind, Gallery,* and *Penthouse.* Vital statistics, unless otherwise noted, are from the U.S. Census Bureau, Bureau of Indian Affairs, or Public Health Service.

Newspapers referred to—not necessarily for information, for they sometimes had more errors than facts—were the *New York Times,* the *New York Daily News,* the *New York Post,* the *Washington Post,* and the *Washington News.* Two papers deserve a great deal of credit. The first is *Akwesasne Notes,* the journal of Indian activism, whose back issues provide an invaluable reference to fact and opinion in the Indian world, and whose staffers deserve every award the journalistic societies could (but won't) bestow upon them for putting out a great paper on a shoestring. The second is the *Shannon County News,* which was burned during the Wounded Knee siege but has since resumed publication. If only for his tremendous courage, publisher Aaron DeSersa deserves many medals.

Following is a list of books that contributed historical background. It is only a partial list, but it should give some idea of the complexity of the situation and the amount of information available.

Andrist, Ralph K. *The Long Death*. New York: Macmillan Co., 1964.

Armstrong, Virginia Irving. *I Have Spoken*. Chicago: Swallow Press, 1971. Anthology.

Barrett, S. M. *Geronimo, His Own Story*. New York: E. P. Dutton, 1971. Reprint.

Beebe, Lucius, and Clegg, Charles. *The American West*. New York: Bonanza, 1955.

Bētzinez, Jason, with Nye, W. S. *I Fought with Geronimo*. New York: Stackpole, 1959.

Bigelow, Lt. John, Jr. *On the Bloody Trail of Geronimo*. Westernlore, 1968. Reprint.

Bolton, Reginald Pelham. *Indian Life of Long Ago in the City of New York*. New York: Crown, 1972. Reprint from 1934.

Bourke, John G. *On the Border with Crook*. New York: Charles Scribner's Sons, 1891.

Brady, Cyrus Townsend. *Indian Fights and Fighters*. McClure, Phillips & Co., 1904.

Brandon, William. *The American Heritage Book of Indians*. New York: American Heritage Publishers, 1961.

Brown, Dee. *The Galvanized Yankees*. Urbana: University of Illinois, 1963.

———. *Action at Beecher Island*. New York: Doubleday & Co., 1967.

———. *Bury My Heart at Wounded Knee*. New York: Holt, Rinehart and Winston, 1970; New York: Bantam Paperback, 1972.

Brown, Dee, and Schmitt, Martin F. *Fighting Indians of the West*. New York: Charles Scribner's Sons, 1948.

Brown, Joseph Epes. *The Sacred Pipe*. Norman, Okla.: University of Oklahoma, 1953.

——— *The Spiritual Legacy of the American Indian*. Pendle Hill, 1964 (pamphlet).

Brown, Mark H., and Felton, William R. *The Frontier Years*. New York: Holt, Rinehart and Winston, 1955.

Buechel, Eugene, Rev. S.J. *Lakota-English Dictionary*. Red Cloud Indian School, 1970.

Burnette, Robert. *The Tortured Americans*. Englewood Cliffs, N.J.: Prentice-Hall, 1971.

Catlin, George. *North American Indians*. New York: Dover, 1973. Original published in London 1844.

Collier, John. *American Indian Ceremonial Dances*. New York: Crown, 1972.

Curtis, Natalie. *The Indians' Book*. New York: Harper and Brothers, 1923.

Custer, George A. *My Life on the Plains*. Lincoln, Neb.: Bison Books, 1966. Reprint.

Deloria, Vine, ed. *Of Utmost Good Faith*. New York: Bantam, 1971. Anthology.

De Voto, Bernard. *Across the Wide Missouri*. Boston: Houghton Mifflin, 1947.

Dixon, Joseph K. *The Vanishing Race*. Rodman Wanamaker, 1913.

Eastman, Charles A. *Indian Boyhood*. McClure Phillips Co., 1902.

Forbes, Jack D., ed. *The Indian in America's Past*. Englewood Cliffs, N.J.: Prentice-Hall, 1964.

Graham, W. A., Col. (ret.). *The Custer Myth: A Source Book of Custeriana*. New York: Crown, 1955.

Grinnell, George Bird. *By Cheyenne Campfires*. New Haven: Yale University, 1926.

Hassrick, Royal B. *The Sioux: Life and Customs of a Warrior Society*. Norman, Okla.: University of Oklahoma Press, 1964.

Horan, James D. *The Great American West*. New York: Crown, 1959.

Jackson, Helen Hunt. *A Century of Dishonor*. New York: Harper & Row.

Josephy, Alvin. *The Patriot Chiefs*. New York: Viking Press, 1968.

———. *The Indian Heritage of America*. New York: Knopf, 1968; New York: Bantam Paperback, 1969.

———. *Red Power*. New York: American Heritage Press, 1971.

Kobler, John. *Capone*. New York: G. P. Putnam's Sons, 1971.

Laubin, Reginald and Gladys. *The Indian Tipi.* New York: Ballantine, 1957.

Levine, Stuart, and Lurie, Nancy O., eds. *The American Indian Today.* Baltimore: Pelican, 1970.

Lighthall, J. I. *The Indian Folk Medicine Guide.* New York: Popular Library, 1973.

Linderman, Frank B. *Plenty Coups, Chief of the Crows.* Lincoln, Neb.: Bison, 1962.

Marquis, Thomas B., M.D. *Wooden Leg: A Warrior Who Fought Custer.* Lincoln, Neb.: Bison, 1965. Reprint.

Marriott, Alice, and Rachlin, Carol K. *American Indian Mythology.* New York: Thomas Y. Crowell, 1968.

McLaughlin, James. *My Friend the Indian.* Boston: Houghton Mifflin, 1910.

Millard, Joseph. *The Cheyenne Wars.* New York: Ace, 1964.

Miller, David Humphreys. *Custer's Fall.* New York: Duell, Sloan, and Pearce, 1957.

Myers, J. Jay. *Red Chiefs and White Challengers.* New York: Washington Square Press, 1972.

Neihardt, John G. *Black Elk Speaks.* New York: William Morrow & Co., 1932.

Parkman, Francis. *The Oregon Trail.* New York: New American Library, Signet Classics, 1950.

———. *The Conspiracy of Pontiac.* New York: Collier, 1962. Reprint.

Powell, Peter J., Rev. *Sweet Medicine.* Norman, Okla.: University of Oklahoma, 1969.

Sandoz, Mari. *Crazy Horse, the Strange Man of the Oglalas.* Lincoln, Neb.: Bison, 1961. Reprint.

———. *Cheyenne Autumn.* New York: Avon, 1964.

———. *The Battle of the Little Bighorn.* New York: J. B. Lippincott, 1966.

Schultz, J. W. *My Life as an Indian.* New York: Fawcett.

Stands In Timber, John, with Liberty, Margot. *Cheyenne Memories.* New Haven: Yale University Press, 1967.

Steiner, Stan. *The New Indians.* New York: Dell, 1968.

Tomkins, William. *Indian Sign Language.* New York: Dover, 1969. Reprint.

Vestal, Stanley. *Sitting Bull, Champion of the Sioux.* Norman, Okla.: University of Oklahoma, 1957.

Vogel, Virgil J. *American Indian Medicine.* Norman, Okla.: University of Oklahoma, 1970.

Washburn, Wilcomb E., ed. *The Indian and the White Man*. New York: Doubleday Anchor, 1964.

———. *Red Man's Land—White Man's Law*. New York: Charles Scribner's Sons, 1971.

Webb, Walter Prescott. *The Great Plains*. Lexington, Mass.: Ginn and Co., 1931.

Weslager, C. A. *The Delaware Indians: A History*. New Brunswick, N.J.: Rutgers University Press, 1972.

———. *Magic Medicines of the Indian*. New York: Middle Atlantic Press, 1973.

Wissler, Clark. *Red Man Reservations*. New York: Collier, 1969. Originally published as *Indian Cavalcade*. Sheridan House, 1938.

———. *Indians of the United States*. Revised edition. New York: Doubleday, 1966.

# Index

## ABOUT THE AUTHORS

ROBERT BURNETTE, Tribal Chairman of the Rosebud Sioux and pioneer Indian activist, has been working to help his people for the past quarter of a century. He served three years in Washington, D.C., as executive director of the National Congress of American Indians, the tribes' national lobby. Born on the Rosebud Reservation in 1926, Burnette lived in a tent for several years as a child. He joined the U.S. Marines at seventeen and served in the Pacific in World War II. His lonely struggle against the Bureau of Indian Affairs (BIA) apathy and tribal corruption is described in his first book, *The Tortured Americans*. Burnette served as national co-chairman for the Trail of Broken Treaties march on Washington during election week, 1972. He negotiated on behalf of the traditional Sioux chiefs after Wounded Knee II. Burnette heads American Indians and Friends, Inc., an organization creating employment and economic opportunities on the reservation. Mr. Burnette presently lectures for the Bantam Lecture Bureau.

JOHN KOSTER is a newsman specializing in Indian matters and Indian activism. His writings have been syndicated by the North American Newspaper Alliance and reprinted in AKWESASNE NOTES, the Indian national newspaper. Born in Baltimore, raised in New Jersey and California, Koster has been a reporter for five years. His interests include the history of the West and parapsychology.